The Prophet:

A Story of Love and Grace

Marian Kerr-Bahin

A wholly owned subsidiary of TBN

Manufactured in the United States of America

10 9 8 7 6 5 4 3 2 1

Library of Congress Cataloging-in-Publication Data is available.

ISBN: 978-1-63769-576-0

E-ISBN: 978-1-63769-577-7

Dedication

I dedicate this book to my sweet mother, Merlene Kerr, my father, Rupert Kerr, to my dear neighbor and friend Irma Gabriel and my only child, my son, Aaron Bahin.

Mom, Merlene, you are one of the sweetest persons I have known, and you never cease to pray for me. Even as an adult, I find great comfort in your hugs and your earnest, heartfelt prayers. Great mother of consolation, thank you for always considering my siblings and me, your babies, even when we were fully grown. You are so selfless, never asking for anything but always trying to find out if your babies were okay. You are a true expression of God's love in my life. Gentle, loving, kind, compassionate, and easy to be around. You are the perfect caregiver and have a servant's heart. You have loved me well and poured into me your love for the Lord Jesus and for the scriptures. Your relentless singing over me has made me a lover of Yahweh and of His Christ.

My dad, Rupert, you are one of the hardest working persons I know. You provided for your family, going above and beyond to ensure our needs were met. You will always be the champion of my life as a role model, protector, and guardian of the home. What you lack in words, you made up with your acts of kindness for your family and your community. You serve well those who were entrusted to your care and set an amazing example of loyalty and strength of character in my life. Now your physical strength has diminished, but your words still resound in my ears and still have the power to shape my world. What a champion you are of courage and grace you are in the eyes of God and of men.

The Prophet

My sweet neighbor Irma, what a blessing you were in my life. You came as an answer to prayer for a friend with whom I could have hot chocolate and tea. You became a part of my neighborhood, home Bible study group, and what an asset you were. You always showed up with the most beautiful fruit salad or a beautiful cake on your best cake platter. You so enjoyed my teaching that even when the homegroup dissolved, years later, you would always call on me to come and study the Bible with you in your house. It was in your house in January 2020 that I received the inspiration to write this book as we poured over the first few chapters of the Gospel of Luke. It was the last time we met for Bible study before you moved to Jacksonville and it was when the book was birthed. You wanted to grow in your knowledge of the word and in the person of Jesus Christ. I suggested the book of Luke, which we never completed because the virus came and remain on the land. You lost your job, and you were forced to move away to be close to your children. Something beautiful happened that night when we spoke of the meeting of Mary and Elizabeth and the supernatural encounter they had. I leaped into the pages of the Bible and began a walk with them, and that journey ended in the writing of this book. I am forever grateful for your interest in my teaching and for pushing me to go deeper in the word.

My son, Aaron, I became an empty nester, and my world seemed so out of sort. You were twenty and was gone off to the Navy. I have tried to share the gospels with you a few summers ago. We poured over the stories of Jesus and his journey on the earth as we read through the pages of the four gospels and the book of Acts of the Bible. I do not know if you enjoyed those mornings as much as I did, but week after week that summer when you were eleven years old, I knew that I had to personally go over these stories with you and be sure you understood my Judeo-Christian worldview. It was that

Dedication

same year you got baptized after giving your heart to Jesus at the "Blink" production. I knew those were the last years I had with you before you were grown into a teen and formed your own opinions about life and the world around you. I have watched you questioned your faith and battle with the insecurities of the teen years. I hear your doubts about your faith as you wrestle with the secular world-view, but I knew that indelible planted in your heart was the truth of God's word and that you would never depart from it. You are forever the one who made me a mom and released in me the God kind of love, the agape love. The kind of love that is willing to die for the other. That is your mother's love for you, my beloved son.

Introduction

It was April of 2020; the Coronavirus was plundering the globe, and fear was at an all-time high. I sat in the den of my girlfriend Irma's home, discussing the current crisis in our land. We then poured over the story of Mary and Elizabeth in the Gospel of Luke chapter two, trying to find comfort in the words. She has been laid off from work because of the virus and was struggling with anxiety; she was now requesting if we could have Bible study again. I was not physically well and have not been well for over five years. My body was constantly riddled in pain, and my energy level was increasingly low, but I have not lost my love and passion for the word of God. It has been since Christmas that I have been revisiting the story of Mary's encounter with her cousin Elizabeth and has been pouring it over in my heart again and again. It had ignited my spirit at a new level, and I just could not shake the majestic moment that had unfolded. I was looking at this story at a different level of understanding, and my imagination was racing through the lines of the story and the era of that day. What a beautiful encounter and an epic moment in the history of mankind. The novel *The Prophet* was birthed. I practically began to walk with my mind's eyes into the depth of the story and imagined what it could have been for two women to be divinely impacted in the area of fertility and the divine unfolding of the Heavenly Father in the salvation of humanity.

In the depth of my own struggle with illness, I had entered into the lives of two women deeply impacted by Yahweh, as revealed in the scripture. It would be a year-long journey to complete this book, for I have been struggling for five years with chronic fatigue, debilitating weakness, chronic bone pain, brain fog, and myriads of symptoms in my body. I was mostly confined to home for two and a half years and only left the house for church, and on the days, I went to the ER or to my doctor to try to figure out what was destroying my body. On the days when the brain fog lifted, I would pour over the four gospels. It was a season in my life that I thought I would die and not get to share the gospel like I always wanted to. I started making small videos and posted them on YouTube and Facebook, tagging them to my family and friends. I had to find a way to fulfill my desire to share the gospel before I die. I was experiencing every symptom of fibromyalgia, but my doctor thought it was all related to menopause. My symptoms were debilitating, and I had not worked in over two years. I had spent all the money I had and had just grown worse. No one had a solution for my condition.

One night in June 2016, while pouring my heart out in prayer to Jesus about my maladies, I had an open vision in which Jesus appeared to be pouring all these red and blue jewels and light into my belly. I came out of the experience with an increased passion for reading the four gospels and a deeper depth and of understanding of walking with Jesus through the gospels. My mini-videos presented me as "The Jesus' Story-Teller." This became an amazing journey as my mind struggled to make sense of the increased pain, fatigue, and weakness that bombarded my body. I remembered five years prior, at my fiftieth birthday, I had prayed a prayer to God to go into full-time ministry. I now felt like I was in the middle of hell. Five years of my life were taken with illness, and I did not know if I would live or die. I may never get to preach, but could I share my version of John and Jesus and the women who were their mothers? I was fifty-five years old; I prayed for one chance to present Jesus. This is how it all began and how God would give me one year in which to write this script I wish to share with the world.

So let me retract this story to 2015 when I turned fifty years old;

Introduction

I was excited to be in my jubilee year and had a great desire to return to full-time ministry. I have been working as a nurse for almost twenty years and have lived in the USA for twenty-three years. Prior to coming to the USA, I had served as a youth pastor on my island of Jamaica for over ten years and felt God led me into nursing school when I came to New York City in 1993. I wanted to go to Bible school. One day while in fasting and prayer, I heard an inner audible voice instructing me to go to a nine-month business school, which later led to all the doors opening for nursing school. I accepted the challenge and followed after nursing with all my heart because it was a childhood dream. At fifty, I was restless and dissatisfied with my life, I loved nursing, but it has not provided the opportunity for evangelism as I had hoped it would have. It was a high-demand job that was a very task-oriented job that served the needs of the sick and disease through medicine, trying to bring them back to wellness. I have worked in hospitals, jails, drug rehab centers, hospices, cancer units and have seen humanity at its worse. I knew the world and medicine did not have an answer for the human dilemma, but that Jesus was the answer.

I was hungry for teaching and preaching the word of God again, and that morning after my fiftieth birthday, having returned from my twelve-hour night tour in the hospital, I dropped to my knees and prayed, asking God to give me the ability to go into full-time ministry. I forgot about the prayer and went about my activities of daily living, but things in my life started to change in a negative way. I began to experience health issues: joint pains and stiffness, anxiety, dizziness, heart palpitations, numbness and tingling in my hands and feet, and severe fatigue and weakness. After seeing my family doctor, it was diagnosed as the onset of menopause and that it would be self-limiting. Within a year, I had to quit the job at the hospital after suffering two near syncopal episodes and was having difficulty coping with the demands of the high stressors of the job in the hospital. I stayed home for five months, had multiple doctor visits and emergency room visits only to be told over and over again that my symptoms were all related to menopause and that I was simply going through the changes of life. I went back to work in a new job less stressful than the hospital but changed two jobs in less than a year each, just trying to find a nursing job I could cope with. I was forced to resign the last job because of ill health and the inability to cope with the demands of the job. I had severe fatigue, suffered from pain all over my body. I lost all my energy; I was dizzy constantly, bloated, and had a foggy brain almost constantly. I had numbness and tingling in my hands and feet. Nothing in my life made sense. My world was turned upside down, and all I could do was pray.

I have been in great health up until this point. I exercised three times weekly, ride my bike, power walked, and swam. I was on no medications and had no medical comorbidities. I had always maintained a healthy weight and ate healthy meals. One year rolled into five years of a roller-coaster life of pain, fatigue, weakness, brain fog, and weight gain. I had not worked for over two years and stayed in bed most days, and the doctors continued to label my condition as menopause. I did my own research because my condition was too debilitating for menopause; no family member of mine experienced such severity of symptoms as I was having. I started hormone therapy which relieved a small amount of my fatigue. I had all the symptoms of fibromyalgia, and it was debilitating. I got tested for autoimmune diseases, I got my endocrine system evaluated, and all the tests came back negative. I had an evaluation with a homeopathic doctor who did a urine test and a multi-system symptoms evaluation which showed I had poly-system inflammatory processes. I was so weakened that if I was in the street and the rain started falling, I could not run to my car. I was always exuberant in worship service at church,

Introduction

and even the smallest attempt to celebrate in church would leave me riddled with pain and exhaustion. I would go home from church and collapse in the bed, disillusioned. I still helped with feeding the homeless on Sunday evenings after church but practically felt myself shaking in pain. At the end of the hour, I would walk slowly to my car without complaint and prayed in tongues all the way home. Up to this point, I had gone to many healing conferences, had more hands laid on me, and more prayers offered than I ever did in all my lifetime. I had been prophesied over and given five different diagnoses during prayer sessions, and nothing changed in my health. I was contending in prayer for my healing, and not even the church had the immediate answers for me. I would not die but live and declare the glory of God; I prayed over myself daily. I read scriptures on healing and played the YouTube healing scriptures twenty-four hours daily. The book *The Prophet: A Story of Love and Grace* was birthed out of my own pursuit for healing and finding the grace of God in my most difficult season of my life. I completed this book in October 2020 and received divine healing in my home on November 1, 2020, and started Bible school in January 2021. I hope this book will be a blessing to you as you journey with me through the pages.

Part 1:
The Angel Has Come

Elizabeth flung the door of the house opened and wandered into the garden in the early morning sunlight. She lifted her head up to the heavens bathing in the sun's glorious warmth from the morning rays. She was fat, and her abdomen was protruding under her dress. These were visible signs that the baby was growing in leaps and bounds. She smiled and lifted her face to the skies and gently rubbed her baby bump. It was time for them to reveal to their family and friends the promise of God fulfilled in their lives. God has been faithful to fulfill the angelic proclamation made to her husband Zacharias five months ago. Elizabeth had hidden away from her family and neighbors for five long months when she became pregnant. She wanted the promise to develop and grow then show herself to the world. She had long resigned herself to the title of childlessness, and now she was going to be a mother by the divine intervention of Yahweh. She pinched herself nervously and contemplated on how God had truly answered their prayers after years of praying without a result for the fruit of the womb. She was now eighty-eight years old and had long passed the years of child-bearing. She had watched the changes in her body curiously, weekly then monthly, as her breast grew larger and her abdomen began to swell underneath her dress. Of a certainty, what Zacharias had written on the scroll and handed to her on that eventful day of his return from Jerusalem five months earlier had come to fruition. With only one night of passionate lovemaking with her husband, the baby named John by the angel Gabriel was conceived and now growing in her womb. Zacharias had returned from temple duty in Jerusalem dumb, but the letter he handed her hastily that day stated that an angel had visited him while he served at the Altar of Incense. The mighty angel Gabriel had announced that they were going to have a baby boy. According to the letter, he was going to be a special Jewish boy, and there were instructions given to raise him a Nazarite to God and that his name should be called John and he will be the prophet before the Christ-Messiah make his entrance into the world. She had smiled and hugged her husband, pondering with joyful amazement at the things she had read. As she passionately kissed her husband that night and intimately lay in his arms, with a deep longing for motherhood, she welcomed him home. She knew that this would be the night the seed would be formed in her womb according to the word of God. He had spent a week in Jerusalem in temple duties, and the house has been lonely without him. They have been the best of friends and lovers for years and have enjoyed their lives together despite their childless state. Her whole life has been one marked by the reproach and the shame of been barren. She was the wife of a priest, yet her womb has been closed for all her child-bearing years. It was a kind of irony and the storyline that has played out in and around in her head for all these years as her neighbors snickered and gossiped behind her back, "There goes the faultless, blameless priest who served God faithfully, yet his wife could not get a child from God." She lived with the curse of been a poor wife who could not give her husband children. In neighboring countries, she would have been called "a useless woman." Her mother-in-law could have by now suggested for her son to take a second wife. Even in Israel, she could have been put away by a letter of divorcement. However, Zacharias had remained a loving, faithful, and godly husband who never blamed her for what he knew only God could give. Now life was growing in her womb, and her neighbors knew not of her good fortune. "How would they receive her? What would they think at her age?" she wondered as she basked in the morning sunlight. She knew God had favored her, and they would rejoice with her. The miracle in her womb would birth eternal joy in many just as it has birthed joy in her heart. She would be forever written down in history to present hope, love, and the redemption of God to others. Elizabeth and Zacharias are parents to John, the prophet to Christ-Messiah.

Zacharias has undoubtedly been a loving and devoted husband but, first of all, an honorable priest to the Most High God of Israel. He did not take his job of priesthood lightly, and neither did he take his role of a husband lightly. He loved doting and fussing over his beautiful wife and best friend and always assured her how sacred and precious she was to him. In his office as a priest, his life was held to the highest standard of the Levitical laws of the priesthood. He was the husband of one wife and had to rule his children well. When he received the angelic visitation and was told they were going to have a baby boy, he immediately exclaimed, "We are stricken in age." He was frightened and shaken to his core. Not once in all his priestly ministration had he had a heavenly visitation. "A child?" The cry of Zacharias was heard by Gabriel—the mighty archangel. Zacharias was doubting and protesting that at their age, they were not willing to care for a child. His complaint in the natural was logical. They are comfortable where they were and have long given up on the dreams of parenthood. They have endured the laughter and the scorns of their neighbors and had long submitted to old age. "We are too old to raise a special child for God. We do not have prior experience, and we just don't qualify! We are not Abraham and Sarah, so we do not have such faith." In truth, Zacharias and Elizabeth had lived impeccable, religious lives before their neighbors and were often called blameless before God. Their family and neighbors did not understand the cause of their childless lives. They were Levites; it was an expectation that their lives were to be a picture of holiness and well-pleasing to God as a priestly household is required to be.

Their families and neighbors honored their position. The heart of God for them has now been revealed, and the purpose of their lives was just beginning to unfold. In reality, they were not forgotten; God has remembered them, and who could imagine at their age?

Year after year, Zacharias has zealously carried out his temple duties, traveling from the Judean hill in Ein Kerem to the temple in Jerusalem. What greater honor was there in Israel than to be born of the priestly lineage of Aaron of the tribe of Levi and to serve Yahweh, the King of heaven and earth, on behalf of His chosen people Israel? According to his Jewish culture, he met all the requirements to be blessed with children. Their songs and psalms of King David chant, "Children are a heritage from God and blessed is the man who has his quiver full of them" (Psalm 127:5). Instead, he and his wife Elizabeth had for years, it appeared, marked with the curse of been barren. Gabriel, the angel, during the visitation, had proclaimed, "Your prayer has been heard." This was a long, forgotten prayer, one he and Elizabeth had prayed for over thirty-five years. Over and again, they had prayed in the days of their youths when their love was new and deeply forged in their hearts, and their passion burned deeply for each other; they had dreamed of having twelve children and hoped it would be eleven boys and a little girl. Like Jacob, the patriarch, as is written in their holy book, the Torah, Zacharias dreamed of raising priestly boys to take his place in the Levitical priesthood. He was an only child, and he wanted to have many children, and so did Elizabeth, who was from a clan of fruitful women.

The first year of marriage had rolled into ten years, and Elizabeth's womb remained silent and unyielding. Their love remained as strong as the day they first met. Zacharias's love for her was kindled from the first day he was introduced to the red-haired girl his mother had chosen for him. Elizabeth was star-struck from the first time she laid her eyes on the handsome, brown-eyed priest in training, who was ten years older, to whom she was betrothed. However, as the years passed into decades and the quietness in her womb remained the same, they would kiss and lay lovingly in each other arms at nights but refuse to raise the subject of a baby. They, having now resolved to leave their unrequited prayer request for a child outside the bedroom door, would then sleep in peaceful slumber, having surrendered their dreams of parenthood to God. They celebrated the birth of their family and neighbors' children and attended many bris and naming ceremonies. Zacharias officiated at many bar mitzvahs and bat mitzvahs of their families and their neighbors. They would welcome babies in the world and celebrated with others as the boys are initiated into manhood at the age of thirteen and the girls coming out to womanhood at the age of twelve but return to a quiet home and into the arms of each other. In Israel, the girls were usually married by fourteen years old. The men can sometimes wait until they were older, like in their early twenties or thirties. Zacharias was twenty-four years old, and Elizabeth was only fourteen years old when they were married. If the woman is fertile, she could start making healthy babies by the first year of marriage and continued to do so until her fertile years were over. However, there were few in Israel that it was said: "God has closed the womb." This was an omen, a curse for which a woman and her husband could appeal to God for mercy. Zacharias had long passed his seasons of prayers, petitions, and bargaining with God as he and his wife grew old. He has sweetly surrendered to quietness of his house and rather reveled in the undying attention of a loving, beautiful wife whom he treasured with all his heart. He was a priest and understood to humbly serve and trust his God, his Creator, and King as all-wise and all-powerful and also to love the wife of his youth.

Zacharias had at sometimes through the years believed that Elizabeth's childlessness was God's will whether he understood it or not. He has resigned himself to questioning it no further. He had even contemplated that he could be at fault and not his beautiful, beloved wife. He had long accepted a quote from Isaiah, the prophet, concerning Yahweh, "For my thoughts are not your thoughts, neither are your ways my ways, saith the LORD" (Isaiah 55:8). His thought during the years of expectation and hope was to often recall the story of Abraham and Sarah, their ancestors, the matriarch and patriarch of Israel, and Abraham's many conversations with God about His destiny purpose for his seed. Abraham was promised that his descendants would be like the stars of heaven and like the sand on the seashore in numbers. Abraham died and was buried, undoubtedly knowing that God would do according as He had promised. For Abraham, it was a waiting period of over twenty-five years after the promise of a son that Sarah, his ninety-year-old wife, finally became pregnant and gave birth to the promised child that God named Isaac, and he himself was a hundred-year-old man. Zacharias would often smile as he thought on how from the one promised son had grown a nation of millions just as God had promised. Israel had had its glory days when Joshua, the mighty warrior, or Samuel, the greatest prophet ever ruled, or when David and Solomon sat as kings on the throne of Israel. There were also some seasons of despair when the nation rejected the ways of God, but the nation had remained a nation unto Yahweh, who had made a promise to a man called Abraham and was faithful to keep the promise. Zacharias had never veered away from the sovereignty of God as Lord of his life and of Israel.

All her married years, Elizabeth kept herself busy with her gardens and her love for nature. She had a garden of herbs, a vegetable garden, and a flower garden. Her green thumbs had produced great harvests. She was also a skilled homemaker who fussed over every intricate detail of her house and was envied for having the most beautiful house in her village. Her songs of thanksgiving to Yahweh could be heard across the Judean mountain, and every now and again, a full soul ballad of life's elusive dreams would escape her lips and be carried on the wings of the wind to the distant ears of her neighbors. They had pitied her condition but loved her generosity and love for others. She was kind, sensitive, and very loving to the children of her neighbors. Her desperate yearning for children often found her volunteering to teach the children her songs, or she was found in the fields playing games of pass time with them. "How she loved the children," the neighbors whispered in pity. "Why has God forgotten her?" they signed. Not only did she love the children, but she was outgoing and generous to her neighbors with whom she shared the vegetable and herbs from her garden liberally. As the wife of the priest, her house was often filled with gifts from off the altars, but she was always giving back to her neighbors. She was dubbed as a woman of many virtues of which many of the women wished for but few possessed. Her loving, gentle, quiet, and unfeigned spirit was evident to all. Her state of barrenness did not make her soul bitter but turned her into a beautiful worshiper of Yahweh, with total surrender to His will. She had many lonely days and nights when her husband was called away to temple duties. She kept her mind and her hands busy by knitting and sewing children's clothing which she gave to women who sold in the Jerusalem market. She made extra money which she gave back for charitable outreaches both in Judea and also in Jerusalem. She took special care of herself with bath in perfumed oils she made from the herbs and flowers in her garden. She would always bathe and perfume herself, waited and relaxed for her special nights with her husband. She made special broth and cooked ancient herbs in the hope of increasing her fertility. She also gave herbs and ancient portions handed down to her husband. After years of praying, working, hoping, and dreaming, she has settled her heart to listen to the sound of laughter or the cries of the babies in the distant hills and had long since lost the pangs of the longing for a child to clutch her own breast and warm her heart and her arms. Soon Zacharias would be gone again. He had, for the first time in his ninety-eight years, chosen by lot to burn incense in the Holy Place; this is the second chamber of the temple, also called the Inner Court. It was a coveted position that comes only once in the lifetime of a priest because there were so many priests. They were chosen by a lottery, and whomever name was drawn got to serve in this coveted position. She was happy for him that his name was drawn to burn incense this rotation. To carry out this holy duty before God was considered the second highest temple duty. She had often heard him wishing to be chosen for this duty and was excited for him as he was for himself.

Zacharias could never have imagined that his life would be forever changed this fateful week in Jerusalem, burning incense in the Inner Court for the first time. As Zacharias traveled into Jerusalem that day, he pondered over his life and how he had graciously served as a priest as outlined in the Torah and handed down through the generations of the priesthood. Some of his fellow priests took bribes and stole from the temple offerings. He, like he had promised his father before him, that he would serve as it was outlined in the Torah and not fall into the sin of disobedience and rebellion against Yahweh. Over his ninety-eight years, he had watched many changes in the Talmud, as men, the high priests appointed regulated the laws and statutes of Yahweh. His father had taught him well. He remained a loyal servant of Yahweh in his own practices, even when apostasy and heresies pervert the priesthood. As he pondered on these things, he knew of a truth that in all his years of praying and serving temple duties, that not once had he gotten the smallest of indication of a promised child. He had never received a prophetic word or had any dream or visions of the hope of a child. Not once had any of the other priests ever given him a word of revelation from God about his childless status. He had cleaned the temple, sacrificed the animals, and placed them on the altar of sacrifice as a sweet incense to Yahweh. He has presented the babies of his nation to God and prayed the blessings over his kinsmen. The season of child baring with Elizabeth was now long over. The will of God for their lives has prevailed against their prayers, but he still felt blessed of God to having served in His people and His temple and looked forward at the end of each temple duty to going home to a beautiful woman. He would have no child to carry his name or to step into his role of priesthood and servant of most the high God, but as a faithful servant, he submitted to the perceived judgment of God. He had not murmured or complained against Yahweh. He humbly prayed that his heart would be without fault as he stood to serve at the Altar of Incense and that his offering would be pleasing and acceptable to God for His people. The path to Jerusalem was easy as his thoughts meandered through the chasm and peaks of his life. Three hours had passed quickly by, and he shifted his thoughts to the task ahead. For the next two weeks, he would be surrounded by the presbytery, and the common people with sweet incense in worship at the Altar of Incense there in the presence of his God.

As he entered the city through the Eastern Gate of Jerusalem and looked at the ancient walls of the city, so often ruined and re-built, and his thoughts once again reverted to its history. He had read the writings of the prophets and had long wondered what time the promised Messiah would come. The words of Isaiah echoed in his heart, "The voice of him that crieth in the wilderness, Prepare ye the way of the LORD, make straight in the desert a highway for our God" (Isaiah 40:3). He wondered if he would emerge on the scene and propel the nation into a new era of grace... Many in the nation had waited for the promised Messiah and the prophet who, like Elijah, would arise and proclaim the coming of the Messiah. This Messiah was perceived by some to be the one to restore the kingdom of Israel to its former glory as in the days of King David and King Solomon. But there was another school of thought like himself who believed the prophet Isaiah's words of prophecy that described him as the suffering lamb born to be a sacrifice to bring redemption to the whole world as Yahweh had promised to Abraham's seed. "And in thy seed shall all the nations of the earth be blessed; because thou hast obeyed my voice" (Genesis 22:18). So much had been lost since the return from Babylonian captivity up until this time; Israel has lost its glory, and it seems that Yahweh has forgotten His people. The glory days, as written, were long gone. It has been four hundred years post-Babylonian captivity since the last prophet Malachi had spoken, and Jerusalem was under siege as prophesied by Jeremiah:

> For, lo, I will call all the families of the king-
> doms of the north, saith the Lord; and they shall
> come, and they shall set every one his throne
> at the entering of the gates of Jerusalem, and
> against all the walls thereof round about, and
> against all the cities of Judah. And I will utter
> my judgments against them touching all their
> wickedness, who have forsaken me, and have
> burned incense unto other gods, and worshipped
> the works of their own hands.

Jeremiah 1:15-16

Five nations have had a monopoly of Israel, and now Rome, with its resident king, ruled over their nation. The sacrificial system was in order, and the priesthood functioned and celebrated the religious high holy days, but as the scribes have written, there seems to be a lack of luster and purity as to what once was. Israel had killed all their prophets, and no new prophet had arisen in Israel. It was not to Zacharias only that Yahweh has been silent. All Israel longed after the voice of God to rid them of their current resident oppressors, the Romans. There were frequent riots in the streets of the towns as many insurrectionists with lofty speeches and talks of revolution pumped the people to think. They spoke of Samson and David, who were great warriors, and their ancestors who fought valiantly and overcame great enemies with the help of Yahweh. The revolts were quickly squashed by the hardened bands of Roman soldiers who occupied the land and roamed around and oppressed anyone with the ideology of revolt or revenge. Fort Antonio was the largest structure to date in Jerusalem, and King Herod's castle had all the grandeur of the Romanesque style and influence. The area they occupied was like had a town within the town and a life separate from Jewish culture. No one dare defy the orders of the Ceasar. They in Israel were tired of the occupation and longed for a more quiet cultural way of living with sacredness and awe that once resonated in its history. They were tired of the taxation and cruelty of the Roman generals. The long walk to Jerusalem had given him time for quiet contemplation and reflection. His steps quickened as he took his final steps up the temple mount. He quickly turned his heart again to the task at hand. Today would be his epic moment in the history of his priesthood. He would perform his best service to God at the Altar of Incense.

The congregation was gathering in the Outer Court of the temple, waiting. It appeared to be a larger crowd than usual for the evening sacrifice. The cries of the animals mingled with the voices of the people in unison. As it was and for always would be until the Messiah comes, the animals would be offered up for the sins of the people of Israel. It was a covenant in writing, given by God to His people Israel. The cry and lament of the sheep chosen would be the last cry to be heard of the animal as it would be killed and burned on the altar of sacrifice to satisfy the requirement for the atonement of the sins of the people. The Outer Court was a place of business with God; it was where the shedding of the animal's blood and the desperate pleading of the people called out for the mercy of Yahweh. All the priests on duty for the evening sacrifice were present, along with the temple helpers. They gathered at the brazen basin and performed the ceremonial washing and were all dressed in their priestly garments. Each took their position as the solemn ceremony began. The sound of the shofar sounded long and hard as the large congregation stood at attention for the seriousness of the evening sacrifice for the sins of the nation. The evening and morning sacrifice were a continuous offering of the yearling lamb for the sins of the people. The animals had to be without blemish and that of total perfection. So pure was the holiness of God that for the people to even stand before him alive, a spotless lamb has to die twice daily to take the man's place in atonement for sin. This was the commandment of God that had been commanded of the nation since Moses led the nation out of Egypt thousands of years ago. The laws and statutes of the land concerning the way of living and religious life were given to Moses in his encounters with God in Mount Sinai and throughout the forty years while Israel lived in the wilderness. These laws were written down and memorized throughout the generations and therefore could not be forgotten. The lamb was slain, its blood drained out, and the animal was placed on the altar of sacrifice. The offering was burned in fire, and the aroma of burnt animal flesh was raised to the heavens. The loss of its life gave men the atonement needed to stand before God. As the flesh was consumed by the burning fire, it was now Zacharias's moment to perform the part of the ceremony he was selected for tonight.

This was a once-in-a-lifetime duty, and it was considered the second-highest duty of a priesthood. Cesar Augustus ruled in Rome, but it was Herod who was King of Judea. In order to promote his influence and favor in Israel, he had given large sums of money to repair and rebuild the temple. His gift had allowed the people to restore the temple to represent its present grandeur, but it could not be compared to the original temple of Solomon. The nation was extremely grateful for the finances, but King Herod took great pride in showing off his influence and prowess in the land under his jurisdiction. He now had power to choose the high priest, and this was never known in Israel. It was Yahweh who chose the first high priest, Aaron, and gave command that the priesthood should continue under his lineage. This was not the jurisdiction of a pagan king, for thee Jews had a system already ordained by God, but an apostate nation continues to fall further away from the ways of Yahweh; therefore, many breaches were made in the commandments of God as men continue to look to the favor of men and not of God. The temple itself was divided into three sections: the Outer Court, where the people gathered for worship and was the house of the brazen altar of sacrifice, and the brazen bason for ceremonial washing; then there was the Inner Court or the Holy Place which was the inner chamber where Zacharias would be working today burning incense at the Altar of Incense; the third room was called the Most Holy Place, which was separated from the Inner Court by beautiful, thick drapes of multiple colors and was only entered in once yearly by the high priest.

What awesome gratitude filled his heart as he collected some red, hot coal from the Altar of Sacrifice. He collected his oils and utensils, then entered the Holy Place to offer sweet incense to Yahweh. The priest and the people in the Outer Court were praying and chanting, filling the atmosphere with worship and the cries of their petitions. Here in the Holy Place, he would put the coals on the Altar of Incense, and he would pour perfumed oil over the coals of fire. The flames and would erupt, and the smoke would rise and fill the room, and the fragrance from the oil would be released, filling the rooms with the most beautiful aroma that was acceptable and pleasing to God. The people would be filled with gratitude and thanksgiving, would wait until the smoke had cleared, and the priest would return to the Outer Court to join the congregation. God had accepted their prayers in heaven, and their hearts would be merry and filled with gratitude. This was no ordinary ceremony; this was their lifestyle and the laws and precepts as given by God. Every tiny detail, from the recipe for making the sacred oil of incents, the furniture in the temple, the dress codes of the priest, the type of sacrifices to be offered, and the time the sacrifices were to be offered were given to Moses by God. The Levites, one of the twelve tribes of Israel, were selected by God to carry out all the works and ceremonies pertaining to God and the temple. The priests were from the direct lineage of Aaron and were selected and were assigned to temple duties, but all Levites were a part of the religious workforce.

The Inner Court or the Holy Place was home to the Altar of Incense, the Table of Shewbread, and the Menorah. Each item was strategically placed and offer symbolism and memorial to God, who has ordered and given every detail for their making and which was documented in the Torah. The Altar of Incense was overlaid with gold and was exactly made as God had given Moses the pattern. The Menorah was a seven-branch golden lampstand that was kept burning continuously, and much care had to be given that the light would never go out. The Table of Shewbread was a table on which twelve baked unleavened bread was placed before the Lord God and symbolic of the twelve tribes of Israel. One of the priestly duties was to make and replace the bread weakly, and once the bread was removed, it was to be eaten by the priests. Zacharias knew all the commandments and the laws and has served at all these temple duties with great joy. Behind brightly colored drapes was the Holy of Holies. Zacharias knew he would never be able to enter this room because only the high priest could enter in once yearly at Yom Kippur, which is the high holy day called the Day of Atonement. He knew in this room was the Ark of the Covenant of God, which was overlaid with gold and covered with the Mercy Seat, which was made of pure gold with two cherubim of gold on both ends of covering. The Ark contained Aaron's rod that budded, which represents life, a golden pot that contained manna which was the bread from heaven that the Israelites ate during the years of living in the wilderness, according to their history. It also contained the two stone tablets on which the ten commandments of God were originally written. These were part of the history of the nation of Israel after leaving Egypt into the promised land of Canaan. It was at the Mercy Seat that yearly the blood of a bull sacrificed was placed, and the fire of God would come down and receive the offering for the people's sins for the year. Yom Kippur, the Day of Atonement, was a high holy day when all Israel traveled to Jerusalem to worship and celebrate in a feast. It was one of the many feast days of celebration in Jerusalem. Zacharias loved his history, his culture, and his people, but above all, he loved his God. All his youth was spent in preparation to serve God and his people; he was born a Levite lineage of Aaron and born to serve God and his country. This was his identity. He was not young anymore, but finally, he was chosen to perform the second highest temple duty. He was honored to have gotten to serve. So little did he knew that his life was about to be changed, and a new chapter would begin for the world and for him and his sweet wife, Elizabeth.

Zacharias prepared the coals of fire on the Altar of Incense. He chanted, "Elohim, Adonai, receive the prayers, petitions, and worship of your people." He lifted the vial with the sweet oil and poured it over the blazing coals of fire on the altar. The flames arose, followed by a billow of smoke that filled the room, and was pouring out into the Outer Court. The glorious fragrance of the oil was released and filled the atmosphere. Zacharias closed his eyes in worship to Yahweh. With his head raised to heaven, he worshiped and gave thanksgiving to God. The experience was glorious, it was like a supernatural exchange had taken place, and God has kissed his face. His heart was filled with unimaginable joy. "Is this what they all experienced at the Altar Of Incense?" he wondered. Tears of joy flowed liberally down his face as the smoke began to clear the air. "Surely, God is in this place," he murmured. He opened his eyes and started to collect his utensils, he had to clean the altar, add oil to the lamp, and then return to the people, but he was not alone. Standing to the right side of the Altar of Incense was a tall and intimidating angel. Zacharias was startled; his eyes bulged from their sockets, his arms flew over his head, his mouth dropped opened widely, but no sound came out. Zacharias began shaking as the angel stood there observing him. "Be not afraid," he said in a booming voice. This was easy for him to say. Zacharias' hands went down to his sides, and his eyes returned to their normal size, but his whole body continued to vibrate, and he felt as if he was about to fall.

"Will I die today?" he wondered. "Did I not prepare myself fully to stand before my God?" While he contemplated these things, the angel put him at ease by saying, "Fear not, Zacharias, for thy prayer is heard, and thy wife, Elizabeth, shall bear thee a son, and thou shalt call his name John." Zacharias shook even more as the angel continued to deliver his message. "A baby?" he contemplated as the angel continued his message. "And thou shalt have joy and gladness, and many shall rejoice at his birth." Zacharias's anxiety began to rise; he could feel himself about to panic as his tremors increased, but this massive angel continued on and on with his speech, "For he shall be great in the sight of the Lord and shall drink neither wine nor strong drink and he shall be filled with the Holy Ghost even from his mother's womb." *What?* Zacharias thought. "This is unheard of in Israel; nobody is ever filled with the Holy Spirit in the womb." Despite Zacharias's nerves and thoughts, the angel continued to deliver the message he was given to deliver, "Many of the children in Israel shall he turn to the Lord their God. He shall go before him in the spirit and power of Elijah to turn the hearts of the father to the children and the disobedient to the wisdom of the just to make ready a people prepared for the Lord." Zacharias was dumbfounded by all that was delivered to him; he finally opened his mouth and asked, "Whereby shall I know this? For I am an old man, and my wife is well stricken in years." The angel looked at him and shook his head. "I am Gabriel," he boomed, "I stand in the presence of God, and I am sent to speak to you and shew thee these glad tidings." Zacharias shook even harder and falling to his knees, helpless. The angel went on to tell him that he would be dumb and would not speak until the birth of his baby because he doubted the word of God. The angel vanished, and Zacharias was left on the floor wondering about what had just happened to him. He tried talking to God, by no sound came from his mouth. He reflected on the words of the angel as he pulled himself off the floor. He was dumb. He could not believe he had such an incredible, amazing encounter and was doubtful and so afraid. He had an encounter that every priest would be envious of, but he had messed up, and now he must face the congregation without an explanation as to why he was delayed. The smoke had disappeared, the coals on the altar were cold, and he had lost his speech. He pulled himself together and took a deep breath, thinking how he would communicate to the people. The ceremony for the evening was over; he could not proclaim a blessing over them. He placed more oil in the Menorah, cleaned the altar, collected his oils and utensils, and exited the Holy Place.

The congregation waited anxiously for him. They were waiting for the blessings, but he waved at them to depart. They were puzzled; he had stayed longer than most priests did. The smoke had settled, but the sweet aroma of the incense still poignantly lingered in the air. Zacharias appeared a little shaken, and they wondered aloud if he had seen a vision. The people broke out in the blessings, "The Lord bless you and keep you; the Lord make His face to shine upon you, the Lord lift up His countenance upon you and give you His peace." Joy and gladness filled their hearts as they hugged each other and departed in the deepening shadows of the setting sun towards their homes. Zacharias washed and put away the utensil of the evening sacrifice. All the temple helpers for that day observed how quiet and subdued he appeared. He indicated to them that he could not speak and later wrote on a scroll to the High Priest that he would not be able to speak until God released him to do so. Like the people, they thought Zacharias had a vision and was covenanted to not speaks, or he was punished for some sins he had committed and appearing before God. Special requests, like a vow of silence from God, were not unheard of, but they knew it was not normal for the priest to come from the Holy Place and be unable to speak. When they met in the priest's quarters that evening for supper, the high priest was immediately given the scroll with the information that Zacharias had lost his speech in the Holy Place that day. It was his first day at the Altar of Incense. The decision was made to draw lot again and choose another priest to continue Zacharias's role of burning incense. Zacharias was reassigned to cleaning duties since he had six-day of service remaining. He was reassigned to the lowly duty of washing and keep the Altar of Sacrifice clean and the fire burning after both the morning and evening sacrifices. He was reassigned to the temple helper's duties, but he agreed with the nodding of his head, for he was dumb and could not serve otherwise. He also gave them no further explanation of what he had experienced in the temple that day.

These quiet times during cleaning gave Zacharias the needed time to go over in his head his encounter with the archangel Gabriel in the Inner Court. He wondered at the beauty and the splendor of his heavenly visitor. He relived the encounter of the fear and awe he had experienced during this heavenly visitation. Having pulled back the image of the angel in his mind, he contemplated that the angel must have stood at about ten feet tall. He was dressed in a white linen robe adorned with a golden girdle around his waist. His wingtip touched the roof of the room. On his head was a golden crown with blue and red jewels, and on his feet were golden slippers. He had a golden scroll in his hand from which he read. His face was like shining light, and his eyes were piercing blue lights; his voice was a deep, steady rumble. He wondered how the people outside the room did not hear the conversation. He shuddered just on remembering Gabriel's response when he doubted his word, "I am Gabriel that stands in the presence of God." His heart broke for thinking he had responded so poorly. Gabriel, one of the greatest archangels, had visited him, and all he could say was that he and Elizabeth were too old to have a baby. He remembered reading the scrolls of Daniel the prophet while in priesthood school and many times after, how this same Gabriel had visited Daniel and told him he was greatly beloved in heaven. He had spoken to Daniel about the rebuilding of the temple and of the coming of the Messiah. He had spoken to Daniel about the Prince, the Messiah, the death of the Messiah for the world, and the birth of a new era into the world. He had shown the whole future of Israel and of the world to Daniel, and Daniel had written it all down and deliver it to his people so they would know what is to be expected.

Yet here, Zacharias had panicked and doubted the messenger even though he knew all the prophecies. This was what a true priest lived for, to have a heavenly visitation and to hear the heart of God concerning humanity. He believed that if a man remained a holy and faithful servant of Yahweh, then prophecy could be fulfilled in their lives. He had the prophecy Isaiah and Daniel revealed to him that he would be a part of the unfolding of the great mystery, and he was so afraid he blurted out unbelief. He was told that God had chosen him to be a part of the realities of the prophecies of the scroll, and he was so scared that he blurted out unbelief. He could not share his encounter with the others; what would they think? Things have been so far removed from the old path of Moses, and the promises had appeared to be so long forgotten that masses of the people no longer believe. Most of the priests, including the high priest, go through the motions of temple duties, but they have lost their hope and faith in the promises of Yahweh. He had lost his voice in temple duty, and it did not move them to curiosity. Most have lost hope in the coming Messiah. The high priest was accepting bribes from the Romans and was involved in many sacrilegious acts in the name of God. It has become an office of regalia and a display of pomp and pride instead of giving glory to Yahweh. The king now appointed the high priest, and Yahweh and His ways were almost forgotten as they write their own creeds and interpretation of the laws. The Talmud was now referenced over the Torah, and none but himself seem to have a problem with this. No one spoke of the coming Messiah anymore, and life was hard, and their Roman taskmasters were very demanding. From the Babylonian captivity till now, nothing has been the same. Tyrannical heathen leaders have capitalized on the land, and the people have been marginalized and dominated in the land. Yahweh had remained silent, it appeared. They had forgotten that their ancestors spent four hundred thirty years in Egypt's slave camps before Yahweh brought them out as a mighty nation as destroying all of Egypt and the wicked Pharoh. He gave them the land of Canaan as He had promised to Abraham. Has God forgotten His people? The Roman occupation has become normative; they dominated more than half of the world. They were tough and sophisticated and left a heavy military presence in the lands they conquered. The oppressed people were reduced to a little more than slaves as the Romans' levy and fines practically took more than half the wealth of each family. It was Israel against Israel as the publicans who were appointed Jewish tax collectors oppressed his brother to satisfy Rome's demand. The forbidden things of Yahweh were mostly forgotten. No one knew who to trust anymore. Many traitors have grown in the nation, and people have gone to the Romans' prison for failing to pay taxes. Some were even crucified on the cross and suffered a cruel death for reports of sedition. For years, Zacharias had cried and prayed to Yahweh for the redemption of his nation, but when the answer came, he was unprepared for such a holy visitation. He would keep his encounter to himself for fear of being laughed at or questioned for hearsay. These high priests appointed by King Herod were tough and cruel and would rather appease Caesar than accept the revelation of God. He had doubted the angel and what did it get him but the loss of his speech. The high priest had questioned his encounter in the temple but was sufficed with what he wrote on a scroll stating that he was placed on an oat of silence. Zacharias was an old priest and was revered for his piety. The high priest respected his answer and reassign him to cleaning duties as a sign of mockery. In a few days, he would be released to return to the mountain of Judea. He could hardly wait to share this amazing encounter with Elizabeth. Remembering he could not speak, he decided to start writing out his encounter to his beloved Elizabeth. It would also be a good way to remember every detail, which he would share later with all who would love to hear of their miracle.

That night, following temple duty, Zacharias lit a candle, and on a small scroll, he began to pen a letter to Elizabeth.

The Prophet

My sweet precious rose, Elizabeth,

You cannot imagine what happened to me at the temple only a day ago. I am forced to write you this letter because this encounter has left me speechless. Forgive your husband for lacking in faith. The angel Gabriel said I would not talk again until his words were fulfilled. We are going to have a baby boy! The angel Gabriel said God had remembered our prayers and we were going to have a boy, and his name will be called John. My dear Liz, you will not believe this, but that which Daniel had spoken of and Isaiah and Zacharias the prophets will be fulfilled in part by our child. Isaiah had seen it and wrote, "The voice of one crying in the wilderness to prepare the way for the Lord." Daniel was visited by this same Gabriel and was foretold about the Messiah's coming. Now, my dear Elizabeth, God has sent this same Gabriel who stands in his presence to tell me of the Messiah coming and to tell us that we will get to be the parents of John who will be the prophet of the Messiah and a mighty prophet like unto the prophet Elijah of old. I am dumb, but I am dumbfounded. Who could have imagined that you and I would be trusted with such a great gift of the promised prophet of the Lord Messiah!

My dear Liz, it is a new day! A new season of God's grace and favor to all men, and I cannot wait to see it unfold. Am I nervous? Yes! I still am. I am still shaking in my sandals. Our son will be a Nazarite. We cannot cut his hair, and we have to be sure he only eats the foods on the list as given in the rules for Nazarites. I still think we are too old, but if God wants to entrust this precious gift into our hands, I say yes! Thousand times, yes! I know you will be elated. Finally, after all these years, God will remove your shame and give you a baby as written in prophecy that will usher the Messiah into the world. The long-awaited Messiah is coming, and I have been given the good news. I will leave it into your hands when you de-

cide to share the good news with the family neighbors, but as with all prophecy, it will come to pass as is told. There is much more to be told, and I will have to get you pregnant; I will write some more again once I get home.

With all my love,

Zacharias

As Zacharias folded the scroll and placed it in his satchel, he gave silent worship to God, who saw it fit to give him the amazing honor of fatherhood and the good news of the Messiah's coming. He could not help but wonder who the virgin would be that would be entrusted with the Lord's child, the Messiah. So long has Israel awaited the promise, and now in his own hearing was the majestic angel Gabriel with the proclamation that the time was now! God would come and live among men. Why was he chosen? He thought there were many more qualified priests than himself who may have been praying and waiting in Jerusalem for the fulfillment of such wonderful prophecies. Stories were told of all the virgin girls that the high priest and his council prepped each year in waiting for the coming Messiah. If they were chosen to be the parent of John, then he was sure the Messiah would not be given to the virgins chosen according to the high priest and his council's choosing. *Yahweh certainly chooses whom He will*, for not in a million years would Zacharias have thought he would have beheld and heard such wonder that he experienced a day ago in the temple. As he slept that night, he dreamed Elizabeth was walking and singing in the garden with her face turned up into the warm morning sunlight. Her face was alighted with joyous glow and a heart that was merry as a canary. Even at her age, she was still as beautiful to behold and to be desired as the day he first married her. He awoke from his dreams, longing to be with his wife. He smiled, thinking how carnal he was. During temple duty, they had to separate themselves from such thoughts until they return home. The dream had triggered his thought, and he knew within a few days he would be home with his beautiful Elizabeth, and for the first time in many years, he would have the good news that would make any barren woman in Israel happy. He prepared himself for temple duty; it was almost time for the morning sacrifice. He counted down the days with joy; soon, he would be home again.

Meanwhile, Elizabeth in Judea had risen early and was thinking of Zacharias. She knew he would be home before sunset tomorrow. This gave her heart a reason to be happy. Although temple duty took him away for only a week at a time at his age, yet she still missed him when he was away. Their neighbors had large families, and even when the children were grown, they sometimes lived close by, and their hands were then filled with their grandbabies. Elizabeth and Zacharias, being married for seventy-four years, were still by themselves. Since her family lived in Nazareth and she sometimes only sees them now when they traveled to Jerusalem on the feast days. Many years ago, when they were younger, they would make the trip to Nazareth for occasions like a bar mitzvah, bat mitzvah, bris, and naming ceremonies. She loved to visit her family, but it was a long trip from where they lived in Judea to Nazareth. Zacharias was an only child, and they have long buried his parents. They live in Judea for Zacharias's religious duties. This was where his father had lived, and this was where he would live out his life also. She decided to weed the rose garden today. As she opened the door of her cottage, she was bathing in the glorious warm sunlight. Her heart rose to the sweet energy, and without a thought, she was twirling and dancing and singing with her face to the sun. "I will bless the Lord at all times; His praise will always be in my mouth." It was a song of David and one she loved singing in the morning. A soft wind rustled in the treetops, and she lifted her head to the air in worship to God. She saw the smoke rising from the fireplaces of her neighbors and heard the stirring of the children as the cries of the babies and the high pitch sounds of the toddlers mingled on the wings of the wind. A new day has dawned; new mercies and melodies already lit the morning sky. The hills were a radiant green as they rise and fall under a clear blue sky. It was a morning like every other day, but somehow her heart held a special melody. Sometimes the mundane and sameness are apparent, yet each day brings its own joys or sorrows. This was a morning she felt a great melody of joy, and the birds could be heard echoing back their own songs of joyful sounds. Elizabeth could not imagine that her life would be changed in a day. She bent her knees to the ground and weeded around her rosebushes until the sun was in the mid sky. She had not taken her tea or morning meal, for so sweet was her communion and worship with her God that she has forgotten to eat.

Zacharias packed his sack and departed the priest holding. He has accomplished his priestly duties but not in the way he had expected to. However, his angelic encounter far outmatched any experience he had hope to make at the Altar of Incense. He got to serve only one day, and that was enough; he had met the mighty Gabriel, and who else had such a story to tell. It was some three and a half hours walk from the temple mount to where he lived in Ein Kerem. Usually, he would have left Jerusalem at noon after stopping in the market to buy supplies from the list Elizabeth had given him. He would usually get home by sunset, but with no speech to bargain in the market and with the good news he had to share, he could hardly wait to get home to Elizabeth. He was actually anxious to get home. He had so much bottled up inside and with no easy way to express it to her. This morning before his departure, he had a request in writing to the high priest that he would not return for temple duty until when his speech returned. The priests and temple helpers had at this time formed some theory that Zacharias got his speech taken because he appeared before God unworthily. He shrugged his shoulder on hearing the mocking and quiet laughter of the other priests and temple helpers this morning. He was dumb, not deaf, how insensitive he thought they were. The long-awaited promise of the Messiah and his prophet was locked up in his heart, and it would be fulfilled in God's own time. Who would believe his story? It would be his for the knowing and theirs for the believing. Zacharias had, however, determined in his heart that he would first share the story with his sweet Elizabeth because it was her story too. He sang in his heart, and his steps were swifter and lighter than usual. He had no provision to take home that day, but he decided he could return to the market another day. What he had to share with Elizabeth this day would be greater than any provision he could bring home from the Jerusalem market. He would not be delayed another day. He had kept this secret for seven days, and now he was bursting to share the good news with his Liz.

Up the mountain, he raced, this glorious Friday morning, vigorously waving his hands to the neighbors with greater enthusiasm than he, as a priest, had ever expressed. They could tell he was in a hurry, but no one knew he could not speak. Elizabeth was usually the happy, cheerful one who was always singing. Even though he was kind and gentle, he was more reserved in the expression of emotions. His neighbors look up to him for his kind wisdom and advice. They admire his patience and deep love for his childless wife. He always praised her openly for the love and care she gave him and her compassion for others. They respected him for his great sense of piety and loyalty to God. It could never be said that Zacharias was found brawling in the streets. He was a priest that stood completely loyal to the teachings of the Torah. He was a good example of the priesthood. He read for many hours and had an hour of prayer and personal quiet time with God each day. This morning he was unusually very happy, smiling from ear to ear, and even though he could not speak, he waved vigorously at his neighbors. They were curiously surprised to see him back home so early in the day. This was going to be a surprise for Elizabeth, who did not expect him home so soon.

He pondered on how her heart would rejoice that in the eternal heaven, God had not forgotten her and that she was going to be mother to the greatest prophet to ever live on earth. God has selected her, a woman of eighty-eight years old, whose dreams of having children had long vanished like the sand on the seashores in the forever-rushing tides. Gone were the days of her youth and the window for conception. He thought back on how often she had dreamed, hoped, and prayed each month as predictable as her circle was. Not once did she missed a period, nor once did a baby formed in her womb. He had listened to her complaints and lamented with her when the miracle did not happen. But once the normal flow of life dictates and her body started to change, Elizabeth had rested her dreams in the hand of God and graciously surrendered to time and seasons of her life. Zacharias opened the door to a startled Elizabeth, who was in the kitchen cooking. She rose to greet him and saw his face beaming like the glowing flames. She ran into his arms, where he held her for a long time in the deepest, warmest embrace. She pulled back for a while, for he still had not spoken a word to tell her why he was home so early. He hugged her again, pulling her against his chest, and planted multiple kisses on her face and arms. He was an amazing husband, and she had no reason to complain, but his actions, she thought, though exaggerated, were a sweet mixture of complete rapture. As old as she was, her body still responded to his intimate embrace. *Had her husband lost his mind in Jerusalem?* she pondered. She pulled back the second time and gently looked deep into his eyes and demanding an explanation.

Zacharias pulled back but this time put his finger to her lips and indicated holding on to arms for her to follow him. A puzzled Elizabeth followed her husband, wondering what strange behavior this was and her husband refusing to speak to her. He sat her down on the bench and sat next to her retrieving the scroll he had written a few nights earlier. He gave her the scroll, and she noticed he wiped tears from the corners of his eyes. Puzzled, she unrolled the scroll and saw the salutation "My dear Elizabeth." She looked up at him, startled, but he indicated for her to continue reading. Elizabeth dropped her eyes to the scroll and did not lift her head until she completed reading his letter. She dropped the scroll to the ground, turned and hugged her husband, and wept unashamedly. They were soft tears of joy, tears of fears, fears of the unknown, but also tears of dreams and prayers come true from a God who remembered. If God had said it, she believed it and received His words with all her heart. She had a million questions to ask, but her Zacharias was without his voice. Her priest was, for the first time, speechless. She wiped her tears, then broke out into peals of laughter of happiness. She arose from the bench, grabbed his arms, and broke forth into a dance of thanksgiving and worship to Yahweh for the words she had just read. She knew her age, but she knew her God. Like Sarah, the matriarch of their nation, she shouted, "God hath made me laugh so that all that hear will laugh with me." She hugged the handsome old man standing beside her as life and health surged through their bodies.

The night has been filled with beautiful intimacy and more passion than they had ever experienced in their youths. As Elizabeth arose up the next morning, many questions flooded her mind. She wondered if that was the night when God would have resurrected her ovaries and cause an egg to be released and the night when the seed of her husband would germinate that egg and the promised life of their prophet child would begin. She smiled with wonder, remembering the night of beauty and passion mingled with a word of hope from God. She gave thanks to God for having kept their love so deeply connected all these years that at the promise of a word from the angel, they could connect on such a level of intimacy to birth to life that which God had spoken.

She had no doubt that John was conceived. However, her mind went into a frazzle to determine what was the next step to be taken. Zacharias was still asleep as she rehearsed the possibilities in her head. He could not speak, so all her questions would only be answered in a timely fashion on a scroll. She knew that if she tried to share with her neighbors or families the miracle that they had been given, she would become the object and subject of their dinner table talks and laughter. An angelic visitation is not an everyday occurrence. There was the risk she ran of being mocked, "Elizabeth has gone mad." She would let wisdom speak for itself. She would allow John to grow until her words could no longer be questioned, and the proof would be in the bump in her belly, the kicking of a living child in her womb, and the increase in her breast size. She calculated that by five months, the baby would be filled with energy, and the joys would be her to share her testimony and Zacharias's encounter in the temple. Zacharias arose from his sleep smiling also; he bowed on his knees and prayed in silent thanksgiving. What a supernatural night it has been. He had mated with his wife like in their youth. It has been years since they have both felt so alive and passionate. He had no doubt that the miracle child had been conceived. Elizabeth busied herself in the kitchen, making his favorite bread and egg meal. As they sat down to eat, she asked him to tell her more of his encounter with the angel Gabriel. She handed him the scroll, and he promised to write again once the meal was done.

The Prophet

Zacharias wrote the description of the angel and the wonder of what he had experienced in the temple. He explained to her how his answer to the angel had led to his mouth been shut. He spoke of how the angel only identify himself by name when he rejected the word spoken and how he had made an excuse because of their age. He explained to Elizabeth the amazement of discovering that Gabriel, the same angel that appeared to the great prophet Daniel, had spoken to him, Zacharias. According to Gabriel, their baby would bring joy to all who witness this miracle. He was no ordinary child, he wrote but would be the prophet who would introduce the Messiah to the nation. He shared with Elizabeth that Israel's redemption was soon to come, and they have been written into the script on Yahweh's timeline. He wrote that John would not drink wine or anything from the vine. He promised that they would review the information written in the Torah on raising a Nazarite boy. He shared with her that the angel said he would operate in the power and spirit of the prophet Elijah. This was the Elijah who shut up the heaven and prevented it from raining for three years when Ahab and Jezebel, the wicked monarchs, transgressed the commandments of God, Yahweh, by allowing the image of the devil called Baal to be brought into the temple of God and had the nation to worship him. Elijah had called for a meeting of the king and the people on Mount Carmel for proof of the true God of Israel who would answer by fire. He stood as one prophet against four hundred prophets of Baal. Yahweh blocked all the prayers of the Baal prophets as they cried and prayed and cut themselves all that day, but their god did not answer. Elijah prayed in the evening at the time of the evening sacrifice, and God the true and only God, Yahweh, then sent fire from heaven and burned the altar of Elijah with the bull, the stones, and the water and declared himself God of Israel. The nation of Israel celebrated by killing all the four hundred prophets of Baal and returned to God with all their hearts. Zacharias shared with her that their son would be filled with the Holy Ghost from her womb and would go before the Lord Messiah and would turn the children of Israel back to God. He expressed gratitude that they were selected and that they would both be obedient in raising John as the angel has commanded. He rejoiced that the promised Messiah coming was eminent, and they were selected to be the parents of the prophet to the Lord. He warned her that he did not know how it would all unfold, but theirs would be the joy to watch daily for the promises spoken by the angel that came from the face of God and spoken of by the prophecies in the scrolls.

Elizabeth read her husband's writings and wept openly. She knew that God had always communicated to her nation by miraculous signs and wonders. Their nation, throughout its history, was always revered for having the Almighty God, Yahweh, who overcomes all the gods of the other nations of the earth during warfare and gives Israel amazing victory as long as they remain holy and loyal to His ways. He has only always asked that Israel obey His commandments and stay away from idols. The scrolls of the prophets and the Torah are filled with many stories of Abraham, Moses, Joshua, Barack, Deborah, Gideon, Sampson, King David, King Solomon, Nehemiah, Daniel, and how God used them for extraordinary purposes to maintain His presence in the world. Some have even spoken and prophesied of the coming Messiah, God's Son, who would be born to a virgin girl that would bring salvation to the whole world. Now the great Redeemer was coming in their lifetime, and that which they have anticipated and read about was now being birthed in the world, and they were getting to be a part of this story. They, who were once called childless and ridiculed for being barren, would forever have their names written in the archive of history, like Sarah and Abraham, Isaac and Rebecca, Rachel whose womb was closed but then brought forth the prince of Egypt Joseph. Hannah, whose barren womb was that which brought forth the powerful prophet Samuel who was one of the greatest leaders of the nation of Israel; she—Elizabeth, mother of John, the prophet of the Lord Messiah. The prayers, tears, pain, and the waiting of many decades were worth it all. She was now endowed with a great treasure that was not given by man and could not be taken away from her. This was her male child, the first to open the womb and forever blessed by God. This baby was named John the Prophet to the Lord Messiah.

Zacharias chose to become the scribe and journal the whole pregnancy experience with Elizabeth. She chuckled as she spoke out his decision aloud, "Yes! You will count the days and the weeks as we take this journey together." She laughed as he came over and hugged her shoulders; how she loved this silent priest, the daddy of her baby. It would be weeks before Elizabeth would know for sure if she was pregnant because, for her, the season of her monthly flow had long gone. In her very soul, she believed the miracle happened last night when Zacharias returned from Jerusalem. She shared with him the desire to keep the pregnancy private until after the fifth month so that they would not have to listen to the scoffers and doubters in their community. They did not want the words of others to attempt to abort their promise. Elizabeth wanted to remain happy and cheerful and to give her seed a beautiful environment in which to grow. Each morning she would place her hands on her abdomen and spoke lovingly and gently to her child, "You, John the Prophet of the Lord Messiah, shall neither drink wine nor any strong drink. You shall eat no dry grapes or anything from the vine. There shall be no razor placed on your head to shave it. The locks of the head of your hair shall grow on your head. You shall not touch anything dead, not even your mother or your father, for you, my son, is consecrated unto the Lord God." By the end of the first month, since Zacharias returned, Elizabeth began to sense changes in her body. She had developed a mild intolerance for spicy food and was craving healthy foods like nuts and fruits. It seemed like she was also more hungry than usual and was therefore eating more often. Her breasts have developed a tingling sensation and were starting to get bigger, but her waistline remained the same. Zacharias smiled each time he came into the room. His wife had a genuine glow, and although he knew nothing about pregnancies, he knew there was a new sense of aura and grace on his wife's face.

Since Zacharias knew carpentry, he decided to make an extra room on to their house for the baby. He had nine months and would only ask for help from his neighbors to put the roof on. He would also build the baby's bed, a chair, and an extra table that Elizabeth would need for the room. They have decided to spend the time quietly at home and only go out if it was necessary. Life in Judea continued as usual; the neighbors waved as they passed by, and a few women occasionally stopped by for small talks while Elizabeth tended the garden. Zacharias had ordered the material for the room, and they were dropped off in the yard. The neighbors observed Zacharias working by himself, adding the room to the house, and this was not normal in Israel. However, Elizabeth told them that it was a small prayer room and that Zacharias has taken a vow of silence for the year, and if he needed help from the men, he would request so later. He was a priest, so the explanation was accepted, so no one questioned his vow of silence. The words, however, got around the little hillside community, and they gave them their space for a time of consecration and piety. Their season of secrecy was a lot easier than they expected. In another four months, there would be enough proof in Elizabeth's womb to publicly announce that she was having a baby. Zacharias's steps appeared to have become stronger, Elizabeth observed as he moved up and around the yard in the building of the room. He accomplished so much in one day that Elizabeth had to remind him to rest and eat lunch with her. She watched him secretly, amazed at how his zest for life and stamina had increased. Her ninety-eight-year-old husband had the strength of a young man. He now walked with his shoulders squared and his stance purposefully. His eyes were intense and shining with happiness. She could imagine him singing as he hammered away. If only he was not dumb; she missed their times of conversation. He had assured her that this was not a permanent condition but a temporary one. The angel had told him his speech would only return after the baby was born. "A priest doubted," she murmured, thinking of the frailty of the human mind when face to face with and an angel of God. She wondered what she would have done if she had a visitation and chuckled when she thought about it. She would have fainted. Somehow, she understood her husband's hesitancy for who could imagine such a thing at such a time. They were certainly stricken in age. But because the stories of their history in the Torah were correct, then they were perfect. It was just the kind of thing their God has always done. He has done the impossible again so none could question His doings. This had His fingerprint on it, and no one could deny this miracle.

It was already two months, and Elizabeth had already gained some more weight. She was naturally gaining weight from all the extra food she was eating. Her abdomen appeared slightly swollen from its usually flat state. She was not a fat woman, but neither was she thin. She was usually told she had big bones. At the age of eighty-eight, she has taken care of herself and had always eaten well. She had no ailments or medical problems and was never sick, not even with a common cold. She used all her wonderful herbs from her garden and always prided herself for the special ability to make many herbal portions which usually make her neighbors feel better. She made special perfumed oils and lotions, which were good for the face and skin to promote health and youthfulness. She often traded her secrets with her neighbors in the name of beauty tips. She had her own morning and evening routine and prided herself in taking care of God's temple. This morning it was the sensation of a mild butterfly touch on her abdomen. She stood still in the place she was standing and lifted her skirt to look at her abdomen. She felt nothing but knew baby John was getting ready to kick. She remained busy in her garden, wanting to stay as active as she could until she was no longer able to do so. The secret of her heart was getting ready to burst open. She had not seen her family in Nazareth for a long while. She was closest to her sister Abigail and brother, Nathan. Their parents had already died, and some of her siblings were already dead also. Their children were married and had families of their own in Nazareth. There were also the children of her uncles and aunts on both sides of her parents' families. Like most Jewish families, they were too numerous to count. Zacharias was dumb, so they would not travel at this time. Moreover, as they had gotten older, they have resigned themselves to traveling to Jerusalem and home again. Her family came down for all the seven God-given feast festivals in Jerusalem, and it was always a wonderful time of fellowship and good food. However, there would be too much explaining to do at this early time in her pregnancy, and she wanted to cherish each moment of her pregnancy like golden nuggets treasured and tucked away for safety. Her unimaginable fortune of having a prophetic child, which was specially handpicked and delivered to her by the mighty angel Gabriel, was going to bring joy to many. When the baby was five months along, it would be a good time to bring the family and friends all together to celebrate with her and Zacharias. This time would also be enough time to overcome the superstitions and omen that many Jews also believed about the evil eye. She had no such fears but would rather not hear the negative comments of unbelievers in the miracle of Yahweh on their lives.

Zacharias had completed the sides of the room. The roof was

ready to be installed. His best friend, Benjamin, heard his friend was on a vow of silence and decided to visit anyway. No words were needed as he hugged his friend. Zacharias agreed and accepted his assistance with the roof placement. They worked together, and Benjamin tried to catch him up on his family stories. They have been best of friends for years, and he always came to Zacharias for advice on religious, social, and family issues, and he trusted the wisdom of his friend. He had twelve children who were already grown and move away from home and a sick wife for whom his daughters help him to care for. He shared the joy of been a grandpa and told him that the youngest boy had twin boys two months ago, now giving him thirteen grandsons. Zacharias nodded his head in happiness for his friend. His heart burned within him, and he wanted to share his own good news with his friend but had agreed with Elizabeth to wait until the fifth month. They would have to plan a special reveal party he thought, not knowing Elizabeth had the same idea. He was not worried because he knew the angel already told him that all who hear would rejoice with them. Elizabeth's pregnancy was going well. She was gaining weight, and he could now see the growth in her abdomen. Pregnancy was a great experience for Elizabeth. She was glowing like a twenty-year-old bride. He, himself, was feeling increased energy and stamina. They both possessed great joy. He was surprised at the speed with which he finished the room and was grateful for his friend Benjamin who came to help with the roof. He knew it had to be divine help from God for the gift He has given them to care for. In another four weeks, they would reveal the pregnancy to the world, and an idea for an announcement was already forming in his head. A dinner invitation to their closest family and friends would be the proper thing to do. He hugged his friend after dinner and indicated his gratitude for his help with the roof. Benjamin left for his home, not having the least inclination that his best friend was about to become a father at ninety-eight years old. As

48

soon as he left, he wrote on the scroll what his idea was for a revealing of the baby. He handed the scroll to Elizabeth, and as soon as she read it, she laughed and told him that it was the same inspiration she had when she was gardening that morning. They decided that she would make the guest list and write out a menu. His responsibility would be to build a booth for the feast and arrange the seating. They would need help with the cooking but knew trusted neighbors who would help them immediately.

Elizabeth did less gardening now that it was now mid-summer, and her abdomen was really beginning to grow. It was already four months, and John was beginning to dance around in her abdomen with joy, or she wondered if it was the Holy Ghost in the child. The baby was always dancing around in her, and this also made her happy. Zacharias had taken over much of the gardening. She kept herself busy making clothes for the baby. She did not have the unknown worries that other mothers had. She was having a boy, and his name was already picked out for her. She had ordered blue, yellow, and white materials and had already made swaddling clothes, diapers, and shirts for her son. She had made warm blankets for his bed and has already decorated his little room with pale yellow fabric mixed with a touch of blue. The yellow reminded her of the sunlight and the blue of the sky. It was a simple living style, but she was skilled with her hands finding a way to make her son's room cheerful, cozy, and warm. John would be due at the beginning of the winter, and she wanted to have everything ready. She had helped many women with the making of their baby's clothing and was knowledgeable on what she needed for her own baby. In four weeks, they would be having a dinner to reveal her pregnancy. She had written out an invitation and send it with a runner to Nazareth. She was only inviting her brother and sister and their families. The neighbors would be informed by word of mouth. The invitation had simply stated: "Hear ye! Hear ye! Zacharias and Elizabeth invite you to the diner on the last day of July and would like to introduce you to their big surprise." The neighbors were curious; they knew Zacharias was on a vow of silence. But what could this be? There was going to be a dinner party, so they were all excited to hear the surprise. He had added a room to their house, and now he was having a party. Their curious minds were bursting with many questions, but they were invited, so they would have to wait for the unfolding of the mystery. Elizabeth made new clothing for herself with which she hid her growing belly well. She arranged with a few of the ladies, and they gathered to discuss the menu for the dinner party. She got lots of support and would pay a special cook to make most of the food they need; she was expecting over two hundred guests. The local music band agreed to bring their instruments and play for free for their social dance. They just needed wine and a good meal. The community folks needed a little excitement in the hill and were more than willing to help at Elizabeth's request. They never suspected the surprise she had growing in her womb. Elizabeth chuckled as she imagined how surprised many of her neighbors were going to be and not to mention her family. Her dearest friend, Midge, had also been kept out of the secret; she just had to wait until she had the proof in her womb to show to her friend who had prayed and waited with her for years for the blessing of a baby. "Hallelujah! Let hallelujah rings to God our King," she sang as the last neighbor left her house. Midge was her confidante and best friend for years. She had missed chatting with Elizabeth since her husband has been on a vow of silence. Elizabeth loved her friend but knew if she told her before the time, she had decided she would have gone back on the promise she had made herself and Zacharias. Midge had commented on how she appeared to have gained some weight and on how her face was glowing and beautiful. Elizabeth laughed as she gabbed with her friend; she laughingly told her that her miracle facial creams were working for her. It was not easy to hide her true feelings from Midge, but the meeting for the day was to discuss the dinner party. Soon she would be able to share her joys with her best friend without doubts and questions about her age. She parted the curtain and entered her room. Zacharias was writing at the table. She told him of Midge's curious eyes and questions. She was happy that in four weeks, there would be the reveal, and the secrecy would be over. The baby moved in her abdomen, and she went over to Zacharias sitting at the desk so he could feel the joyful life in her womb.

Zacharias's hand pressed gently on the warm abdomen of his wife, where she had felt the baby moved. He felt the kicking sensation against her skin. Joy bubbled up in his soul. For the first time, he has felt and beheld the wonder of a life growing in his wife's womb. He wished he could talk to his baby, but he could not talk, so he prayed a silent prayer of protection over his prince and over the beautiful woman carrying his child. This was his own flesh and blood, his own seed, and a male child after his own kind. He knew that John would be more than a priest but a prophet to the Lord Messiah and a Nazarite unto God. He wondered at amazement that the child was already filled with the Holy Ghost and destined to walk out the life Yahweh had given him. In their culture, the Holy Ghost usually comes upon a person; usually, a Nazarite, a priest, a prophet, or a king who was assigned for special purposes, and when the assignment was completed, the Holy Ghost would be lifted until they were ready for another assignment. Some were anointed by prophets while others had angelic visitation, but Yahweh had always sent His Spirit to equip man to do exploits in the world filled with evil demons and devil-driven men. Most prophets in the Torah had this experience, but he could not find one that was filled with the Holy Ghost from his mother's womb. He had documented the full encounter in the temple and now daily documented anything significant with Elizabeth and the baby's growth. He measured her abdomen each month and marked the difference on a string with different colors of ink. His boy was growing rapidly, and the joy had not left his heart since the day he realized the child was conceived. He would certainly be a dad and father to the prophet of the Lord Messiah. As would be expected, John would have to complete his training as a priest like all Levite's boys from Aaron's lineage, but his son would be different. He was already assigned a prophet by God. He would start very early to teach him all the expectations of a Nazarite. He knew his son would have supernatural knowledge and power because the Spirit of God would be upon him throughout his lifetime, even from his mother's womb. He focused his thought on the present, remembering he had to get his friend Benjamin to get a few men to set up a booth and make some rough benches for the dinner party. He wrote a note to his friend, and Elizabeth would get one of the boys in the neighborhood to run it over to Benjamin's house. He was happy it was almost time to share their secret with the world. "I, Zacharias, after the priesthood order of Abia, a descendant of Aaron, of the tribe of Levi, father of John, a prophet unto the Lord Messiah."

Zacharias was amused; there was no one with the name John from the priesthood lineage of Aaron. It was certainly a new era, and the patterns were shifting. The name John was a very common name among Jewish boys of his days. The meaning of the name was "Jehovah has been gracious, has shown favor." Yes, indeed! God has been gracious to him and Elizabeth. He had to be sure no one would try to change his name or force tradition on them. He wanted to be obedient to God. For how often was a child given a name by God? His blessings were amazing, but he stopped and wondered who would carry the Messiah and to whom would his fatherhood be entrusted. *Would it be here in Judea or in Jerusalem itself?* He had the revelation of the words of the prophets; God did not need his help to unfold them. He had to focus on his task of raising the child God had entrusted to him. He felt a small tinge of pride but quickly dismissed it. He felt rather humbled that the Creator of the universe, Yahweh, had sent His mighty angel Gabriel to him, Zacharias, to reveal the unfolding of a new day and a new dispensation on the face of the earth. God will finally kiss the face of the earth and reconcile man unto himself through His Prince the Messiah. It was difficult not to be able to speak; he sometimes felt so useless in the plans concerning the celebration dinner. He had the greatest news to share, and as the father, he would not be the one to share it. God could have abandoned him for his doubt and chose someone else to have the prophet, John. If his dumbness is the only price he had to pay for being doubtful, then he would rather be dumb and still get to have his son. Did an old priest feel like dancing? This exactly was how Zacharias felt. He was an old man as happy as a young man when he first hears his wife has delivered a son.

Elizabeth was excited; it was only a week away, and this would be on the first day of the week. Her family had agreed to travel into Jerusalem from Nazareth. They would visit the temple for Sabbath, stay in an inn that night then travel on Sunday to be there on time for the dinner party. She was told that a party of twenty was coming from Nazareth. Her brother and sister would be coming with their spouses and about sixteen children and grandchildren. It was a short notice, so not everyone was able to come. She was happy that both her siblings were coming. She could only imagine the shock and joy that would be expressed that day. Gratitude mingled with thanksgiving, and great drops of tears fell from her eyes. She felt the baby stir within her. She hugged her swollen belly and sang a lullaby to her child. He kicked around a little harder, causing her to laugh. He was such a bundle of energy and joy. She now knew what it felt like to have a baby growing on the inside. Her energy level was still very high, but she was getting heavier each day, and it was now more difficult to bend over or sit on the ground. Zacharias encouraged her to rest more, and she did not have a choice. He had taken over the gardening, and she was still able to cook and take care of the house. Zacharias had Benjamin bought all the wine supplies for the dinner. Midge, her friend, would meet with the cook to go over the menu and pay her to buy and prepare the food. The food would then be delivered on the day and time of the dinner. Midge and her youngest daughter Rachel had volunteered to help with setting up the food and sharing.

The booth was ready; makeshift seats were already in place. An area was arranged with tables for the food and a place set up for the music men to sit. There was lots of room in the yard to accommodate everyone to dance and be happy. They anticipated a great celebration. She could only imagine how happy everyone would be after they announced the news of the baby.

They had both agreed that Zacharias would write the baby's announcement on a scroll and some detail of his encounter in the temple five months ago with the angel Gabriel. When everyone had gathered and seated, he, Zacharias, would stand up with Benjamin, who would welcome the guests and tell them why Zacharias cannot speak. Elizabeth would remain behind the door and only come out when Benjamin read from the scroll concerning her pregnancy. He had already written the speech, and Elizabeth had read it a couple of times and approved.

"My dear family and friends, it's with great joy and thankfulness that you are gathered here with us to be told that God had remembered my dear wife Elizabeth and me and has blessed us with a child. She is now five months pregnant, and we think this is the time to share this good news with you knowing you would not have believed it if we have told you earlier." At this point, Elizabeth would join him and Benjamin under the booth and give the people some time to react to the news of her pregnancy. Then Benjamin, if able to, would continue to read the writings on the scroll.

"Five months ago, while called away for temple duty, I was burning incense in the Holy Place as by lot I was chosen to do. An angel named Gabriel appeared to me and told me that God has heard my prayers and that Elizabeth was going to have a baby who would be a prophet to the Lord Messiah and he will turn the heart of Israel back to God. It is for this reason that we call you to celebrate with us because we that are old are chosen to be parents to this son who shall be a Nazarite unto God. God has looked on us and taken away our shame. He has favored us to reveal his mystery unto us and to include us into His story of redemption, which is also your story of redemption, so eat, drink, and be merry and give thanks to God on our behalf! For once again, God has visited Israel. Hallelujah!" he laid his pen down and walked out into the garden, where he lifted his hands in worship to Yahweh, who was faithful. He bowed on his knees in the dirt and worshiped the God who created him from dirt and chose to bless him with a son even in his old age.

Zacharias and Elizabeth had decided to wait until his circumcision, eight days after birth, to announce his name as was customary. A pregnant mother had to wait until they give birth for the reveal of the sex of their child, but Elizabeth and Zacharias already knew they were going to have a son because this was God's doing, and He had given them all the details of the child's life. Elizabeth wandered out into the yard and walked into her rose garden. Zacharias was doing a great job with the gardens. Thinking her hands are going to be busy with the baby, she could see that Zacharias was going to spend more time in these gardens than she would ever do again. John's entry into the world would change their lives forever and, even so, much more hers. She was going to be a mother. She imagined herself breastfeeding, singing, and rocking her son to sleep. She would spend weeks, months, years watching this baby grow; this was her son: her own son, the child of her old age. God had silenced her shame of barrenness and, even at her age, given her the grace to bear a child. This has not been seen in Mount Ein Kerem or in this generation. God had kissed her face and taken away her shame, and has made her heart glad in this season. The messianic era has arrived, and John, her son, would herald his day. She meandered through the twists and turns of her gardens, smelling the fragrance of the roses and the herbs, and a sweet song arose in her soul. She opened her mouth, and instead of a woeful ballad—it was a song of joyful adoration of Yahweh, her God, that has shown her great favor. Her voice was carried by the wind downhill, and her neighbors stopped to listen. This was no lamentation but the sound of a joyful heart. Soon the mountains and the valleys and all who would travel from Nazareth would rejoice, for she who was called barren was bringing forth life.

It was Sunday, and the big day was here. Sabbath celebration was quiet as it always was. They had lit the Menorah, and she did the blessings as she had always done since Zacharias became dumb. They both spent quiet times to themselves in prayer and deep contemplation. Both were praying that Sunday would be a good day without ill feelings and that all who came would experience the joy they have had since the visitation. She was up early Sunday morning to bake a few cakes she had left over to bake. The dinner was to start at 4:00 p.m., and the neighbors and the hired cook would start bringing in the food by 3:00 p.m. Everything was in its proper place for the dinner; she had gone over every detail, being the perfectionist that she was. The morning was cool, with a soft wind rustling in the trees. The sky was blue except for a few scattered clouds around the hillside. There was no indication of rain, and she hoped it stayed that way. A sense of serenity and peace hung in the air. She loved the mountain air and scenery and looked forward to the celebration of her pregnancy so long anticipated. Zacharias and Benjamin had done a great job preparing the yard and the booth. Midge, her daughter Rachel, and Benjamin would be coming by an hour early to help set up the food. Elizabeth had a special dress made that would accentuate her abdomen. The fabric was green and gold stripes with a golden waist band that pulled back the cloth above her abdomen, then flowing to the ground. The bodice was close-fitted with sleeves that were large and long. Her head regalia was a mixture of green and gold with a touch of orange. She added some pearl to her neck and ears, and she looked like a real Jewish princess. Zacharias would put on one of his newest robes, and he had bought a new tallit and yarmulke. For now, she would cover her body with multiple loose clothing as she helped with the preparation of the ground. It was 3:00 p.m.; the food had arrived, and with her friends, everything was arranged on the tables, and the list was checked off; everything was in abundance and in order. They were expecting over two hundred guests. Zacharias checked the wine and put out what they were going to use for the evening ceremony. There was a lot of food; the neighbors had been kind. There was gif filefish, chicken soup with matzo balls, brisket, roasted chicken, multiple potato dishes, kugel, latkes, apples, honey, bagels, cream cheese, lox, tomato slices, pickles, artichokes, challah, rugelach, chocolate babka, matzo covered in chocolate and sufganiyot, along with fresh fruits and vegetables. It was an abundance of food and fit for a king's table. Elizabeth was pleased with her neighbors and friends; the abundance of their gifts reflected the love that they were pouring out on her today.

Their guests were beginning to arrive—some tired from their

long travel. They waved them welcome, but those formal greetings would be done later. Elizabeth was so happy to see her siblings and their families, but she held back from embracing them until later. She, therefore, kept busy yelling at them as they took their donkeys to the back of the house and secured them. Enough water and basins were set up for them to freshen up, and the house was opened for anyone who needed to come in. The sound of chatter was already building up to a crescendo as people met and greeted in the yard. Elizabeth escaped the crowd and disappeared into the room, where she freshened up and got herself dressed. Zacharias had earlier return to dressed himself and has returned to Benjamin's side under the booth. Benjamin had just greeted his guests. His neighbors knew he was under a vow of silence but wondered why he was having a party and not breaking his silence. The families were a little surprised Benjamin was talking for him. Zachariah was never lost for words; he was usually well-spoken and often sought after for his wisdom, knowledge, and understanding of matters concerning Yahweh and life. Benjamin got their attention and requested that they settled down. He announced that he was speaking for his friend, who was still under a vow of silence and would be reading from the scroll all that he had written. The eyes of the women darted around, looking for Elizabeth; her sister Abigail still wondered how she had not gotten a hug and the usual kisses since she arrived. Elizabeth was still behind the curtains of her door, waiting for the reading of the letter to be started before making her appearance. Benjamin unrolled the scroll, not knowing what to expect. His friend, the priest, had not spoken for over five long months, so it has to be exceptionally good news. He read: "My dear family and friends, it is with great joy and thankfulness to Yahweh that you are gathered here with us today to be told that God has remembered my dear wife, Elizabeth, and me and has blessed us with a child." Benjamin dropped the scroll and looked at his friend with alarm and puzzlement. There was not a sound as a hush settled in the atmosphere. The crowd looked on completely in awe. Elizabeth emerged from the doorway beaming like a beautiful princess, and certainly, her abdomen was round and full. The people let out a glorious scream, hugging and kissing each other in complete amazement. The eyes of every woman were filled with tears. They rushed in unison to Elizabeth, gently touching her abdomen and planting kisses on her face. Some broke forth in thanking and praise to God, while the others were looking on in wonderment, still not believing what they were seeing. The musician broke out into beautiful rhapsodies of praise, and everyone started dancing around in circles and singing in the grass. No sweeter sound was ever heard in their yard before. The reason for such happiness was more than anyone could ever imagine. After all these years, a child would be born to the elderly priest and his wife. "It is a miracle!" they exploded. "God had come down and kissed their face." Yahweh has blessed this land! Benjamin turned and hugged his friend so hard and lifted him up from the ground in gladness. "My friend! My friend! God has remembered you. The men all came up hugging and kissing Zacharias while the women continued to gently hug and placed kisses on Elizabeth's cheeks. There was no question from the lips of anyone; the evidence was there. Elizabeth was pregnant. As the music settled, Benjamin encouraged the people to return to their seats. He had retrieved the scroll and quickly read the remainder of the address to himself. Hugging his friend again, he turned to the people and told them they needed to hear the rest of the story. Elizabeth returned and stood by her husband, who hugged her gently and pulled her to his side. Elizabeth could see the shock and wonderment on the faces of her family; they all appeared in a daze, wiping tears from their eyes. Abigail, her sister, was held up by her two oldest daughters. She was still overwhelmed by the content of the news. Everyone was still all hugging their own families tightly as they beheld a miracle in their eyes. Benjamin read again from the scroll, telling them about Zacharias angelic visitation in the temple five months ago and how Gabriel had told him that God has heard his prayer and was going to give him and Elizabeth a special child, who will be a Nazarite unto God and a prophet before the Lord Messiah. The people wept the more and hugged each other with joy. "God has remembered! God has remembered! Messiah will come, and His priest is here." Most of her neighbors were now grandmothers and great-grandmothers; her own siblings were great-grandparents, and she was going to be a mother for the first time at eighty-eight, and Zacharias was ninety-eight years old. They all knew that this was a miracle and a sign and a wonder from God that would not be soon forgotten. The sound of the coming Messiah resonated in the air, and the people were glad and celebrated. Benjamin explained that Zacharias would be on a vow of silence until the baby was born. They clapped and cheered and received the news with great gladness. Benjamin prayed, giving thanks to God, who has blessed Judea with great news of a prophet and the news of the coming Messiah by sending His great angel Gabriel to His faithful priest Zacharias. He blessed the food and invited the people to eat, drink, and be merry.

Midge, her friend, and her sister Abigail gathered Elizabeth in their arms and gently lead her back into the house. They gently sat her on a chair and begged for further explanation. The women were bursting with excitement and wanted to hear the full story. The baby kicked inside her womb, and Elizabeth placed their hands on her abdomen as his tiny feet pumped into her side. "He is a very strong boy," Abigail exclaimed with joy. They wanted to know if she was feeling well and what the experience was for her seeing she was already so old. They complemented her skin and her dress and just hugged and loved her. Elizabeth tried to explain to them Zacharias's account in the temple five months ago. She was frequently interrupted as the other ladies came in the house to greet her, and the teen and the children looked in and stared at her with twinkles in their eyes. They did not all understand the extent of the miracle and the odds of this happening, but the adults were excited, and so were they because they all loved Aunt Elizabeth and the priest. The teens started a traditional dance, the boys with boys, and girls with girls going around and around in a circle as they go chapping their hands and moving in rhythm to the music they loved. As the music picked up its rhythm, other guests shared out the food, bottles of wines were open, and they all ate, drank, danced, and celebrated the miracle of life. Surly, God has visited this Judean hill community, and they got to be a part of it. The was no doubt in anyone's mind as to how special this baby was going to be. It is only in the Torah that they read of such wonderful miracles given to women who were once barren and of old age. Every child like Isaac, Joseph, Samson, and Samuel was given to women who suffered the curse of barrenness and bore men who became great leaders in Israel. They heard the words of Benjamin, "He is a Nazarite unto God and a prophet to Lord Messiah." Every rabbi in Israel taught on the promised Messiah, as written in Torah, and everyone in Israel has at some time heard of the coming Messiah, as written in the scrolls of the prophets. Even King David, in some of his prophetic songs, prophesied of the coming Messiah. The prophets Isaiah, Jeremiah, Micah, Zachariah, and Daniel all wrote and gave a vivid description of the coming Messiah. Prophet Isaiah was the most prolific in his writing of the coming Messiah. He gave a subtle but detailed description of a virgin having a child after the great apostasy and exile of the nation of Israel. Some in Israel believed the Messiah would be a sacrificial lamb to bring true redemption to the earth, and others believed he was to become a king like unto David and free them from all their enemies, their current resident Roman oppressors. They thought on these things as they ate and danced into the evening and celebrated the great miracle that they got to be a part of that day. Elizabeth smiled in wonder as she recollected the words spoken by Gabriel the angel to her husband, "You will have joy and gladness; many shall rejoice at his birth." She could already see the joy on the faces of her family and friends.

As the night shadow fell, the party came to an end. Everyone helped to clean up the grounds and collected the leftover food. Now that they knew Elizabeth was pregnant, she was forbidden to help with cleaning up. The ladies all agreed she needed to have a young maiden working with her for the next four months into the pregnancy and when the baby arrived. All the mothers fussed over her telling her what to be expected and what not to do. She now had a whole community of girls fussing over her. The local midwife Huldah was also at the party and already gave Elizabeth strict instructions to fetch her immediately if she had any pain or health issues. Elizabeth smiled; she loved all the attention she was finally getting but reassured them that she had never felt stronger and knew that the baby was going to do well. Her best friend, Midge, suggested that her youngest daughter Rachel, who was still unmarried, would become her daily helper and would then stay with her a few months after the baby arrived. They all agreed this would allow Elizabeth to rest for the birth of her baby and get some help during the first few months after the baby's birth. They all thought she needed it because she was not a young mother.

The shadows deepened as the sun completely disappeared under the hill. The families slowly bade goodbye and dispersed down the hills to their home with joyful sounds of a miracle in Judea. Elizabeth's family from Nazareth would camp out under the booth with their sleeping bags. They were used to camping out when taking a long trip to Jerusalem. The stars began to shine out of a thick blanket of the darkness of the night sky. Millions of stars could be seen by the children lying on the ground; the magic of the night has fallen.

Part 1: The Angel Has Come

The sky was cloudless, and the moon began to rise up and appeared to have come and rested over Elizabeth's house, and the children cheered as they crawled into their sleeping bags and welcomed the moonlight snuggles and kisses. Laughing and filled with joy, Elizabeth made her way inside the house with Abigail and Midge. She showed them the baby's room, and they were both delighted with her work. The ladies expressed no disappointment in just finding out about the pregnancy; they both knew that if Elizabeth had uttered such a thing to them before she was visibly pregnant, they would have said she was gone mad. They have been all young and have prayed and waited for Elizabeth to get a child, and now they were all old and grey-haired, and Elizabeth was pregnant. They have never seen or heard this in all Israel, not in their lifetime. But Torah has taught them God still moves among his beloved people. They marvel at the great wisdom that was visible in the decision she and Zacharias had made not to share until she was well advanced in the pregnancy. She also revealed to them that the real reason Zacharias was made dumb was that he doubted the words of the angel. They had shared that he was on a vow of silence with the neighbors to ward off suspicions and gossips. Abigail wanted to know what Elizabeth wanted her to do for her. She could not return to Nazareth without knowing her sister would be properly taken care of. Midge assured her she would take care of Elizabeth, so it was safe for her to return to Nazareth with her family. Elizabeth agreed that Midge's daughter would only come if she needed her in the last two months of pregnancy but would need the help after the baby was born. Elizabeth insisted that when Abigail and Nathan return to Nazareth with their children. They, however, were to keep her pregnancy among themselves until after the birth of the baby. They would prefer that the questions and gossip be kept at a minimum since this was a great blessing from God. They would then invite all the aunts, uncles, and cousins down for the circumcision and naming of the baby. Abigail knew it would be hard; this was too good a news to keep, but she also knew the skepticism that this would draw. With that been said, the women then sat and had girl talks of baby joys. Abigail would sleep in the bed with her sister tonight and arise in the morning to travel home with her heart filled with wonder and joy.

Meanwhile, Zacharias, Nathan, and Benjamin sat out in the moonlight and watched the children crawled into their blankets. The two men talked while Zacharias nodded his head in agreement with what they were saying. They discussed the prophecy of Isaiah and what that would now mean for their nation Israel. They had all hoped and prayed that they would live to see the fulfillment of such marvelous things but knew they would possibly be dead and buried before the prophecies would all be fulfilled, but tonight they rejoiced because the messianic era was emerging and the glory of God would touch the earth. They were all men in their eighties and nineties and would forever treasure in their hearts what they heard and have seen tonight. They were made to behold and participate in this miracle of the prophet of the Messiah. They were the carriers of the story now written in their hearts. They could not help but to also contemplate on who the parents of the Messiah would be and that he would be born in Bethlehem of Judea also as was prophesied. The men were all faithful followers of Yahweh's word and the prophecies of old. Despite the apostasy that the nation was in, there were a few good men, the torch bearers, the ones who carried the light and fire of Yahweh, who remained loyal and faithful to the ways of the Torah. "Time will reveal," Benjamin stated. Zacharias, his friend Benjamin, and brother-in-law Nathan were all believers in the Messiah coming as the suffering lamb as written in the scroll of Isaiah the prophet. There was the other belief that the Messiah would become like unto King David and would rule in Jerusalem and rid them of all their oppressors. The men talked deep into the night, pouring over the Torah and all they had learned through the years in their history. Much effort has been taken to preserve the scrolls during the Babylonian captivity period, and it was greatly believed that Yahweh, Himself, had protected the sacred writings. They all went to sleep pouring over in their hearts what was happening and spoken of in Israel this night. Zacharias did not wish to reveal his encounter in the temple or to share his wife's pregnancy any further with the priestly order in Jerusalem. It would be kept among their family and friend here in Ein Kerem because he believed the prophecy would fulfill itself without having others speak against it or having him and Elizabeth be called into question by the high priest on such matters. There was so much corruption in the temple. He preferred for the child to be raised in obscurity until the Holy Spirit chose to release him and propel him into ministry. He knew it would be another thirty years before the prophecy would be completely fulfilled when John became a man. Zacharias, like his friends, knew he would also be dead before John became the great prophet as foretold by the angel. But he would go to his grave a happy old man knowing that God has given him a son and that God would also fulfill His every word concerning John. The years of doubting himself as a priest and servant of Yahweh were now laid to rest. In the realms of heaven, Yahweh had determined a beautiful gift for him in his book of destiny and had sent Gabriel the archangel on special delivery. He knew that he was also greatly loved in heaven, and here he repented and confessed the doubts he had carried for years. There on the ground in the silence of his heart, he vowed to God that with all the energy he had left, he would raise John according to His orders. He prayed that Elizabeth would also live many years in health to enjoy the God-given fruit of her womb. His birth would always remain a wonder and amazement to their village. It appeared he had just fallen asleep when he was awoken to bustling footsteps in the yard. It was still dark, but Nathan and Abigail would be traveling back with the children to Nazareth. Under the fading moonlight, they have gathered their belongings and placed them on the donkeys to start the long journey home. Elizabeth was also up. Abigail had slept in her bed while Midge and her daughter Rachel slept in the guest room. After long hugs and joyful tears, they waved goodbye, and the traveling party started downhill before dawn. They would cover a good three hours into Jerusalem before the sun came up. Benjamin joined the group from Nazareth; he would go on home since he was also awake. Elizabeth and Zacharias returned to bed when, finally, the last beast disappeared down the hill and out of their sight. Midge and Rachel were soundly asleep and had not awoken to the excitement of the morning. He gently led his wife back to bed, and they both collapsed in bed, still tired from all the excitement of the previous evening. No words need to be spoken; they were still overwhelmed and very happy from yesterday's gathering. Finally, they were able to share their story with the ones they love. Everyone and even more family would join them for his circumcision and naming party eight days after the baby's birth. But now they could rest, and Elizabeth would accomplish her months of pregnancy in joy and rest under the watchful eyes of her neighbors. While they slept, Midge and Rachel awoke and made their trip home, still amazed about the events of the evening. Rachel had many questions for her mother. She was excited about her mother's best friend's pregnancy but was amazed by her age and what they have spoken about. This is the first miracle she had experienced.

The sun was high in the sky when Elizabeth awoke to John dancing around in her abdomen. His movement had startled her out of her sleep. She had dreamed a rather disturbing dream. In the dream, she saw a rough man in a coat of camel's hair been brought before Herod the King. The king was displeased with the man and had ordered him to be put in prison. The dream puzzled her as she reflected on it, but she soon dismissed it. She was not a dreamer, and the kick in her abdomen had awoken her. Later if she remembered, she would discuss her dream with Zacharias. She smiled down at her abdomen and started praying a blessing over her son. She got up and walked to the kitchen. From the window, she could see Zacharias in the vegetable garden. She wondered how she had gotten so blessed, for she had the best husband a woman could ever ask for. He had always believed in their love, and when they thought God had forgotten them, he had blessed them with a special anointed boy child. She smiled about the events of yesterday and how happy everyone was with the surprise pregnancy reveal. She noticed many gold coins were left on the table from the previous night. She laughed out loudly, recollecting how Benjamin's jaws had drop opened and the scroll falling to the ground and the cries of the women in unison on hearing of the pregnancy. There was not one eye that was without tears of joy, including her own. She cried because everyone else was crying. She saw that her sister Abigail almost fainted, and two of her daughters had to grab her, and then they all ended up laughing and crying together. All the hugs and kisses were warm and sweet as she received their love and attention. She made breakfast and called Zacharias to the table. She talked about the success of their dinner and the joys of the celebration. Zacharias nodded his head in agreement. Elizabeth shared her thankfulness for Benjamin and Midge, and all they have done to help them celebrate, and how accepting everyone was of her pregnancy. They thank God for such faithful friends who promised to be there for them to see them through the birth of their child. They both agree to rest for today and clean up tomorrow. They would just enjoy each other's company today and spend some quiet time with God. Zacharias took out his scroll. He had so much he wanted to write down today. Elizabeth had chosen to knit a cap and sweater for the baby and did so relaxing comfortably in the rocker in his room. She had brown and white wool she would use. She could hardly wait to count down the months until the baby arrived. How little did she know that she would be getting a beautiful surprise within the next month?

Zacharias was up early this eventful day and was busy in the garden. He knew Elizabeth was too big and was no longer able to care for the garden. So with joy, he labored in her garden. It was a good place to think. With the arrival of his son and the promised Messiah, his thoughts were filled with deeps sadness on the state of his beloved land. The land was split into pieces as to what the men believed. There had been all these rival sects that projected that they knew what was best for Israel; there were the Pharisees, Sadducees, Zealots, Essenes, and the Herodians. This had led to much debating and arguments on who was wrong or right and who had the interest of the land of Israel at heart. The Zealots were a radical extremist group who desired nothing but to see the land be rid of Roman tyranny. They wanted to cease power and crown one among themselves as king of Israel. The problem with this group was that they did not make Yahweh a part of their solution. They were self-made bigots who were even resistant to the laws of God. They would plot and plan treason to burn the garrison and cause great disturbance in Jerusalem. They spoke boldly of the coming Messiah but were renegade in their actions and disrupters of the peace in the land. This led to their blood spilling in the land and pulling out the wrath of the Roman on the law-abiding citizen. Many that led this group of insurrectionists find themselves usually in the Roman garrison or crucified on the hill of Golgotha. The Essenes, on the other hand, were on the side of peace and piety. They had separated themselves in the desert of Judea and live in the caves by the Dead Sea. They pride themselves in the practice of religious consecration. They deemed themselves to be the keepers of history and spent their lives rewriting the sacred scrolls. These men chose to live in piety, poverty, and some lived even in celibacy, none of which was a requirement of Yahweh's law. However, they were driven by these practices, which they believed made them feel closer to God. Their religious pursuit drew many to their group, but their way of living was the most isolated, and that made them the least popular of the sects. The Sadducees were the rich socialites, and they fought for political and religious influence in the land. They participated in the Sanhedrin council and tried to balance the Jewish lifestyle with the regulation of the Roman monarchy. They were a proud group who did not believe in life after death but lived their lives to their fullest potential of political and social influence. They were, however, foolish to think that they did not have an eternal soul and had lost the essence of who Yahweh truly was. The Pharisees were from a school of thought that naturally propel them into religious life. They prided themselves in studying the laws of Moses and raised up the rabbinical schools in an effort to preserve the religious history and Jewish culture, but they were proud and astute, ever teaching the laws but never themselves living out the commands of Yahweh. The Greek's influence in philosophy in the world had crossed over into the Jewish lifestyle, and the Pharisees were considered the thinkers and shakers of the land. They held on to religious autonomy and debated everyone, and largely ran the temple. The majority of Israel seemed to favor the Pharisees because of their love for the laws of Moses. The Herodians, on the other hand, were the sect of Jews who were somehow deemed the most loyal to King Herod. There was the belief that these men even considered Herod to be the messiah. Their dream and purpose were to somehow return Israel to a true theocracy. Zacharias thought they were gone mad. Herod had no Jewish lineage, his ancestors were Edomites, and Herod the Great had converted to Judaism to impress the people of the land of Rome had made him the king of Israel. *How far removed could a people be?* he wondered. They have forgotten the commands of Yahweh.

However, as a nation, they have all manage to unify in the worship of Yahweh and continued with the sacrificial system as commanded by Moses. Zachariah himself did not have allegiance to any one sect. His priestly lineage had survived since the return of Zerubbabel to Jerusalem to rebuild the temple as was prophesied by Zechariah. His great-grandfather had survived the Babylonian captivity and had returned to Jerusalem, where they rebuilt the temple walls and restarted temple services. Zacharias upheld the law of Moses, read and memorized large portions of the Torah and studied the prophets, and knew that his nation was a long way from the consecration Yahweh desired. In his own heart, his land was still in a state of apostasy as each was drawn away by his own belief and interpretation of the law thereof. Where the nation once stood as twelve tribes, the sons of one man Jacob, the son of Isaac, the Son of Abraham, was now divided into sects and philosophical thinkers, making a mockery of Yahweh's commands. Many of his fellow men in priesthood were driven by greed, power, and political ambitions, and he had no desire for such. There deep in his contemplation in the garden, he heard the voice of a woman behind him. He turned around, and to his amazement, there alighting from a donkey was a young maiden. He squinted his eyes to adjust to the sun, and as he looked closely, he recognized Mary, who was Elizabeth's aunt's granddaughter. It makes her Elizabeth's second cousin. He arose from the ground, smiled, and rushed over to her, taking the beast and indicating for her to go indoors. He wondered if she had traveled to Judea all by herself from Nazareth. She was fourteen years old and still unmarried. They had told Abigail that Midge's daughter, Rachel, would be helping Elizabeth if she needed help. *Why had they sent this girl so far away from home?* He took the donkey to the backyard, gave it water, and tied it near the grass where it could graze. He would give the women some time to greet and talk.

Part 1: The Angel Has Come

Mary hurried to the door with her sack across her shoulder. It has been a long way from Nazareth to Judea, and she had traveled for two days with a group of women coming into Jerusalem market to sell their summer produce. Her mother and father had agreed for her to visit her cousin Elizabeth when she told them she had a dream that her Aunt Elizabeth was pregnant with a baby and was inviting her to come. She could not relay to her parents and did not want to tell them about her angelic encounter four days ago. She was going to be the mother of the promised Messiah, and she had agreed with the angel who called himself Gabriel. He was the one who told her that Cousin Elizabeth was pregnant with a child in her old age. Somehow, she believed the angel wanted her to visit Elizabeth since he told her about her pregnancy. Her parents, Anne and Joachim, agreed on her visiting Elizabeth. They, themselves, had heard the whispering of a possible pregnant Elizabeth. Her niece Abigail and her brother Nathan with their families had made a trip to Judea a month ago for some dinner to which no one else in Nazareth was invited. Since they returned, there have been rumors about the miraculous pregnancy of their cousin Elizabeth. If she was pregnant as Mary had dreamed, then when she returned, the rumors would be confirmed. Mary had been engaged to Joseph, and in three months, it would be a year, and they could plan an extravagant wedding, and Mary would move to live with Joseph and consummate the marriage. These were her final free months as a single woman. They agreed she could spend three months in Judea and return in time for her own wedding. They arranged for her to travel by the donkey with a band of women traveling down to the Jerusalem market. They would have to stopover in Samaria, then travel on the next day to Jerusalem where she would then make the journey by herself to the hills of Judea into Ein Kerem, where her cousin Elizabeth lived. This journey would be safe because many traveled back and from Judea to Jerusalem. Mary was happy they had both agreed without any further questions. The only times she had seen this elderly couple was during her visits to Jerusalem during the feast days. She always had great respect and love for the elderly priest and his wife, cousin Elizabeth. She would politely greet them and would listen in to the conversations with Elizabeth and the older ladies. However, here on their doorstep, her little head was filled with the thought of what she would tell Joseph when she returned pregnant to Nazareth. She was hoping and praying that Elizabeth, with her miracle pregnancy, could help her young cousin understand the gift that has been given to her. She believed God would give her some answer for Joseph. He was a mature man thirty-five years older than herself, but he was kind, gentle, and generous, and she loved him. What would she tell her beloved Joseph? She was hoping her wise older cousin and her husband, the priest, would have some real answers for her concerning this mysterious child she should carry. She knocked timidly on the door, hailing, "Hello, cousin Elizabeth!"

Elizabeth heard the voice of the maiden, and the baby started jumping in her womb with more excitement than Elizabeth had ever experienced. Elizabeth opened her door to a frightened girl, her young cousin Mary from Nazareth. "Mary!" she cried, extending her arm and welcomed her in her arms. While they hugged, Zacharias had returned from tending to the donkey. He watched the ladies with the intent to listen to their conversation. As they shifted out of the embrace, he beheld as Elizabeth's eyes closed, head lifted, and a glow like a radiance was on her face as if she was enraptured. She began speaking in a high beautiful sing-song voice like the priests would do in worship. Zacharias came to the door and beheld in amazement the words his wife uttered. He knew the Holy Spirit had come upon her. He stood in awe at her utterances as she stood transfixed, holding on to Mary's outstretched hands.

Blessed art thou among women, and blessed is the fruit of thy womb. And whence is this to me, that the mother of my Lord should come to me? For, lo, as soon as the voice of thy salutation sounded in mine ears, the babe leaped in my womb for joy. And blessed is she that believed: for there shall be a performance of those things which were told her from the Lord.

Luke 1:42-45

Zacharias looked on in amazement. *Elizabeth was a prophetess!* And before he could fathom what he Just heard, Mary's head rose to the air, her face shone in greater brilliance, with her eyes closed. He realized that the Holy Spirit was now coming upon Mary; he knew something significant was taking place. He fell to his knees in quiet worship as Mary prophesied.

My soul doth magnify the Lord, And my spirit hath rejoiced in God my Saviour. For he hath regarded the low estate of his handmaiden: for, behold, from henceforth all generations shall call me blessed. For he that is mighty hath done to me great things; and holy is his name. And his mercy is on them that fear him from generation to generation. He hath shewed strength with his arm; he hath scattered the proud in the imagination of their hearts. He hath put down the mighty from their seats, and exalted them of low degree. He hath filled the hungry with good things; and the rich he hath sent empty away. He hath helped his servant Israel, in remembrance of his mercy; As he spake to our fathers, to Abraham, and to his seed for ever.

Luke 1:46-55

The Prophet

Zacharias wept, tears coming down his face unchecked. Here, in his house, two unlearned women of humble beginnings had prophesied of things too amazing to behold. His Elizabeth has affirmed that there was to be a conception; she was the mother of the Lord if she believed the words spoken to her. The girl Mary, the Holy Spirit came upon her and overshadowed her, and she had prophesied of the seed of the child in her own womb. He was beholding a miracle of eternal significance, and all heaven must have stood at attention. It was the unfolding of the conception of the Messiah. How could two women with no prior experience in prophecy speak so eloquently the mysteries of God? And Mary—she was so young. Her words were of prophecy foretold and now fulfilled in her, the virgin birth of the Messiah. He has never seen it this way in Israel, and he had gotten to be an eyewitness of it all. The Holy Spirit lifted, and both women looked at each other in amazement at what they had just experienced in the house. Zacharias came over and looked at the women in amazement. He was dumb and could not speak but have heard the utterances of God concerning his child. The women hugged and cried. Zacharias went over, putting his arms over their shoulders, silently saying amen and blessings on them both. The double blessing of the new era had started in his house. He would document it all and watch its unfolding. This was the story of the next dispensation, and he had to be sure to keep an accurate record. The ladies collected themselves as Elizabeth led Mary to the table. She had come a long way and; she must be tired and hungry. She would serve lunch, and then Mary could tell them her story. Mary marveled at how important Elizabeth was to her child's coming into the world. She had never had the Holy Spirit come upon her before, but the angel had told her that this would happen to her, and the moment was so precious, she Mary was chosen and was carrying the Lord Messiah. This was one experience and the one with the angelic visitation that she would never forget as long as she lived. She knew then that she was pregnant with the child she would name Jesus according to the angel's words. She could not wait to share her encounter with the angel with them. She, a nervous little girl from Nazareth, was going to be the mother of the long-awaited Messiah of Israel. How she needed Zacharias and Elizabeth's words of wisdom at this time in her life; What did she know about a holy mandate? This was an edict from Yahweh, from the throne room of Heaven. If anyone knew the prophecies, it would be the priest Zacharias. Zacharias was excited as a priest should be in the light of the revelations he had just witnessed. He wanted to hear her story and to document it also on a scroll. They had chicken soup with bread, some dates, and dry figs. Mary's fears were abated, she knew that her cousin and her husband were a part of her story, but she did not know how the baby in Elizabeth's womb recognized her as the Lord's mother. There was so much to be told, and so much she needed to know. The task seemed like an impossible one, but God, Yahweh, who was faithful, would unfold this story He had begun to write in her life. As the angel had told her, "For with God nothing shall be impossible," she had come to a house of rest and revelation. Yahweh had led her here.

They finished their lunch, and Elizabeth cleaned up the kitchen and rejoined them at the table. Zacharias was busy writing on a scroll. Mary had noticed he has not once spoken to her. She had become a little nervous and hoped he would welcome her into their home. Elizabeth appeared to have read Mary's thought because, on returning to the table, she immediately told her that Zacharias was on a vow of silence. She said she would explain it to her later but now wanted her to share what brought her here from Nazareth, and they would discuss the meaning of that which happened to them both today. She also pointed to her abdomen and smiled, stating, "We will also talk about this baby and your baby." Elizabeth could not have imagined that the Messiah would also be born to her family. The unwed virgin daughter of her cousin was going to be the mother of the Messiah so fulfilling the prophecy of Isaiah. "Therefore the Lord himself will give you sign; Behold, a virgin shall conceive, and bear a son, and shall call his name Immanuel" (Isaiah 7:14). She, Elizabeth, was mother to the prophet who would go forth to announce the Messiah. The blend was perfectly supernatural; only a God so full of surprises and wonders could have orchestrated this beautiful unfolding in their home. *He never ceased to amaze his children who love him*, Zacharias thought as Elizabeth gestured for Mary to begin her story. Mary was not afraid anymore. All the way from Nazareth, she had prayed to God for her story to have some meaning to her cousin Elizabeth and her husband, and now she knew they understood. The angel had highlighted cousin Elizabeth to her, and she was driven as by divine prompting to take the journey. Mary started by stating how she was alone at home four days ago, praying with her eyes closed and lifted up to heaven. She was to be married to Joseph in three months, and she was anxious because he was so much older than her, and she was praying to be a good wife for Joseph and that he would be the good husband for her. She then said she immediately sensed a presence in the room. She opened her eyes, and there, to her surprise, was the most magnificent angel just standing there. She startled, falling face down to the floor, when the voice of the angel boomed, "Hail, thou that art highly favoured, the Lord is with thee: blessed art thou among women" (Luke 1:28). Mary described how troubled she was and wondered what kind of salutation this was. The angel then said, "Fear not, Mary!" She slowly lifted herself from the floor and sat up looking awed, struck at this majestic messenger as he continued speaking,

> Thou has found favour with God. And, behold,
> thou shalt conceive in thy womb, and bring forth

> a son, and shalt call his name Jesus. He shall be
> great, and shall be called the Son of the Highest:
> and the Lord God shall give unto him the throne
> of his father David: And he shall reign over the
> house of Jacob for ever; and of his kingdom
> there shall be no end.

Luke 1:30-33

Frightened, she looked up at him, asking, "How shall this be seeing, I know not a man?" (Luke 1:34) She was shocked at his answer.

> And the angel answered and said unto her, The
> Holy Ghost shall come upon thee, and the power
> of the Highest shall overshadow thee: therefore
> also that holy thing which shall be born of thee
> shall be called the Son of God.

Luke 1:35

He then mentioned Elizabeth's name, and Mary was amazed at his words.

> And, behold, thy cousin Elisabeth, she hath also
> conceived a son in her old age: and this is the
> sixth month with her, who was called barren.
> For with God nothing shall be impossible.

Luke 1:36-37

Mary went on to describe how overwhelmed she was by the presence of this heavenly visitor but how she also felt a holy boldness that propelled her to cry out, "Behold the handmaid of the Lord, be it unto me according to thy word" (Luke 1:38). She then said the angel disappeared, and she was left there shaking on the floor and think-ing about what she had just experienced. She described the angel in every detail, and Zacharias knew it was the same angel Gabriel that had visited him six months earlier. Mary continued to speak, "It was this encounter that had made me asked my parents to travel down and see you." She had told her parents that she had a dream that her cousin Elizabeth was going to have a baby in her old age. They had heard rumors of the pregnancy themselves and were curious to know if this was true, so they willingly agreed that Mary would come and spend her last three months before marriage in Judea with her cousin Elizabeth and Zacharias. "I did not know how to share the angelic encounter with them," Mary said. There was so much she did not even understand and needed a voice of wisdom to help her understand and navigate the holy responsibility that was given to her. Elizabeth held her hands across the table and comforted and consoled her, assuring her that God had divinely led her to them to guide her in the journey to mother of God.

Zacharias wept openly. Tears of joy poured not only from his eyes but from his heart. The Messiah was here; the long-awaited Messiah was sitting at his table in the womb of a little maiden who was not even old enough to know and understand all the prophecies and the words written in the Torah that talks of the eternal king who would sit on the throne of David, the seed of Abraham, Isaac and Jacob, the one who would crush the serpent's head. This girl was so bold that she agreed to take on the role of mother to the Messiah without so much as a full understanding of her assignment. She was a courageous girl who took the road all by herself, carrying a secret so dear that she did not even dare to share with her own parents. This girl was so wise that she understood she needed priestly guidance. The Virgin Mary—the mother of the son of God—was a guest in his house and was cousin to his wife, Elizabeth. He scribbled on the scroll that Elizabeth should give her an unfolding of their story of her pregnancy and about the beloved child, John, she was carrying and how their baby would be linked to her baby in life. Elizabeth, too, was crying. Mary watched them both in wonderment. They knew something that she did not know and would be able to answer the questions in her heart. Elizabeth then composed herself, and sitting across from Mary; she shared with Mary how that six months ago, the same angel she described, whose name was Gabriel, had visited Zacharias while he burned incense in the temple at Jerusalem. The angel had told Zacharias that Elizabeth would conceive and have a son and that he should be called John. She shared how Zacharias doubted because of their age, and because of that, the angel told him that he would be dumb and would not speak until after the baby was born. Mary looked at Zacharias, who shook his head in humility. He was the priest, but he doubted the words of the angel. Mary re-assured him that she did the same thing; she had asked, "How could this be, I am but a virgin?" Mary voiced that her cousin's husband, Zacharias, received a punishment because he was an experienced priest who knew and waited for these prophecies to be fulfilled and should have known better than doubting the messenger from God. She, on the other hand, was a young and inexperienced girl and was therefore given an explanation by the angel. Zacharias nodded at her wisdom, and he could sense why God would have chosen her to be the mother of His child. Elizabeth continued to explain to her that after Zacharias came home that day, they were intimate that night, and that was the night the baby was miraculously conceived. She also told Mary that God has given her baby the name John and that John should be raised a Nazarite and would be the prophet who would go before Her son, Jesus Messiah, to prepare the way for His ministry to unfold. She told her that according to the angel, John would make the hearts of the people ready to receive her son, Jesus. Mary sat amazed as Elizabeth recounted their story. Now it was her time to cry, and large tears flowed unabashedly down her face. They were all in a true moment of the epic unfolding of God's love and grace on humanity. God has divinely planned out the path for her life, and here were the wise people, her own cousins, who would instruct her on the journey that she was beginning to take as the mother of the Messiah. Zacharias wrote on the scroll that he would be praying and would write out some instructions for her on how to proceed from here on. Mary shared with them that she would stay with them for three months because she wanted to grow in the knowledge of the prophecy concerning her child and would know how to handle her pregnancy when she got home. The sun had set in the sky; they have spoken for a long time. There was much more to be said, but Elizabeth suggested that Mary must be tired and needed to rest after such a long trip and all the excitement for the day. She would sleep in the guest bedroom on the opposite side of the kitchen. Mary did not want to sleep but withdrew to the quiet of the room, where she rehearsed the events of the day. She laid there immersed in her thought of Yahweh on how He completely planned the dawning of a completely new era unlike any other and for placing her in the helm and bringing it all together by allowing her to take this journey into Judea to see her second cousin, Elizabeth. How could she have understood such amazing things? Unless she had made the journey to find the older woman that the angel had given reference to. She reflected on home and imagined how stunned her own parents would be had they been eye-witnesses to today's happenings. If she could conclude anything from today, it was that the ways of God are deep mysteries that He unveils on His own time-line. She was glad that even though it was a complicated mystery unfolding before her eyes, she was glad to be a part of it and wanted to see its unraveling and celebrate each moment with heartfelt joy. As she pondered on these things, a warmth engulfed her abdomen. She placed her hands on her lower abdomen and silently whispered,

Part 1: The Angel Has Come

"I, Mary, daughter of Joachim and Anne, mother of the Messiah." She laid there and reveled in the gift that she has been given to her. Elizabeth also rose from the table to make dinner because it was already late in the evening. As she cooked the dinner, adding spices and vegetables to the stew, she allowed the aroma to mesmerize her, and she praised God for making an old woman's heart glad. They later all ate in silence that night, each immersed in his own thoughts and savoring the meal and the events of the day. A tired Mary bade good night and retired to bed after taking a bath. Zacharias made himself comfortable at the writing desk. He still had much to write of the days happening before turning out the lights.

Elizabeth also went to bed. She just realized how tired she really felt. It had been a long and exciting day, and there was so much to think about and give worship to God for. Zacharias indicated he would come to bed later; he wanted to write an account of today's happening in the scroll he had started. Elizabeth laid there meditating on the events of the day. Mary was young; she was fourteen years old, the same age she was when she got married to Zacharias. She had said she was engaged to be married to Joseph, who was her fifty-year-old cousin. In another three months, it would be a year since her father agreed to give her to Joseph. She prayed, holding her own abdomen, that Mary would be granted great wisdom to carry the Lord Messiah and that Joseph would still be willing to marry her when he discovered she was pregnant. She expressed to God her confidence in His all-knowing, all-wise ways and that it was far more beautiful and beyond what man could even imagine. Who could have orchestrated the convergence of mother of the Messiah and mother of John, his prophet? Yet here, in this quiet Judean community with only them three as eyewitnesses, the divine Creator has chosen to bring the prophecies foretold into a living reality. The greatest moment that Israel had waited for was happening in her house and not in Jerusalem, not in the high priest's house but in the home of a humble elderly priest, living on the top of the hill in Ein Kerem. Her little cousin Mary traveled all the way from Nazareth to Judea to merge the promises and confirm the prophecies foretold. Elizabeth fell into a restful sleep following the leaping and dancing of the child in her womb. Tomorrow was another day when she would have time to talk with the young maiden concerning scriptures and the prophecies and to see her understanding of what the baby she was carrying symbolized. God had chosen to send her to them, so both Zacharias and Elizabeth understood that they had much to teach her before she returned to Nazareth. Zacharias could not speak, so most of the instructions would be left to her. She was happy that all these years, as the wife of a priest, she had paid attention to the conversations of her husband. He was displeased with the political climate and the compromise of the Levitical priesthood. He often vented that they had a form of godliness but denied the power and authority of God. The nation, in general, now ran on man-made ideologies, and that the Talmud now took over from the commandments of Yahweh as written by Moses in the Torah. The Roman's infiltration brought further decay to the concept of separation from the heathen nations. Zacharias usually complained that the Babylonian, Persian, and Hellenistic ideology had infiltrated their culture since the post captivity era; Israel has been mesmerized by the idol nations around them and has tried to pattern their philosophy like unto those nations and had forgotten the ways of God. Yahweh had been silent for more than four hundred years, and since the prophet Malachi, there have been no prophetic voices in the streets of Jerusalem. Rome had grown in influence and power for over nine hundred years. Their history spoke of these things, and former prophets had written of the destruction and rebuilding of Jerusalem and of the Messiah coming to restore all things. Elizabeth smiled in amazement as she recollected her prophetic experience earlier that day. She had never prophesied before. She wondered about the word of her husband concerning her baby, "He shall be filled with the Holy Ghost from his mother's womb." The baby had danced in her with such intensity, and then that bubble up in her own soul and those words of affirmation spoken to Mary. Goose pimples rippled all over her arms and neck. She had experienced the Holy Spirit's presence, and He had spoken through her words that Mary needed to hear to embrace her call for the conception of the Lord's child. Then the Holy Spirit fell upon Mary as she broke forth with exuberance and exaltation to God, embracing the gift she was given to bless the world. Elizabeth fell asleep and dreamed she was floating on a perfectly white cloud, drifting into nothing but the glory of God.

Zacharias sat at the table, writing into the night the events of the day. He knew another part of the puzzle had all come together today, and he wanted to be sure to document it all. He knew they were also chosen to guide Mary into her journey of motherhood of the prophesied Messiah. He knew that no prophecy needs interpretation and that what God had given to man by an angel cannot be refuted. Even the psalms of David spoke expressly of God, magnifying his words above his own name. Mary will now have to learn to keep the word of God in her heart and allow God to fulfill what He had promised. Zacharias clearly understood that man is the conduit through which God will operate in the world, but man once he says yes to God's will, he would have to trust God daily for the details of his plan. He knew that God would not put the young maiden's life in danger. He had sent her to them to build up her faith, so when she goes back home, she will go back with the confidence that she can birth the promise of God into reality and that God would be with her all the way. *She is young and pregnant, so she will need lots of courage*, he contemplated. He believed that Joseph would be a good man for her. He was one of her older cousins, so he prayed that God would also visit him and share his plan for the Lord's child, the Messiah, with him. He knew that in his Jewish culture, the headship of the home and the family falls on the father. Every boy needs a strong man to teach and guide him through the journey to manhood. These boys are on special assignments, and God had a perfect plan. For the first time in earth's history since the fall of man in the Garden of Eden, God will walk with man again, and he, Zacharias, in his old age, had beheld the unfolding of the words spoken to him by the angel Gabriel. He would comfort the maiden and give strength to her by having Elizabeth pouring over the prophecies of the Messiah with her. He now knew why he had always shared in-depth the prophecies with his beloved wife because now she will be his voice to the maiden. He dipped his pen in ink and wrote on his scroll:

The wonder of wonders has occurred here today, and all who hear and receive it will be glad. The Lord's child, the Messiah, is conceived this day. From this day forward, things will never be the same. God has visited man again, and this time in the flesh, and there is hope for all humanity. Instead of this violence and bloodshed, there will be a new day of peace, joy, and hope; a new order in Jerusalem for the Messiah has come.

Overcome with exhaustion, he arose and went to bed. He drifted off into a peaceful sleep and dreamed of playing in the garden with a ruddy cheek boy, his son John. Mary rose from her sleep and was at first affrightened by her surroundings. She then remembered that she was not in Nazareth but in the house of cousins Elizabeth and Zacharias in Judea. Although they were her family, she knew very little information about them personally. She lived in Nazareth all her life and knew her second cousins Abigail and Nathaniel and their family very well, along with all her mother's family. Three times yearly, when they all came down to Jerusalem for the major feast days, then they would meet and greet and eat together with cousins

Part 1: The Angel Has Come

Elizabeth and priest Zacharias as a family. Cousin Zacharias was revered as a priest, but she knew they had no children of their own, and her cousin Elizabeth was pitied by her mother and grandmother, who often called her the barren wife of the priest. This was not done in meanness but in irony as if to say God is sometimes not fair. Mary, being the last child of her parents' twelve children, was to be married off, then her parents would be free to enjoy their freedom. Mary had always felt close to God. She paid attention to the Torah being read each Sabbath and to the songs and psalms being sung in the synagogue. Her father would often read from the Torah of the stories told of Israel's journey from Egypt to Canaan, and the many battles fought. She had learned to read the scrolls from her youth, and, as the youngest, she was not was hassled with house chores. The boys often got formal training, but everyone had to learn Torah because it contains their way of living. Her father often recounted the story of Esther during the week of Purim, and she learned about Esther and her boldness to go and stand before King Ahasuerus even though she was not called, having taken the risk that she could be put to death. She, however, found favor with the King she loved, and her life and the lives of all the people of Israel living in Medo-Persian provinces were spared from the wicked plot of Haman, who desired to have all Jews killed. She had always hoped in her heart that she would be bold if called to defend her people and her God. Now, here, she was entrusted with the Son of God; what greater service was there than that to carry Messiah into the world. Yesterday was so surreal, and the beautiful memories flashed through her brain. She remembered that light that came upon her and seemed to flow through her whole being. She remembered hearing herself utter beautiful words of things she knew not of. "For he that is mighty hath done to me great things; and holy is his name. And his mercy is on them that fear him from generation to generation" (Luke 1:49-50). She had always enjoyed listening to the priest giving the

85

reading in the synagogue and in the temple when she went down to Jerusalem. Yesterday she sounded like another person, and that sensation of light, a pure light that flooded her, still made her shudder. She laid there in the bed, flooded with happiness and unafraid. She had felt the holiness of Yahweh and found in herself great strength to take on the world and was happy to be alive and to be chosen to be mother to the Lord's child. Her thoughts reverted to her parents, *What will my mother and father think of me when they discover that I am pregnant?* She knew that without a revelation from God, they would be heartbroken, thinking that she had brought shame to their names by been wanton. The community could call for her stoning if Joseph denied the child was his. She knew she would have to convince him of her encounter with the angel and that he would believe in her, and then they would get married immediately on her return. She prayed that God would also visit Joseph and that he would say yes, like she did, and become the father to the Lord's child. She knew she would need to have a plan before she returned to Nazareth, but somehow, she knew that God would protect His own Child. She loved Joseph, and she knew he loved her, so in her heart, she hoped that this would not change the love between them but make their bond even stronger. But she knew now that her earthly mission was to now carry this male child who would become the world changer, Savior, and Redeemer of Israel and of the whole world. She would be forever written in the history books for her youth and bravery like Esther. She stumbled out of bed and worshiped and praised Yahweh that had chosen her and blessed her above all other girls in her village and in all of Israel. The aroma of freshly baked bread drifted into the room and filled her nostrils. Her guts rumbled, and she arose up with a smile. "Jesus needed nutrients," she murmured. On getting up, she washed and wandered into the kitchen, smiling. Sitting at the table was her cousin Elizabeth and Zacharias, who greeted her smiling. Elizabeth welcomed her to the table and arose to get some breakfast on the table for her. Mary could see clearly this morning how very pregnant Elizabeth was. She would, from now on, help her with the cleaning and cooking and give her time to rest and relax for the rest of her pregnancy.

Breakfast was eaten in silence as both ladies savored the food. They needed to eat to make their babies grow. The young Mary was thin, with a beautifully framed face and perfect slate-colored eyes; Elizabeth observed. Her hair was covered, but she could not help but see the strands of golden-colored hair spilling from under her head covering. She was beautiful to look upon. She knew any man would be pleased to call her his wife. She would teach her to knit and sew clothing for her baby if she did not have these skills. They would sit in the rose garden and talk today while Zacharias continued to harvest the herbs and vegetables in the other gardens. Elizabeth had seen her cousin Mary with her family at the temple in Jerusalem and the few times she had traveled back to bar mitzvahs or the circumcision of babies in Nazareth when she was a little girl. It has been a few years since she had not traveled down to Nazareth and had missed Mary's coming-out party a year ago. She and Zacharias have resigned themselves to going no further than Jerusalem these days. They had grown old, and a whole new generation had grown up who hardly knew who they were. Since they did not have children nor grandchildren, they had never had any grand ceremonies or parties in their home. However, as a culture, they kept up with the birth and death of each family member, and accurate records were always kept. She knew Mary was the last child of her second cousin, Anna, who was blessed with twelve children: six boys and six girls. Now God had fused their lives together by the babies in their wombs. It was a three-generational gap between her and the maiden. But God was joining the generations together, the old and the young, the prophet and the Messiah, long woven in the tapestry of their history and mysteriously written in their scrolls. They went and sat under an oak tree across from the rose garden; here, they could delight themselves in the many colors and fragrances of the garden. Elizabeth's hands had been very good at cross-pollination, and this had resulted in a large variety of colors in her rose garden. She had even nicknamed it her "rainbow rose garden." The fragrances were unbelievably heavenly. The birds sang in the trees, while butterflies and bees seem to meander in and out of the rosebuds collecting nectars. A light wind sprang up, rustling in the top of the trees, seemingly whispering their names. Here sat an old woman and a young girl sharing their souls. Mary was the first to break the silence as she questioned Elizabeth about the state of her health and the challenges of carrying the baby at her age. Elizabeth laughed lightly, holding on to her baby, who was dancing around again in her abdomen. She gathered Mary's hands and placed them gently over the place on her abdomen where her little boy danced. She reassured Mary that God had given her grace and would finish what He started. He is a God that gives strength to weak things to accomplish His will and purpose. She shared her years of pain and the scorn she endured when she and Zacharias thought God had forgotten them and how their prayers only stopped when her season of child-bearing waned and died. Their dreams they had surrendered to God and lavished their love on God and on each other. Never in a million lifetime had she imagined that God would have kissed their faces and given them a child in this old age. Elizabeth shared with her that her health had been perfect and her energy level unstoppable. It was like she had supernatural help to carry the child. She had to agree with the prophets that God makes the impossible possible. "He made a highway in the wilderness and rivers in the desert places," she murmured, quoting the prophet Isaiah (Isaiah 43:19). Elizabeth shared her wisdom with Mary. If it was of a natural occurrence, it would not be called a miracle, but when God shows up in the earth realm, He does that which is contrary to the natural to make a statement that cannot be denied. She shared with Mary that her purpose was of the highest order ever. She was the virgin called to be the mother of the Messiah and would, as she so rightly prophesied the night before, "All people shall call me blessed" (Luke 1:48). Mary sat looking at her older cousin, whose face shone with such intense passion and radiance as she began to talk to her of the prophecies that tell of the Messiah's birth and destiny. Zacharias, who was a passionate scholar of the Torah, the prophetic scrolls, and the psalms, had shared with her the mysteries written all over the scriptures that pointed to a perfect Christ, the Anointed One, who would finally reconcile the nations to God. She spoke to her of the brokenness in Eden's Garden that would now be restored, and man would have free access to God through the redemption by a Savior as Isaiah prophesied. "All we like sheep have gone astray; we have turned every one to his own way; and the LORD hath laid on him the iniquity of us all" (Isaiah 53:6). She explained to her how Israel was the nation called to present the picture of God to a broken world but how as a nation, Israel has failed miserably. Although their history was filled with many triumphant stories of God's intervention and favor, yet it was also riddled with the rebellion of a people as generation after generations forgot their God and turned to idols and devils, which opened the doors to the curses and desolation that had plagued them as a nation. Prophets like Isaiah had cried out to the people to repent and return to God's way, but how a rebellious nation would lock the prophets of God in prisons and accuse them of cursing the nation and the king. In prison, the prophets would continue to write and lament that stiff-necked people would go into captivity but that God would send a deliverer. This deliverer He proclaimed would be anointed and gifted as a true deliverer to the people who would have an ear to hear as proclaimed by Isaiah,

> The Spirit of the LORD GOD is upon me; because
> the LORD hath anointed me to preach good tid-
> ings unto the meek; he hath sent me to bind up
> the brokenhearted, to proclaim liberty to the
> captives, and the opening of the prison to them
> that are bound; To proclaim the acceptable year
> of the LORD, and the day of vengeance of our
> God; to comfort all that mourn; To appoint unto
> them that mourn in Zion, to give unto them
> beauty for ashes, the oil of joy for mourning, the
> garment of praise for the spirit of heaviness; that
> they might be called trees of righteousness, the
> planting of the LORD, that he might be glorified.

Isaiah 61:1-3

This child would be born from a virgin girl as a sign that could
not be denied. Even Moses wrote of a star that should come out of
Jacob and the scepter that would rise from Israel. She assured her
that her child was no ordinary child, but the King of Kings as declared by the prophet Jeremiah; "Behold, the days come, saith the
LORD, that I will raise unto David a righteous Branch, and a King
shall reign and prosper, and shall execute judgment and justice in
the earth" (Jeremiah 23:5). She also warned her that he must first
suffer like a sacrificial lamb then be raised up by God. Elizabeth's
eyes burned like a fire, and her voice was like a piercing sword into
the heart as the young Mary sat transfixed by her every word as she
continued to quote from the scriptures as written by Isaiah.

> For he shall grow up before him as a tender
> plant, and as a root out of a dry ground: he hath
> no form nor comeliness; and when we shall
> see him, there is no beauty that we should de-
> sire him. He is despised and rejected of men; a

man of sorrows, and acquainted with grief: and we hid as it were our faces from him; he was despised, and we esteemed him not. Surely he hath borne our griefs, and carried our sorrows: yet we did esteem him stricken, smitten of God, and afflicted. But he was wounded for our transgressions, he was bruised for our iniquities: the chastisement of our peace was upon him; and with his stripes we are healed. All we like sheep have gone astray; we have turned every one to his own way; and the Lord hath laid on him the iniquity of us all. He was oppressed, and he was afflicted, yet he opened not his mouth: he is brought as a lamb to the slaughter, and as a sheep before her shearers is dumb, so he openeth not his mouth. He was taken from prison and from judgment: and who shall declare his generation? for he was cut off out of the land of the living: for the transgression of my people was he stricken. And he made his grave with the wicked, and with the rich in his death; because he had done no violence, neither was any deceit in his mouth. Yet it pleased the Lord to bruise him; he hath put him to grief: when thou shalt make his soul an offering for sin, he shall see his seed, he shall prolong his days, and the pleasure of the Lord shall prosper in his hand. He shall see of the travail of his soul, and shall be satisfied: by his knowledge shall my righteous servant justify many; for he shall bear their iniquities. Therefore will I divide him a portion with the great, and he shall divide the spoil with the strong; because he hath poured out his soul unto death: and he was numbered with the transgressors; and he bare the sin of many, and made intercession for the transgressors.

Isaiah 53:2-14

The Prophet

Mary sat enthralled; Elizabeth recited all the scriptures from memory. She listened to the words concerning her son, and heaviness of sorrow and also a joy gripped her soul. She had experienced the dual emotions of His suffering and His kingship. He will suffer; He will die but will live to live forever with the many sons and daughters of His Father. How amazing and lyrical the words of the prophets were written. As they had seen so, they had penned the great mysteries of Yahweh wrapped up in words not easily understood. It takes keen eyes and a heart open to Yahweh's will to receive the unveiling of the great mysteries written there in the scriptures. Zacharias has seen this revelation of the Messiah and had shared it with Elizabeth many times over the years. His heart had burned, and his heart had longed for the Messiah. Here she who was an ardent student of the word now unveiling to Mary an understanding of the role she was given. She reassured Mary that she would experience great joys but, as the prophecy is sure, she would also experience great sorrows, but her sorrows would be temporary because as seen by David in the psalm, "For thou wilt not leave my soul in hell; neither wilt thou suffer thine Holy One to see corruption" (Psalm 16:10). Mary sat spelled bound as she continued to listen to all that Elizabeth had to share with her from the prophecies. Now she knew why she had to be here with her. The angel had specifically made mention of Elizabeth's pregnancy, and she had felt the compulsion to come on a visit. Now that she understood her purpose and she would now be unafraid and would always know that God would be with her to fulfill His words concerning His child. She would gladly serve her God and bless His name for choosing her to be a part of His story of redemption. Elizabeth left Mary in her thought as she went back to the house to make lunch.

As she prepared the chicken soup loaded with vegetables, she now wondered how, for years, Zachariah had poured over the Torah and read through the prophecies and shared with her the interpretations he believed were revealed in his heart. It was like he always knew more than was told in the temple meetings. She had always enjoyed listening to him as he shared with her the promise of Yahweh to the world as promised to Abraham and to David and now was fulfilled before their very eyes. At first, she had thought Zacharias had taught her these things because he had no son with whom he could share his wisdom. The prophecies were so amazing that she was always enraptured as her husband poured out his understanding of the scriptures with her. His passion was like she was an audience of a thousand people. His eyes held this spark of a million ambers of flaming fires, and his voice, though low, was as a piercing sword into her very soul. She now understood why they were trusted to share in the annunciation of the conception of the Messiah. They had been prepared for the most epic moment on earth, and little did they know that they were chosen and blessed more than their fellow men. All her tears and pains of yesteryears vanished in the eyes of the mercy and grace of God now revealed in their lives. Midge stopped by to visit and broke into her thoughts as her voice sounded at the door. Elizabeth opened the door and greeted her friend with a hug. As she helped her with the preparation of lunch, she shared with her best friend the new things that had happened in her house. Midge's eyes welled up with tears, she had never seen her friend so happy and aglow, and as she looked out into the rose garden, she saw Mary, the young maiden, the mother of the Messiah, sitting with her face turned up towards the sun. She also, a pious woman who looked for Messiah, hugged her friend and cried, "That which Israel had long waited for was now here! How my soul does extoll the Lord." They looked at each other, asking, "Who would have imagined that in this little hilltop in Judea such wonderful prophecies were unfolding?" The ladies finished making lunch, and Mary and Zacharias joined them at the table. They had vegetable and chicken soup with bread and was topped off with a coffee cake Midge had brought for them. Midge greeted Mary with open arms, kissing her on both her cheeks and calling her the blessed of the Lord. Mary hugged her cousin's friend, for she felt great love in the embrace of the older woman also and knew that she would be a part of the storyteller of the events of the season. Zacharias offered his smiles and nodded his head in agreement with their discussions throughout lunch. He was a happy man, knowing that all those years he had poured out his heart and his passion for the prophecies and the stories of the Torah were absorbed by his beloved Elizabeth. He listened in awe, and he was incredibly pleased with her wisdom and understanding of prophecies as she shared with Midge her conversation with Mary that morning. She was such a patient and good woman and had always enjoyed his passion for the scripture. Now he did not have to attempt to write out that information for Mary. His wife was now a passionate teacher of scriptures, for he was dumb. After lunch, he would write on the scroll the few instructions he would need to give to Mary. Elizabeth had expounded the scriptures to her well, so he only needed to reassure her to trust God to fulfill all he has started in her life. He knew that God would always lead her and would also bring Joseph into full knowledge of what He was doing in the world. He signaled himself excused from the table and went by his writing table where he made himself comfortable and started writing a letter to Mary.

Dear Mary,

Cousin Elizabeth has explained well the prophecies concerning the Messiah to you. I hope you understand well the blessing you will birth in the world. Do not be afraid but trust God to protect His seed and the promises of the prophecies. This is my instructions to you:

Part 1: The Angel Has Come

1. *Do not share your story with everyone; not everyone will believe you or be happy for you.*

2. *Your parents should be told but do not be afraid if they do not believe you.*

3. *If God did not reveal this mystery to Joseph when you get home, do not be afraid God will eventually do so.*

4. *God's mission on earth is never without pain, but the greater blessings will come.*

5. *God will put the right people in your life and give different signs to guide you on this journey of the mother of the Messiah.*

6. *Always keep joy and happiness in your heart, and cherish this baby always.*

7. *Read the Torah with Joseph and remind yourself often of the promises of God.*

8. *Guard your heart always, and never let anyone speak negative words in your life.*

9. *Your rewards will be great, and you will experience great peace and eternal joy.*

10. *He that is Yahweh has called you for this task; you are to be strong and bold.*

Kindly remember that Elizabeth and I will be praying for you when you return home. All will be well; just continue to believe that the God, who has chosen you, will be with you, always my bold warrior.

With all my love and blessings,

The Prophet

Cousin Zacharias (priest of the Most High God)

He would save this letter for when she was ready to go home. He arose from the desk and went out into the garden. He did not have much to write, and words were not needed where God has moved. He knew she would forever have grace and that Joseph would be placed alongside her to fulfill all that was written concerning this promised child. He smiled, thinking of his own child growing each day graciously. Elizabeth seemed to have grown bigger and bigger each day. He was so happy that the love of his life was doing exceptionally well with the pregnancy. She never once complained and remained as radiant as a girl in her youth. He himself was blessed with increased strength and a new passion for life. The sky appears to be a sparkling blue, the songs of the birds sounded sweeter than he could remember them. The wind seemed to whisper his name each time it rustled in the trees. He could spend the whole day in the garden working and was never seemed to get tired. He had gotten a new zest for life, and all his senses seem to be keener and more alive to life around him. He would worship God in the silence and marvel in wonder at the butterflies and bees that stopped by. The color of the roses and the fragrance of the air made him nostalgic when as a boy, he would wander in this garden in search of his own mother. These gardens had now been his wife's sanctuary and have now become his own place of solace and worship. He never knew he was so sentimental; he had grown old and soft. He would now stop to smell the roses and distinguish the different scents and now look deeply at the veins of a leaf, amazed at its intricacy and wonder at the creator of such beauty. He was getting so emotional, and he wondered if the gift of fatherhood has made him soft. He will be a dad in his old age and the face of his own son, his eyes would see. The tear rolled from his eyes and fell unto the leaves and sparkled like a diamond in the afternoon sunlight. He wiped the tears from his eyes and went over to the vegetable garden. He was almost finished with reaping the cucumbers, potatoes, beans, and tomatoes. A few grapevines needed to be harvested, and plums and figs also needed to be picked. After six months, he was accustomed to not talking out loud but always talking to Yahweh. He, however, missed his conversations with his friend Benjamin. He had always loved their time of fellowship when they discussed the political climate of Israel and the problems in the priesthood. It would have been a sweet blessing to talk with his friend Benjamin about the arrival of Mary to their house. He would have loved to share with him the amazing story of her visitation with the angel Gabriel and her pregnancy and when the Holy Spirit came upon her, which he had witnessed with his own eyes. Benjamin's visits were fewer these days; he could not blame him for he was no longer a conversation buddy. He could not do any talking, and it was difficult to write so much in response to Benjamin's questions. However, he hoped he would come by soon so Elizabeth could fill him in on the good news. They had spoken so much of the coming Messiah and his mandate on earth that he wanted to be the one to tell his friend that he was here. He had work to be done, so he left his thoughts behind him and got busy with his hands. There would be enough vegetables for the winter and even some to share with the neighbors.

Elizabeth bade goodbye to her friend Midge; they had agreed that since Mary would stay for three months, then her daughter would only come when Mary left for Nazareth, and then she would stay with her for as long as she needed her after the baby was born. As Midge trudged down the hill, she contemplated on the events of the day. She would continue to make her weekly visit to her friend who was no longer coming out of the house. The whole village knew about Elizabeth's pregnancy, and everywhere there was amazement as the women recount the story in the market and at the wells. Even the men in their gathering were speaking of the mystery and miracle of the elderly priest and his wife getting a child in their old age. Now, what would they think of the miracle of Mary, Elizabeth's third cousin from Nazareth? She was a young unmarried maiden now pregnant with a son after having a visitation from the same angel Gabriel who visited Zacharias in the temple. What would they think? Would they believe? An unmarried pregnant maiden was no easy thing in Israel. Stoning was the commandment in the Torah. Would they believe this was the promised virgin birth Isaiah prophesied about hundreds of years ago? The people were so far removed from the prophecies and promises of Yahweh. What would they think? In three months, Mary would return to Nazareth, and they would maybe never see her again. She decided to let the story be Zacharias and Elizabeth's to share. If they choose to share it with others, it was their story to tell. She also knew that the prophecy would fulfill itself. Her prayers were that she would live to see the fulfillment of the birth of these prophesied boys, and if she died, she would go to her grave knowing the Redeemer of Israel was here. However, she knew in her heart that she would share the story with her youngest daughter Rachel, and she would therefore have to talk to her children and grandchildren that when the prophet John and Messiah Jesus come into their callings in their generation, they would believe and celebrate them remembering her stories. Midge had a strangely warm feeling in her soul. The God of the universe has not forgotten Israel. Tears of joy rolled down her cheeks, and her steps quickened. Her heart held a beautiful melody of the wind of grace on the season she was living in. The Messiah has come. It was no longer a story bound up in the books of the prophecies and hid away for safety. The great one Yahweh has come to walk with a common man again in the person of His Son. The mysteries of heaven were revealed in this little hill country of Ein Kerem. Who could imagine the King of the universe wrapped

98

up in a little girl's womb, and she was sitting in the house of the very pregnant elderly priest wife who was mother of the prophet to the Messiah. Her tears were tears of joy for seeing this day. She entered her house with jubilation and shared the story of the day with her beautiful, sweet, kind-hearted daughter, Rachel. "Messiah is here," she whispered. Startled, the girl looked at her, collecting her in her arms, leading her to hear the whole story. Meanwhile, Elizabeth and Mary got busy with canning cucumbers and tomatoes for the winter months. Elizabeth agreed that Mary would take over the cleaning of the house and the washing of clothes. She would also help with the canning of the vegetables, but Elizabeth would continue to cook as her beloved Zacharias loved her cooking. Elizabeth showed her the baby's room and all the nice clothes she had made. Mary was greatly impressed by Elizabeth's sewing skills even at her age. The baby clothes were beautiful. She expressed to Elizabeth that because she was the youngest child, she had not learned to sew and knit, but that her mother and sisters were exceptionally good at sewing, but she had preferred cooking and baking over sewing. Elizabeth offered to take an hour before noon and early evenings to teach hers some sewing skills if she wanted to learn.

Mary was resistant to learning sewing; she just did not have the patience for it. She would rather have Elizabeth tell her the prophecies in the scrolls repeatedly and asked her questions concerning the laws. She was, however, very sharp and witty with canning the fruits and vegetables and was a great housekeeper like her cousin Elizabeth. She liked to decorate the table with flowers from the garden. Elizabeth knew they die too quickly and rather enjoy them walking in the garden but encouraged her decisions. She knew that in a few months, Mary would be married and would be a mother in six months after marriage. Elizabeth knew this was a tough case viewing it in the natural eyes but knew that God would give her grace for the task He had given to her. Elizabeth asked her about Joseph, and Mary blushed. Her eyes, however, sparkled as she shared with her how good a man Joseph was. He had paid a handsome dowry to her father for her. He was a carpenter and the absolute best in Nazareth and made good money for his work. She shared that he was older, but she had always loved and respected him. He was a distant cousin on her father's side of the family and had not married early. She went on to share how her father was having problems raising money for taxes due on the land. He has been pressured by the publican tax collectors repeatedly, and they threatened that if he did not pay his taxes, he could be put in the Roman jail for defying Caesar's edict. Her father, desperate for money, had gone to his cousin Joseph and promised him his youngest daughter if he could give him the money for the taxes as a part of the dowry. Joseph gave him the money to prevent him from losing the land and had agreed to marry Mary, but only if she agreed to be his betrothed. Mary shared how peaceful she had felt when her father first informed her of his decision. She had known her cousin Joseph for all her lifetime, and he was always a good and generous man in Nazareth. The first time they met and spoke at the betrothal, they both knew that they had found love and honor, and they both had a deep love and fear for Yahweh and His Laws. He had given more money than was requested by her father, and she would wait out her year at home, and then they would be married in a traditional wedding ceremony with seven days of celebration. Elizabeth's heart felt warmth and light; she was glad that Mary had found the love of her life and prayed in her heart that the man Joseph would forever love and cherish his princess wife Mary, mother of God. She had experienced great love from the man she married. They were a perfect match and adored each other. She always respected Zacharias for his continued love and kindness to her even though, year after year, she could not give him children. She knew it could not be easy, but Zacharias showed no displeasure in her. He was always a loving and kind man who always treated her like a princess. She knew how blessed she was because her neighbors sometimes complained about the insensitivity and even abusive ways of their husbands. She had married a wise man, a godly man who loves and honors God above everything else, and showed this by the way he lived out his daily life. Her husband was the godliest man she knew. He lived out his life as mandated by the commandments and statutes of the Torah. He would never dishonor God by treating his wife poorly. He knew that the two had become one flesh and her problem was his problem, and their problem was God's problem to solve. If they did not have children, then it was both their shame and not hers alone to bear. He, however, encouraged her that they would celebrate each other and keep the love in their lives strong each day as God expected of them. She knew that God had chosen this man for her, and she somehow knew that Joseph was the chosen man for Mary. John was suddenly leaping around in her abdomen, and she felt a little exhausted. They would continue with preserving some more vegetables tomorrow. They ate a light dinner as the night shadow cast itself against the disappearing sun, and the stars began to slowly dance in the darkness of the sky. The locus had joined the music of the nightlife and the fireflies danced by the window frames. Zacharias had risen from the table and was now at his desk laboring away in writing; she really missed the voice of her husband and was happy Mary was here with her. The young girl made a great conversation partner. Kissing Mary good night, Elizabeth refreshed herself and climbed wearily into bed. She was about to fall asleep when she heard Zacharias pulled himself into bed beside her. She snuggled in his chest as he curled his arms under her head and around her swollen belly. Since that night she became pregnant, he has not touched her again with desires of burning passion. He instead handled her like a precious jewel as if he was afraid he might hurt her or the baby in some way. He treated her like a beautiful treasure box with the precious jewel of their child, and she was to be nurtured, loved, and handled with care. She missed his voice but needed no words to feel the love he communicated through his eyes, his loving embrace, and warm kisses. The unspoken harmony of their love was stronger than words, and with a gift so precious, their hearts had become more entwined in the sweet anticipation of parenthood. His touches were more frequent, more tender, and his eyes had become deep, soft, and often moist as he spent time looking into her eyes in wonder and amazement. This was her new Zacharias; he had gotten so much softer and attentive. She had always known in her heart that he would be a great father. She asserts that his tears were to make up for the fact that he could not speak. He was always such the talker, and how happy she always was to listen to him. They both drifted off to sleep in their own happy thoughts of tomorrow.

It was early morning, and Benjamin decided to beat the morning sun and was on his way to see his friend Zacharias. It has been four weeks since the dinner, and he had not seen his friends. He walked up the hill smiling to himself as he reflected on the news that they all received four weeks ago. It has been the talk of the neighborhood and had not died down. He knew his friend Zacharias could not speak, but he wanted to talk and to see how Elizabeth was doing and to see if they needed help with anything. His knock sounded on the door, and Zacharias arose from the breakfast table; with haste, they were finishing up with breakfast. Zacharias found his friend Benjamin standing there in the doorway, grinning. With open arms and a wide grin, he greeted his friend with a hug that was returned. Benjamin entered the house, and sitting at the table was a beautiful wide-eyed young maiden. She was not one of the locals because he did not know her. Elizabeth urged him to sit down her face was aglow; she was glad to see him, and she had good news to give him, knowing he was a lover of the prophecies. "Elizabeth! How are you and the baby doing? I see you have gotten a lot bigger since I last saw you. Has Zacharias been a good boy?" His burly voice filled the room. "Yes! Very well," Elizabeth responded with full laughter as the baby juggled around in her abdomen. "Come and sit; we have good news for you." Elizabeth introduced her cousin Mary who greeted the older man and then excused herself as she offered to get him coffee and bread. Benjamin appeared puzzled. He had never seen this cousin visited before but thought that it was nice for her young cousin to be visiting to help her pregnant cousin. As Mary returned with the coffee, Zacharias winked across the table at Elizabeth as if to say, "Do not keep him in suspense any longer." He wished he could tell his friend the story, they had discussed these prophecies so often and had frequent talks of their wait for the Messiah's entrance in the world, but he was dumb, but Elizabeth had become quite the storyteller. Elizabeth started, "Benjamin, this is my little cousin Mary, and she is visiting from Nazareth." Benjamin raised his head to acknowledge her, and Mary avoided eye contact and bowed her head in acknowledgment. She knew the conversation would be about her, so she asked to be excused from the table voicing she would continue the canning for the day. Elizabeth immediately rushed on to fill Benjamin in on the wonderful details of Mary's visit, her angelic visitation, and that she was now pregnant with the Lord Messiah. Benjamin was dumbfounded. The bread fell from his mouth that popped open, and his eyes grew as large as a lemon. Zacharias looked on his friend with a grin plastering his face and nodding his head vigorously in agreement with the story his wife was relaying. He thought they wanted to give him a heart attack. Every time he came to their house, they had stories so miraculous and beautiful that they took his breath away. It took him a while to gather himself together and regain his composure. He believed her because it all made sense. She was pregnant with the prophet, and Mary was pregnant with the Messiah. God had brought a culmination of the fulfillment of His word in their house, and Benjamin knew that if there was any righteous man left in Israel, then he knew his friend Zacharias certainly was one. Who deserved such favor from God? He could see how his beloved friend was greatly loved by Yahweh. After all the years of waiting and not receiving a child, his friend, the priest, was blessed to be father to the prophet of the Lord, and the mother of the Lord was a guest in their house. Benjamin bowed his head in worship for all he had heard and witnessed in that moment. Mary smiled from the kitchen. She was happy to be surrounded by such lovers of Yahweh. He had received the news with such reverence and awe. She felt so blessed to be around people who nurtured the seed now growing in her womb, and they showed no unbelief or disbelief in the grace of God unfolding. They had studied the Torah and the prophets and believed in the Messiah that would come and were ever in expectation. It was not difficult for them to believe. No, not with cousin Elizabeth's story. She was an old woman and was now very pregnant, so no one could question her miracle, but she was a young girl, engaged, and waiting for her wedding day. Who would believe her story? Only a few righteous who still believe and wait for the Messiah's coming, only those who remain faithful to the promise of God and serve Him and obey His laws and precepts. Only an old woman with a miracle of her own would believe her and her husband, a righteous priest, who looked for the promise of heaven, the virgin birth of the Messiah. He was visited by the same angel that visited her and would believe her story because it was also their story. They have all been chosen to be a part of the same unfolding and fulfillment of the prophecies concerning the Lord Messiah. She was filled with thankfulness and gratitude to God for the angel's words that had prompted her to come away to Judah. Here she had found so much nurture and understanding awaiting her. Her days were filled with happiness and joy, whereas on her way there, she was filled with doubts and anxieties.

Part 1: The Angel Has Come

Benjamin invited his friend Zacharias to take a walk with him down the hills and across the vale. He needed to walk and talk to his friend and process all he has just heard and seen. The friends left the house, and Benjamin bubbled up with excitement. He talked about the prophet Isaiah's true description of a virgin who would birth a son after the destruction of the temple in Jerusalem, and the nation taken into captive had to return to Jerusalem. He voiced how as a nation, they had returned to rebuild Jerusalem and the temple when Cyrus was king of Persia as prophesied by Jeremiah. King Cyrus gave money for the rebuilding of Jerusalem and the temple and returned the golden treasures of the temple that Nebuchadnezzar had taken seventy years prior. He thundered on about how Ezra, Nehemiah, and Zerubbabel all made attempts and had rebuilt the walls of Jerusalem and started repairing the temple. But Jerusalem had been attacked fifty-two times, captured and recaptured forty-four times, besieged twenty-three times with complete destruction once before. Herod's repair on the temple was only forty-six years in its making. Sacrifice was now where it belonged. He, like Zacharias, looked for the promised Messiah, the suffering lamb who would bring redemption to the whole world and restore God's way of doing things. Zacharias loved his friend; he was such a history prodigy, and that was what started their great friendship. Zacharias would walk by his house on his way from temple duty in Jerusalem, and Benjamin always had a hundred questions for him to engage in a discourse. They would sometimes sit for hours at a time and talked away into the nights about beliefs, values, and the interpretation of the scriptures. They both had a deep love for Yahweh and the old ways and rejected the heretical teachings of Pharisees and the Sadducees. They were a sect to themselves and enjoyed the company of the other in their off days. Benjamin was a tentmaker by trade. He had retired and turned over his business to his oldest son. He now took care of his livestock and farmed his land. His wife, Anna, had been sick and bedridden for over ten years and was taken care of by one of his daughters. Zacharias was good ears and a fountain of wisdom for him to draw from and to speak his own rhetoric without being ostracized. He continued to rave about what Jerusalem would probably look like in thirty years when the prophet and Messiah came into manhood and into their appointed offices. He looked at his friend Zacharias shaking his head. He was five years younger than his friend Zacharias and voiced out loud that they probably would be dead and buried by then. Zacharias smiled, looking into his friend's face. How he wanted to tell him he was praying for long life to see his son become a man. He had to settle with remaining silent while his friend continued to prattle on, "I can only imagine what the Messiah will say to the Pharisee and the Sadducees. He is going to put them in their places and correct the errors of their ways. They have gone a whoring after the ways of the Greek and the Romans arguing about philosophies and viewpoints instead of returning to the ways of Yahweh." They were both disgusted with how each sect has promoted their sects to be the only voice of wisdom in the city and have manipulated the laws and creeds of God. Post captivity Jerusalem has become Hellenistic and Romanistic in its approach to political life and was filled with philosophical thinkers who have given precedence to the Talmud—their books of manmade laws over God's laws. He nudged Zacharias in the side and smiling broadly, and said, "If your son is going to be like Elijah, they got some trouble coming their way." The prophet Elijah was no pushover prophet; he was remembered for his no-nonsense ways of ministering as God directed him. He challenged King Ahab and Queen Jezebel when they turned Israel over to idolatry. He stopped the heavens from raining for three and a half years. He got fed by birds by the brook Cherith, then lived with that widow woman and her son in Zarephath, where he multiplied the oil and wheat flour for the remainder of the famine. He then challenged four hundred and fifty false prophets of Baal and killed them all on Mount Carmel when they were not able to call on their gods to produce fire. He rebuilt his altar and called on Yahweh. The people became enraged at the false prophets and helped Elijah to kill them all. They then turned back to the true God of Israel. Elijah then ran faster than the chariot of King Ahab when he prayed for the rain to come, and the rain came. He ate two meals prepared by an angel and traveled for forty days to Mount Horeb to talk with God. He completed his assignment as a prophet and was the only man written in history that was then taken up to heaven in a chariot of fire. "Those are big shoes to fill," he laughed, jesting with his friend. *Is anything too hard for God to do?* Zacharias thought. His thoughts had raced along with Benjamin as he recounted the stories of the prophet Elijah. He was seeing a season of miracles, signs, and wonders and wondered if the hearts of the people of Israel would return to God. *God does have a sense of humor,* he thought. He and his wife had been without a child for all their married lives, and now in their old age, they were given a son and told the life history of the child, and now the mother of the Messiah was visiting with them. Zacharias knew at that moment that he would not live to see the story unfold but that he already knew how the story would end. He has had a sure word from God, and like Abraham, he would embrace and cherish this child he was given until his eyes closed in death. The friends had made a full circle around the hill and had made it back to Zacharias's house. Benjamin assured his friend that he would share the stories with his family. This was the story that was spoken to Abraham, Isaac, and Jacob to David and Isaiah and Jeremiah and Daniel and to all who look for the redemption of Israel. There were a few who were wary of the demise of the ways of Yahweh and longed for a pure Jewish way of living where Yahweh was King. They longed to hear the prophet's voice in the street again. Of a certainty as a nation, they have failed God in the bearing of His light to the dark world. But

God had not forgotten His promise. Though He had been silent for a long time, His spoken word, now His written word, has now been fulfilled. Two boys would be born to fulfill the heavenly edict. He bade his friend goodbye and departed to his own house filled with joy. Zacharias entered his yard feeling refreshed and energized. He certainly could not talk, but his friend had engaged his mind on their favorite subject. The sweet joys of life now awaited him at the end of his journey. What other men experienced in their youth was given to him in the fading years of his life, and he and Elizabeth could take no credit for it. Yahweh had favored them and granted them the joy of becoming parents to the prophet of the Messiah, and sitting in his house was the virgin mother of the Messiah. He decided to spend the rest of the day in prayer and meditation. As he entered the door, Elizabeth entered the room and greeted him. She was big in the abdomen, and her pace was slower than usual. He was so happy Mary was with her, for what companion has he been to her. He was speechless and felt inadequate. He went over and gave her his special long hug. The woman of his dreams and the mother of his child so gracefully carrying the gift of life they were given. Not once had he heard her murmured or complained. For an old girl, she carried the baby well.

Elizabeth returned the hug to her husband, and he then released her and entered his sitting chamber to the prayer mat where he intended to spend the rest of the day. Elizabeth made herself comfortable on the chair with her knitting kit. She had helped Mary just a little that morning with canning peaches and some more tomatoes from the garden. She was a little tired from standing. She noticed a mild swelling to her ankles as she pulled her feet up on a wooden stool to rest. John was simply getting bigger; she would soon not be able to see her feet from a standing position. She knitted a blanket for herself and sang the shepherd's psalm. The melody drifted through the house and was pleasant to the ears of those who heard. Zacharias paused from his prayer to listen. Mary in the kitchen smiled and joined in at the last stanza. "Surely goodness and mercy shall follow me all the days of my life: and I will dwell in the house of the LORD for ever." Elizabeth thought immediately went back to what else needed to be done before the baby's arrival. She had completed all her preparation for baby John's room and clothing. *John!* She then pondered on the meaning of his name. "God has been gracious and showed favor," she murmured. God could have chosen anyone else, but He had specifically chosen them in remembrance of their prayers to favor them. Zacharias may have been shocked and spoken out in doubt, but he had never had an angelic visitation. He had only read of such encounters in the Torah and the writings of the prophets. But God had intended in the courts of heaven to make them in their old age parents of the Lord's prophet. God had favored them a long, long time ago. Zacharias and Benjamin had often spoken of the promised Messiah and what that would mean to Israel. He just did not know that he was written in the script of God coming to live with men again. Hot tears welled up in her eyes and fell onto her abdomen and warming her skin, and the baby gave a gentle kick. The realities echoed in her heart. God had favored her, and because of her age, everyone knew it was God's grace and favor. She also knew that it would be forever written down in their scrolls of memory and spoken of long after she was gone. Her mind, pulling out of her reprieve, went back to the tasks to be done. She needed to arrange with Midge for the preparation of the baby's birth, and within eight days following, it was customary to have a circumcision, according to the covenant made with Abraham. This was also usually the time for the naming ceremony of the baby. Huldah, the village midwife, already knew her baby was due in another two months. He should be due at the beginning to mid-November. It would be slightly cold by then with lots of rain but mostly sunny.

Huldah lived half an hour away, and she would have to get a runner to fetch her when her time came. A slight tinge of anxiety rose in her chest. Yes! She would be giving birth and experience birth pains, but she rested her fears and put her trust in Yahweh, who had given her this gift of life. She had spent so little time thinking about the birth of the baby and the baby's aftercare, but now she must turn her thoughts to these matters. Mary would return to Nazareth at the end of October to fulfill her promise to her parents and be married to Joseph. It was also not wise for her to stay any longer because, by then, she would have begun to show outward signs of the pregnancy. She was young and thin. The baby's growth would be evident even by the second month. Midge's daughter would be with her as previously arranged. Elizabeth wondered what the birthing of John would be like for her. Her health has been great, and she knew it was by the grace of God that she was sustained and in good health. Some women her age had complications with their health. Benjamin's wife, after the last baby of twelve children, was not strong anymore, and her health had rapidly declined. Her older girls had to care for her to take the burden off their father. But most Jewish women were strong and quickly bounced back from the delivery of the babies. She was eighty-eight years old, and it could be scary, but today she knew she had to decide to completely trust God that she would have the baby and remain in good health to care for him. The dream of motherhood was hers, and she wanted to savor every moment of the experience. She prayed for Yahweh to give her strength and no complication in the process of birthing.

The weeks passed quickly, and Elizabeth grew bigger. Mary was still in the mode of waiting to see her fruit grow. This was the second month, and she shared with Elizabeth that her breast had grown almost twice their size. She had also missed her monthly flow and was sincerely alarmed at the changes in her body. Her face had grown round and fatter, and she was putting on some more weight on her hips and on the buttocks. She was not protruding in the abdomen, but her waistline had definitely expanded in inches. "Cousin Elizabeth," she asked, "you may have to make me a few new dresses to go home and make them bigger so I can keep myself hidden as you did." Elizabeth chuckled, remembering her decision not to tell until she was in the fifth month. She reassured her that she would have the local seamstress make her three new dresses and headbands of the same material to be worn with them. Mary would go with Midge into Jerusalem and select the fabrics she loved. Midge would then take her to the seamstress to get some beautifully embroidered dresses in a loose style that would be befitting for a new bride and a mother-to-be. It also had to be arranged with the ladies she came down with to the Jerusalem market. She needed to let them know she was almost ready to travel back with them to Nazareth at the end of the month. This could all be arranged on the day she went into town with Midge. Mary already knew their schedule. They usually return to Nazareth on Friday before sunset to celebrate Shabbat. If she went to Jerusalem on Wednesday before noonday, then the arrangement could be made. Midge would be visiting tomorrow, and there was so much she needed to discuss and work out with Midge. She really missed Zacharias's voice of wisdom when so many decisions had to be made. She would, however, talk with him later and see if he was in agreement with her plans. It was only four more weeks to go, and there were decisions to be made, a party to be planned, and Mary to be prepared to go home to Nazareth. She could tell that Mary was a little anxious, but she reassured her that God, who had blessed her with the gift of the mother of His Son, would prepare the way for her when she returned home. She reassured her that she would remain in prayer for her. She encouraged her to keep a healthy heart before God. Therefore, she had to learn to shut unhappiness and unkindness outside of her heart. Mary came over and rested her head on the older woman's shoulder. Elizabeth hugged her and said, "The same God who gave an old woman strength to carry a baby and the wisdom to know how to process the journey is the same God who gave a young unmarried girl His Son to carry and will also give her great wisdom how to process her own journey. May Jehovah go with you and give you His peace." They walked hand in hand into the kitchen, and Elizabeth started supper with Mary assisting. As they cooked, they sang the psalms, "The Lord is my light and my salvation; whom shall I fear? The Lord is the strength of my life; of whom shall I be afraid?" (Psalm 27:1) Zacharias rose from his prayer mat and stretching his arms towards the ceiling. He was stiff in the legs from kneeling so long in prayer. He looked at the women in the kitchen. His Elizabeth was doing a wonderful job preparing Mary and building up her confidence for the journey ahead. God has favored her twice. First, she got to carry a child, and then she got to be a mentor to the mother of the Messiah. She had such love and empathy and a gentle nurturing spirit. He thought, *What a safe place for the Messiah to have begun his life, right here, in the arms and under the watchful eyes of Elizabeth.* She had taken on the role of the mother to the teenager and has done so well with her young cousin. In a few weeks, she would be mother of John, their own beloved son. Certainly, God had given her a double blessing in one year. He always knew she would have been a great mother, and he was already an eyewitness of her love and kindness to her young cousin. Times and seasons were changing as God's timeline was being fulfilled, and he was in the middle of the mix and a partaker of the blessings of Yahweh.

Midge arrived as usual just before lunch and had one of her many delicious cakes for her friend. Elizabeth was excited; there was so much to plan with her friend and so little time in which to do so. As they sat after lunch, she shared with her friend the clothing needs for

Part 1: The Angel Has Come

Mary and the arrangement needed for Mary to travel back to Nazareth at the end of the month. Midge agreed to take Mary into Jerusalem the following day. They also made plans for the baby's birth. Midge's daughter Rachel would come to stay with Elizabeth the day that Mary would leave for Nazareth. She would go and talk with Huldah, the midwife, and arranged all the necessities for the birth and also for the circumcision eight days after the birth. She would get a group of women who would help again with the cooking and preparation for the circumcision and naming ceremony of the baby. Midge expressed that she did not want Elizabeth of Zacharias to worry about any of the planning for the baby's ceremony but that she should be relaxed and focused only on the baby's birth. She would prepare the food and give the announcements once the baby was born. She also wanted to be right by Elizabeth's side when the baby John came into the world. She wanted to be the first hand that held that baby after the hands of Huldah and the mother. She had helped in many birthing of her own grandchildren and wanted to be present for her dear friend, who was blessed in her old age. "I think God is going to let you push this boy out quickly with very little pain," Midge chided. "Why would he want to give this old girl pain? You have had enough pain in waiting for a baby." Elizabeth squeezed her friend's hand fondly. "I hope you are right, friend; I could not stand too much pain," Elizabeth retorted. She had often heard her friend Midge lamented about her own births and the ones that were more painful than the others. She had always seriously exclaimed that the boys' birthing was more painful than that of the girls. She, herself, had been mother to six children. She had four boys and two girls who were all grown and had families of their own, except for Rachel, her youngest, who was still unmarried and lived with her. Her husband had died when Rachel was only six years old, and that was twenty years ago. She had chosen to stay at home to be a companion to her mother, but Midge had insisted her health was good and that she did not need a caregiver. She, however, secretly loved having her as her companion because she had missed her father dearly. She hoped Rachel would finally accept the proposal of Rabbi Levi. His wife had died in child's birth over two years ago; his eyes have been on her Rachel, whom he thought would make a great wife and a mother for his two little boys. He was a good man and was trained and worked as a rabbi with a good character. He was from a good family and had a position in the school in Jerusalem. Midge's hope is that she would finally accept the proposal, and with the dowry, she could be comfortable for the remainder of her life. Her daughter was a good woman and did deserve happiness. She could tell that love was blooming in her daughter's heart. She hoped the engagement would take place in a few months. But for now, she would help Elizabeth until after the baby was born. She emerged from her thoughts to hear her friend assuring Mary, who had entered the room, that she would take her to Jerusalem in the morning. Mary came over to hug Midge and thank her for her kindness and friendship to Cousin Elizabeth and now to her. Midge hugged the girl pulling her in her arms. "This is one special girl," she said, "mother of the Lord, what would I not do for you, woman, blessed of the one Yahweh." She agreed to pick her up in the morning, and for more speedy travel, they would both ride their donkeys into town. Mary smiled; she had forgotten about the donkey. Cousin Zacharias must be doing a great job caring of the creature, for she had not heard him cried once since she has been there.

Mary was excited about going to Jerusalem. She knew it was almost time to go home and face her parents and Joseph, her beloved. She would have loved to have stayed for Cousin Elizabeth's baby's arrival, but if she stayed longer, she would risk the chance of getting too pregnant before going back to be married to Joseph and to unveil her secret blessing. Even if her parents did not believe her story, she hoped that Joseph would believe her story and understand why she had gone away to Judea. She had received so much strength and courage having talked with Elizabeth over these two months that she was ready to face her world and challenges unafraid. She spotted Midge coming over the hill on her donkey. She mounted her beast and headed towards the trail. Elizabeth waved at them from the door and watched as they made their descent and disappeared out of view. The trip to Jerusalem is usually an all-day occasion. Elizabeth would keep herself busy by finishing the blanket she was knitting. Now that she had discussed all the needed done with Midge, her mind was at ease again. While she sat at the breakfast table with Zacharias that morning, she discussed with him what needed to be done. Again, he would get together with Benjamin and had a booth rebuilt for the party for the circumcision and naming ceremony. He was in total agreement with the plans for Mary's travel back to Nazareth and retrieved the letter he had written for her. Elizabeth read his letter and nodded her head. They both wanted to keep it simple for Mary. Her stay with them has been one of building her faith in the task God has appointed her for. She was a stable young lady and had a great grasp of the meaning of her divine calling. Elizabeth believed Mary would be able to face any challenge and that God would give her the wisdom and grace to overcome any obstacles. Zacharias wrote that he was convinced that God would give a revelation to Joseph, and the two would be married without hesitation. Elizabeth voiced her concern that Mary had gotten fatter, and it was already visible that she looked different than when she came. Zacharias signaled for her to hush her fears; he wrote, "Let God take care of His daughter." Elizabeth agreed, knowing that they would be incapable of doing anything for the girl once she went back to Nazareth. She would be busy taking care of her new baby boy, and Zacharias would return to temple duty once he could speak again. She knew Abigail and Nathan would be returning with most of the family for the baby's circumcision and naming ceremony. Only then will they know the outcome of Mary's return. Elizabeth rose from the chair with some effort. It was becoming difficult for her to sit on the lower benches. She has grown so huge in the abdomen that it was difficult to stand up. Zacharias quickly rose up and helped her to find her balance. Elizabeth laughed out loudly, "So, this is how the ladies felt at eight months?" Her pelvic area had widened significantly, and she waddles when she walks and now at a very slow pace. *Welcome to motherhood,* Zacharias thought, kissing her on the top of her head. Elizabeth went towards the kitchen while Zacharias moved towards the door. Silence has become much harder for him these last few days. He wanted so much to encourage Elizabeth and pray over her in these final weeks of her pregnancy. He really felt useless. Elizabeth had to be making most of the planning. He was thankful for the friendship of Midge and all she had done to help them. Except for his silence, the months had gone peaceful and quickly by, and Elizabeth had no complication and remained relatively highly active and strong. For a woman of eighty-eight, he knew that only Yahweh could have determined and orchestrated this birth. He had lived long enough, and at ninety-eight years, he was blessed to have so much stamina and drive. He vowed as soon as his voice returned, he would shout out all that his eyes had beheld. The walk he took with Benjamin yesterday had so exhilarated him that he found himself going down the trail following the path he had walked with his friend yesterday. His strides were long and steady. He could only now understand what eighty-year-old Caleb felt when he said,

> Now therefore give me this mountain, whereof the LORD spoke in that day; for thou heardest in that day how the Anakims were there, and that the cities were great and fenced: if so be the

Part 1: The Angel Has Come

LORD will be with me, then I shall be able to drive them out, as the LORD said.

Joshua 14:12

Even though Caleb's promise was delayed for forty years, he got the land his eyes beheld and lived to enjoy it. Zacharias had no doubt that he would enjoy many days with his wife and his son. He made the circle around the hill in a shorter time than he did with his friend yesterday. So, lost he was in his thoughts that he had not felt the hotness of the mid-day sun on his back. When he walked into to house, Elizabeth looked at him, shocked. He was dripping wet with perspiration. He motioned that he had gone walking, and only then did he realized the sweat he had worked up. He went into the room to freshened up and changed his clothes. *My dear prince,* Elizabeth thought, *he has been silent so long it must be now too much for him today.* They ate lunch in silence. Elizabeth really missed Mary today. She had grown so fond of the maiden and had shared some much with her these eight weeks that today the house was really too quiet without her. She did hope she was having good success with what she set out to do today in Jerusalem. In four weeks, she would return to Nazareth, and shortly after, Elizabeth would have a crying baby to care for.

Elizabeth felt slightly tired after lunch and told Zacharias she would take a little nap before dinner. She overslept and was awoken by Mary and Midge on their return from Jerusalem. Elizabeth was shocked that she had slept away most of the day. Midge told her it was normal and that she would get more tired as the time drew closer for the baby to be born. She encouraged her to rest as much as she wanted to and that she deserved to rest, for after the baby arrives, her hands and feet would be busy all the time. Elizabeth laughed, gathering her strength. She looked over at Mary, whose

117

face was glowing. Her skin was so flawless and radiant that even after a long trip, she still appeared fresh and full of energy. Midge assured her they had eaten in Jerusalem and bade them goodnight. Mary thanked her deeply, and the women waved her goodbye. As her donkey disappeared down the path, Mary joyfully recounted the day's trip like a six-year-old on her first visit to Jerusalem. She had found beautifully dyed fabric and the seamstress gave her detailed information on how she would make her dress. With instruction to make them loose because she was soon to be married and become a mother. This was the first time she had gotten her clothes tailored because her mother had always made her clothes which were usually plain clothing, worn every day. Her mother was very practical when it came to clothing since she had raised so many children; she never wasted money on frivolity. They had met the ladies from Nazareth in the market, and they had agreed for Mary to travel back with them the last Wednesday in October. They all gloated over her appearance, voicing how Mary had gained so much weight and was glowing like a new bride. They voiced that the mountain air must have been good for her because she now looked like a woman and not that thin little girl who came down with them two months ago. They all knew Mary and her family well. They were jesting with her, "Joseph will be happy to see you; he can't wait for his bride to return." Mary was beaming; she was happy to have heard that Joseph was thinking of her, for she had a big and wonderful secret to share with him. The women in the Jerusalem market had no idea the wonderful treasure she carried, which was the cause of the transformation in her body. The seamstress had agreed to have the dresses delivered in three weeks just before the day Mary was to return to Nazareth. The details of the day were shared with Elizabeth, and then the ladies headed to the kitchen. Elizabeth decided on a very light dinner. Mary had eaten in Jerusalem with Midge and was not very hungry. For the first time, Mary felt just a little home sick; this was the first time in eight weeks that her heart has wandered back to Nazareth. She cleaned the kitchen after dinner and went immediately to bed. "She must be tired after all the excitement in Jerusalem today," Elizabeth had spoken aloud. Zacharias looked over at her knowing she was hungry for conversation. *She had slept all afternoon and would be up until late,* he thought. He would be no use to her for conversation, so he gave her the scrolls with the psalms and asked her to read their favorite ones. He closed his eyes while she read the writings of King David.

> Oh LORD, our Lord, how excellent is thy name in all the earth! Who has set thy glory above the heavens. Out of the mouth of babes and sucklings has thou ordained strength because of thine enemies, that thou mightest still the enemy and the avenger. When I consider the heavens, the work of thy fingers, the moon and the stars, which thou hast ordained; what is man that thou are mindful of them of him? And the son of man, that thou visitest him? For thou has made him a little lower than the angels and hast crowned him with glory and honor. Thou madest him to have dominion over the works of thy hands; thou hast put all things under his feet. All sheep and oxen, yea and all the beast of the field; The fowl of the air, and the fish of the sea and whatsoever passeth through the paths of the seas. O LORD our Lord, how excellent is your name in all the earth.

Psalm 8:1-9

"The LORD is my shepherd; I shall not want" (Psalm 23).

"The heavens declare the glory of God; and the firmament sheweth his handywork" (Psalm 19:1).

"God is our refuge and strength, a very present help in trouble" (Psalm 46).

"As the hart panteth after the water brooks, so panteth my soul after thee, O God. My soul thirsteth for God, for the living God: when shall I come and appear before God?" (Psalm 42:1-2)

"The LORD is my light and my salvation; whom shall I fear?" (Psalm 27:1a)

"Make a joyful noise unto the LORD all ye lands" (Psalm 100:1).

"He that dwelleth in the secret place of the most High shall abide under the shadow of the Almighty" (Psalm 91:1).

"Praise ye the LORD. Praise God in his sanctuary: praise him in the firmament of his power" (Psalm 150:1).

"By the rivers of Babylon, there we sat down, yea, we wept, when we remembered Zion" (Psalm 137:1).

Her voice was like a sweet melody of the wind in the corn fields in his ears. There was just something so beautiful about the psalms, which, when read or sang, would move Zacharias heart to worship Yahweh. David was such a poet and songwriter. His writings, whether poetry, prose, ballad, or litany, usually moves the heart whether he was in worship to Yahweh, recounting his personal triumphs or defeat or contemplating the struggles of his people Israel; his writings touched deep chords in the soul. They both had often had to draw comfort from the writings of David to help them with their everyday struggles. But tonight was a beautiful night of joyful thanksgiving for all that Yahweh had done. He never dreamed they would ever have had a child again. But here was his very pregnant wife; they were both stricken in age but with a joyful heart because God had remembered them and has shown favor. Elizabeth was openly weeping and laughing together as they relived and recounted the many blessings of the past eight months. A screech owl sounded in the distant tree, and the cry of a polecat on the prowl resounded in the air. It was late in the night they have drunk themselves happy in the psalms. He assisted his wife into bed, and he prepared himself also for bed. The priest and his wife fell happily in bed. Elizabeth felt the baby dancing around in her womb for joy. The Holy Ghost inside the baby was responding to their joy and worship. She wondered to herself, *A prophet is here*. She sank into bed, overjoyed. In a few weeks, she would be holding John the prophet. Jehovah has been gracious more than she could have even imagined. Her prophet son would be remembered forever in the book of history and in the eternal archives of heaven. She vowed to share her story with anyone who would listen, of how God had visited them and given them a son in their old age. Israel would have to wait and see what would happen. The prophet of the Lord is coming soon, and so is the Messiah right here under her roof. She fell into a blissful sleep and dreamed angels were flying over her house. Zacharias turned in the bed, careful not to awaken his wife. With the psalms still ringing in his ears, he also fell asleep in peaceful bliss. They both felt so in complete harmony with God, Who has kissed their faces and brought them a gift of life, their own son, John the Prophet to the Lord Messiah. Now what they had read about others in the archives of their ancestry has become their reality. Eternity has entered their humble home. The Messiah lies in the womb of his sleeping mother, Mary, and his prophet lies in the womb of his wife, Elizabeth, and in time to come, they would take on the cause for the salvation of the world. The Israel they now knew would be forever changed because of the two babies growing in the wombs of their mothers in his house. What greater blessings could any man ever asked for? Zacharias was full and content. He would die a happy man, for God has remembered him and remembered His promise to Abraham and to the seed of the woman Eve. "And I will put enmity between thee and the woman, and between thy seed and her seed, it shall bruise thy head and thou shalt bruise his heel" (Genesis 3:15). He would sleep with the ancestors knowing that redemption is come to the sons of men. They could now be rejoined to Yahweh and Yahweh to His sons and daughters.

In one week, Mary would be leaving for Nazareth. Elizabeth and Zacharias were at peace with her trip to go back home to Nazareth. They had done all that God has put in their hearts to do for her. She has matured beyond the frightened girl who came into their house three months ago. Mary now had a tiny bump in her belly, and it was with joy that Elizabeth now watched her with great joy, singing and praying over the child in her womb as she had seen her done. She had learned so much from Elizabeth, and she was ready to take this joy home with her, having been fully persuaded in the gift that was given to her. The dresses Elizabeth had given her the money for had arrived, and they were beautiful and fitted her perfectly and so much better than her old dresses now did. The seamstress had done a beautiful work of art on the dresses. She tried them on for Elizabeth and danced around the room like a beautiful princess dancing at her coming-out party. Elizabeth watched her in wonderment. "May this joy forever be hers to keep," she prayed silently. Elizabeth had no idea what would await this child turned woman when she returned home to Nazareth but knew that God would be with her in her wilderness or in the red seas of her life. Her face was lifted to the sky; she had a beautiful glow, her eyes sparkled with complete abandonment, and her movements were with fluid ease. She was dancing and singing to the Lord Yahweh and has forgotten herself. Her tears mingled with her laughter as she collapsed to the floor, crying out in complete surrender to God's will for her life. No one could have prepared her for a baby from God, but this is the life that God had chosen for her, and she knew she would be strong as Esther and bold as Ruth, and courageous as Rahab to fulfill Yahweh's will. The God who favored these women had favored her, Mary, above all else. She was chosen to be the mother of the Messiah. Elizabeth had done well on her Journey, and the baby would be due anytime. She was bigger than most pregnant women she had known, and her baby was a highly active boy in the womb, but this had been a beautiful joy to watch Mary and the treasure she was carrying in her womb. "My Lord, my King, my Jesus Messiah! Welcome to our troubled world." Mary had not learned much in knitting or making baby clothes, but she was an excellent housekeeper and a great cook. She also showed great skill in canning and preserving food which she said she learned from her mother and also loved doing it. Mary was also a beautiful worshiper of Yahweh, and even at the moment like this, she had abandoned herself on the floor in worship and complete consecration to God. She now knew why God had chosen her. She was a pure, innocent soul, a lover of Yahweh with all her heart, her soul, her mind, and her strength, and this is what Yahweh has seen. She sat with the girl until she had fully composed herself and pulled up from the floor. "Cousin Elizabeth," she whispered, "I am ready to go home and to face my family and the man I love with this truth of God. The God I love, the God of Israel, has entrusted me with His greatest possession, His gift to men, the Redeemer of the world, His precious son, Jesus. Now I will go back to Nazareth and nurture Him and raise Him and present Him to the world when His time comes. I am now ready to see this beautiful promise unfold, for I know His name and His destiny, and I am unafraid for Yahweh has given me strength." Elizabeth looked on in amazement. This was not a child anymore but a woman, a strong one with the fortitude and strength of a warrior. She would defend this King's child and guard Him with all her heart. He was not hers to keep. She would one day have to release Him to His destiny and His God's purpose of coming into their world, but for now, she was the guardian of the seed of God growing in her womb. "The great unfolding of the mysteries of heaven," Elizabeth murmured, hugging her young cousin to her chest, "Yes! You are ready, my dear cousin."

The week had ended too quickly, and now Mary was ready to go back to Nazareth. She collected her few possessions and the gift of a few gold coins given to her by Zacharias. He handed her the scroll he had written for her and tell her to read when she got home. Elizabeth had a small basket with bread, honey, boiled eggs, some figs and dates, and water for the journey. Zacharias chose to accompany Mary into Jerusalem to meet with the women in the market. He knew he did not have to talk, and the walk would be good for him. Before they departed, he got the olive oil and blessed it, and poured it on her head. Elizabeth repeated the blessing of Aaron over her seeing Zacharias could not pray aloud, "The Lord bless you and keep you, the Lord cause His face to shine upon you, lift up His countenance upon you and give you His peace." She hugged Elizabeth, and they kissed each other goodbye, wishing each other blessings in the months ahead. She got up on the beast with Zacharias following behind her. Elizabeth stood by the door waving until they disappeared down the hill. She went to her room, holding her abdomen, and cried. She had no reason to cry, but the departure was too emotional for her. What she knew would forever be in her heart. She wished she could keep this girl forever in her house, but now she had to go back to Nazareth to fulfill the next season of her life, and she had to get ready to birth her own child in the world. The baby danced around vigorously in her abdomen. He almost knocked her breath away. She challenged him laughingly, "You, John, will be out of here soon enough, for you are getting too big for the inside." She rested quietly in the bed, for she did not think she would have the courage for any kind of work today. Mary and her Lord were gone. She would lie quietly there until Zacharias returned, and then they would have lunch together. Midge and her daughter would be coming over tomorrow. She was glad she had asked them not to come until the following day after Mary had departed. She had no idea she would have been so emotional, but she knew that the bond she found in Mary could never be denied. Their babies were already bonded by their destinies as already outlined for them by God. How many women get to know the destiny of their children before they are even conceived? She knew the answer to that was very few, but she and Mary did; they were kindred spirits united in life by the seeds they bore. These were babies on specialty assignments, and Mary, sweet Mary, was the carrier of the Lord Messiah, Savior of the world, and she, Elizabeth, carrier of His prophet John. Elizabeth laid there reveling in the truth she knew. "May all who hears this story believe," she murmured. Elizabeth drifted off into a peaceful sleep. She dreamed of walking in a field of green grass by the sea of Galilee. The boats were out on the lake, rocking to the lull of the waves. White birds flopping their wings were dipping in and out the water with the fishes they had caught. It was a brilliant day with a gentle wind blowing across the bay. Across the other side of the field was Mary yelling and running to her with a man and a child in her arms. "Mary, Joseph, and Jesus," she whispered, picking up her pace to reach them. She awoke out of her dream before she could reach them. Elizabeth smiled. She knew God wanted her to rest, knowing Mary would be taken care of. She had slept for a few hours, and again, she contemplated that she was taking more naps than usual. It was also because she had gotten up earlier than usual to see Mary off. She hoped they had at least gotten into Jerusalem because Mary had a long, long journey home. Elizabeth wandered into the baby's room. Her eyes looked over everything to be sure she was well prepared. She heard the voice of her friend Midge at the door, surprised she turned and went to open the door. "Midge, why are you here today?" Rachel was standing behind her with a large grin on her face. Midge scolded her, "Elizabeth! You cannot be by yourself again, not until the baby is born. The baby is due at any time, and someone must be with you at all times. You do not understand the ways of the babies; he can choose to come at any time now. You need us here." Elizabeth knew she was right; she had not thought of that, and Zacharias had followed Mary into Jerusalem. She hugged her friend, surrendering to her wisdom and kindness.

Midge observed that the baby was already extremely low in the abdomen. She sat down with her friend and discussed what will happen and what Elizabeth will need to do when the midwife arrives. Elizabeth was more than happy to have her friend take over; she had experienced the birthing processes of her six children and her many grandchildren. Rachel listened on with a smile. The women loved each other so much, and she just watched in amazement as they sat there talking. Elizabeth was six years older than her mother and was having her first child. She was intrigued because she knew that the baby was a miracle by the sovereign will of God. Her mother had told her of the angel visit to Uncle Zacharias while in the temple and that Aunt Elizabeth had gotten pregnant almost immediately. She wanted to be a part of this great miracle. She had not chosen to marry early because then her mother would be alone. Her mother had insisted that she accepted Levi's proposal, and in many ways, her heart had gone after the rabbi and his two handsome young sons who needed a mother. She knew if she married him, she would also love to have children of her own. She pondered on the mystery of Elizabeth's pregnancy, and she hoped her mother's beautiful friend would have no complications during birthing. Midge instructed Elizabeth on how she needed to breathe when she started having contractions and to listen and cooperate with the midwife to push the baby out. She reassured her that Huldah was an amazing midwife and had delivered all her grandchildren and also that she had helped with the delivery of her own Rachel when she was a student midwife to the midwife who attended to her. Elizabeth was comfortable with Huldah. She had served the community well, and only once was a baby dead on delivery, and it was suspected the baby had died before the delivery. The villagers, actually, praised her calmness and peacefulness even with a breached baby. She had skilled hands and coached the mothers well through the delivery process. God had gifted her well to help women bring their children into the world. For the first time, Elizabeth was going over the process of her own child's birth. She had thought so little of the birthing process, having lost herself in the miracle of her pregnancy. She gave full attention to Midge and felt at peace that Midge, her best friend, would be assisting Huldah with the baby's delivery. Rachel fixed lunch, and the ladies ate lunch as Midge recounted stories of her own deliveries to Elizabeth. Elizabeth had heard these stories before, but it was a long time ago. Rachel was the last child and was already twenty-six years old. Elizabeth smiled; how odd it to be having a baby at her age; her friend was a grandmother and great-grandmother many times over. She hugged her friend, knowing that it was going to be well and, in a few days, she could be holding her baby boy in her arms. Midge talked about breastfeeding and caring for her breast before and during feeding her baby and assured her that Huldah would also go over this with her. Elizabeth thought, *So much to learn.* She was glad she would have this widow woman she called her best friend to be with her. She also knew many other women in the village that she had babysat for and love on their children that she knew would be willing to help her if she ever needed help. It was so beautiful to have a dear friend who can sit with her through the journey of motherhood and see her through to the end of this miracle. Elizabeth knew, in her heart, the birthing process would be smooth for her. Zacharias had not returned home by lunchtime. The ladies cleared the table, and Midge made know to Mary that both she and Rachel would be staying with her both night and day until the baby was born. Elizabeth was moved to tears; she felt so blessed to have her friend Midge who had so much love and concern for her. She was blessed to have her as her friend. Midge also warned her that she would not be in the kitchen anymore. She would do the cooking, and Rachel would clean the house and do the laundry. She went over the clothes and bedding Elizabeth had made for the baby and discussed what she would need to get for the midwife visit. Zacharias would have to make a booth and would remain outside until she was clean again before he could return to the room with her according to Jewish laws. Elizabeth laughed. She reminded her friend that she had been clean for over thirty-eight years before the baby came. Her period was already gone a long time before the baby was conceived, and not to forget, this was by a pure miracle from God. But according to the laws of the Torah, Zacharias would sleep outside for seven days after his son was born. Elizabeth was sure she would not be bleeding much after the baby's delivery, but according to the laws of purification, Zacharias had to stay on the outside of the house. They would have to raise this special child God had entrusted in their care. Midge laughed, knowing her friend. She and Zacharias had always been so full of love and display of intimacy, even at their old age. She did not doubt that this was going to be a new but wonderful season for them both. She threw her head back, looking at her friend laughingly, and said, "Elizabeth! How could this thing be that you, a grandmother, are having a baby?" Elizabeth laughed out loudly, having been totally caught off guard by what her best friend just stated. She was questioning her veracity of motherhood. "It's Yahweh's decision," she laughed, poking her friend in the side. "He decided for us, don't you see Zacharias went dumb questioning His sovereign will; do you want your mouth shut also?" They collapsed on the chair, laughing with Elizabeth clutching her abdomen. Rachel watched the women in amazement that they could still have so much fun even at their age. Elizabeth was worn out, and Midge, sobering up, told her friend to go and rest. They both could do with the laughter. Midge has not had so much fun in a long time. Elizabeth agreed that Midge could do the cooking. Midge was a great cook, and Zacharias has had plenty of meals from her hands. They all hoped Zacharias would come home soon. Elizabeth worried because since going dumb and with her pregnancy Zacharias has not ventured out of the house very much. Midge prepared the evening meal, and they waited for Zacharias.

Zacharias and Benjamin were on their way back from Jerusalem. Benjamin had chosen to travel with his friend that morning, seeing him accompanying Mary alone to Jerusalem. He wanted to be sure his friend had some company after Mary was safely on her way to Nazareth. Therefore, he took his own donkey with the intent to shop for a few items and joined them in the journey to Jerusalem. Zacharias was grateful for the company, knowing his friend would keep him entertained all day. Mary was delivered to the band of merchant women who were packed and ready to go. The men waved goodbye as the women with a few men started their journey to Nazareth. Mary waved back after graciously thanking them for delivering her safely to the vendors. Benjamin was excited. He wanted to go shopping with his friend. He wanted to buy the baby's crib for Zacharias. "You don't have to worry about the evil eye; your baby is special delivery. None will be able to touch him." He spoke this in the knowledge of the Jewish custom not to buy gifts for the babies until they were born. "Your son is here to stay and to become the prophet to the Lord," Zacharias grinned at his friend. He was right. John was a gift that could not be touched. The little sleeping box rocker was suitable for the baby to sleep in up until the first year of life. It would fit at the bedside of the mother's bed until the baby was older and could sleep in his own bed. Zacharias decided to get the holders for the mezuzah; he had spent some time writing out the blessings for the baby's room. He would also buy a basket that would be used to hold the baby when outdoors in the garden. Zacharias had made a bed and a table for the baby's room, but it was not customary to buy other things until the baby arrived. He knew that John was a gift from God, so he would go along with his fiend's wish, and he had no such belief in the "evil eye" superstition of the day. So, a crib and a basket he agreed his friend could buy for the baby. He bought some seeds for the vegetable garden for next spring and bought some honey and dried nuts to take home. Benjamin bought the items on his list dragging Zacharias around the market and filling his ears with the excitement of the prophet and the Messiah. The people, the colors, and the noise in the market were pulsating. It was almost nine months since Zacharias had not ventured into Jerusalem. A band of soldiers was seen in town. Their brightly colored uniforms and headdress were an overly dramatic contrast against the plain clothing of his kingsmen. The bartering of the merchant calling out their wares was overstimulating and harsh to the ears of Zacharias. He only came to the Jerusalem market when he had to. He often bypasses the market on his way to the temple. Now he had been away for too long from the town, and the stimulation was too much for him. His world has been so quiet for so long that the vibrations of the market were overpowering. He, however, tagged along with his friend until he got what he came to buy. They shared the load until they returned to where the donkey was tied up. They loaded up the beast with the purchase of the day. The two men started out for Judea after having lunch in Jerusalem. Benjamin drove the ass ahead, and he and Zacharias walked behind the animal, where he filled Zacharias in with the latest political news. There have been rumors of new taxations regulations and that Caesar was changing the rules about where taxes would be paid. He told Zacharias that he heard on the grapevine that everyone had to go back to his original hometown of their birth. Benjamin laughed, "Everyone has been so long removed from their original hometown and lived where they pleased and what is that to the Caesar, this would never become a rule." Rome had already collected so much tribute money that the nation was tired of the hassle and the constant demand of Rome. Until the Messiah comes and makes all things new, they were obliged to be subject to the demand of Caesar. The mercenaries were getting themselves killed or thrown in prison, and no one seemed to have a plan on how to effectively remove the Roman presence from the land. *We forget the strength and reach of the Roman Empire,* Zacharias thought. *We are but a speck of dust in the reach of their dynasty.* Both men have never traveled out of Jerusalem, but there are those who have traveled to Rome and other regions of the Empire and came back with stories of grandiose palaces and cities with highways, brick walls, and aqueducts much more fascinating than anything seen in Israel. Their military prowess was very present in their land, and the groans and burdens were heavier than any former oppressors their ancestors had served before. Benjamin, as if reading his friend's mind, continued, "It will take divine intervention to bring down Rome. It was a powerful empire, and no one had been able to stand against them in all these years." Zacharias groaned within himself, "If only Israel had remained faithful as a nation to Yahweh, then we would have saved ourselves from such disaster." He shook his head in disdain, thinking to himself, "We wear the tallit, wrap our hands and forehead with the tefillin, wear our kippah, hang the mezuzah on our doors, light our menorah, keep the Sabbath, and the high holy days, but yet God is so far away from us. We carried out the rituals, but the people had forgotten to love God. They wanted His blessings but not the relationship. Yahweh! We have failed you." How he wished, he wished he could talk with his friend. Benjamin walked the last mile in silence, both men deep in their thoughts. The Messiah and his prophet were here, and they could not help but imagined what life would be like in thirty years. They had returned to Ein Kerem safely, and Benjamin unloaded the goods onto Zacharias's doorstep. He would not stay, for they had eaten in Jerusalem but would return to take care of his animals. Zacharias opened the door and was greeted by a chorus of women. He smiled and nodded at them. Elizabeth was in good company. Midge had been a good friend to his wife Elizabeth, and he was happy that she and her daughter were here to take care of his Elizabeth. The evening sun set as they settled down for dinner. The meal was quiet as the women seemed to be engaged with the thoughts in their own heads. Zacharias excused himself from the table. He would write his thought on the scroll and retire for the night. It has been a long day.

The sun burst out in all its glory that day. Midge stirred to the sound of the cock crowing in the distance. She turned in bed and realized her daughter was lying there. Startled, she arose and adjusted her eyes to the room. She smiled, remembering that she and her daughter were at Elizabeth's house. She laid back quietly on the bed. She had not heard a stir from her friends. Her mind rumbled with thought. It was Tuesday, and she hoped that Elizabeth would have the baby before Friday. It was too complicated when the baby came on the Sabbath. There were too many rules to be remembered, and the midwife is usually delayed in coming. Everything was considered work that could not be done. Most people forget mercy and common sense. She would have to talk with Huldah again to ensure she would be prepared to serve Elizabeth even on the Sabbath day. She would also need to find out what she needs to prepare in the room for the delivery of the baby. Elizabeth would have the baby in her room, and Zacharias had already made a small booth in the back of the house and moved in. He had to use an extra blanket and straws to keep warm for the eight days he would be separated from

Elizabeth. He could build a fire if it got terribly cold. Midge felt her aching knees and fingers tingling. It was beginning to get a little cooler, and her joints hurt. Tears sprang to her eyes as she thought about Elizabeth getting ready for delivery. She, herself, had been so long removed from the child's birth process but has somehow remained useful, helping with the delivery of her own grandchildren. She looked at her own daughter, Rachel, lying there sleeping peacefully. She has been such a good daughter and a beautiful girl who has given up her own happiness to stay at home as a companion to her mother. She was happy she had finally decided to marry Levi. He was a good man for her and already came with two boys. She hoped Rachel would also bear him daughters and sons. She was happy for the season she was living in and all the experience she has had in the last nine months. With all assurance, she knew the Messiah was here and that in a few days, his prophet would be delivered into her own arms. She prayed that she would live to see him grow and help her friend Elizabeth to raise her prize child. How blessed she was to partake in the greatest promise God has given to men and was in the process of fulfilling it. She had lived to see the day. She broke out with silent praise and thanksgiving. Rachel also turned in the bed and awoke; she was startled seeing her mom beside her. "Mom, why are you in my bed?" she queried. Sitting up, she also realized she was not home but in the house of Elizabeth waiting for the baby. She hugged her mom, seeing the tears in her eyes. They were both a part of the miracle. Elizabeth was eight years older than her mother. She was the last child of her mother and was already twenty-six years old. She was a baby that was a surprise to her parents. She was fifty-four years and thought she was finished having babies when she found herself pregnant with Rachel. Rachel had spent many days with Aunt Elizabeth, who has been friends with her mother for a very long time. Her mother had shared with her the miracle of the baby and also of the visit of Mary, who was carrying

Lord's child. Her heart has become soft with all the miraculous news she had received. She promised her mom to pay attention to the readings of the Torah and to keep these things in her heart. In another year, she will be married to Levi. She will need to talk with him to see what he believed and what was dear to his heart. What would he think of all this talk of the prophet and the Messiah? She hoped with all her heart that he, too, was a believer in the promises of God to send the Messiah to forever change the face of the earth and to restore righteousness and access back to God the Creator.

Meanwhile, in the other room across the hall, Elizabeth and Zacharias stirred. Elizabeth could only lie on her back with multiple pillows propped under her head and shoulders. Zacharias turned and looked at his wife and raised up to sit by her. He kissed her on the cheek, thinking how huge she really had become. He knew it would be any day now. He could not ask her how she was, so he stroke her abdomen gently with his hand. Elizabeth smiled at the father of her child, the man who had bravely stood by her and never stopped loving her even when she remained barren. God had always had a special plan for both of them, so they were getting to live out the miracle they were born for. This was their destiny; they were parents to the prophet of the Lord's child. Elizabeth tried to pull herself up but could not. The baby was a lot lower in the abdomen this morning, and she was having difficulty even moving her legs. She smiled over at Zacharias and said, "I think he is ready; John is ready to come out; your boy wants to be in your hands." Zacharias smiled, nodding his head in agreement. Elizabeth did not appear to be in any pain, so they lie there in silence. He knew Midge was here and would exactly know what to do. He was going to be a father, and he would do a great job raising a Nazarite child unto God. Elizabeth has always been good with preparing the food they ate, so it would not be difficult for her, sticking with a meal plan for their son John.

Part 1: The Angel Has Come

He squeezed her hand and got out of bed. Elizabeth told him she was having difficulty getting up so he should get Midge so she could tell her what to do. Zacharias opened the door and found Midge in the kitchen making breakfast. He indicated for her to go see about Elizabeth. Her heart skipped a beat as she quickened her steps to the room. "Elizabeth! My friend, how is your morning?" "I think the baby is ready to come," Elizabeth chirped. Midge took one look at her friend's smiling face, and she knew it was not quite yet. "I think this baby has gotten a little lower in the abdomen; I just can't get my feet off the bed this morning." Midge smiled and informed her friend that her baby was getting ready. She got her daughter, and they both helped Elizabeth to sit up. Midge encouraged Elizabeth to walk as much as she could but to rest often. They would call the midwife only when she started active labor. Elizabeth's abdomen was hanging low, and John was kicking with enthusiasm. Elizabeth stood in the spot; she was unable to move until the baby had quieted down again. Midge assisted her friend to the table, where she completed breakfast and set before them all. Elizabeth ate with quite a gusto; she had a healthy appetite. She was surprised at her appetite and the amount of food she had eaten that morning. The morning sun had risen high, and the wind rustled in the treetops. The sweet singing of the birds could be heard in the trees. *How sweet the cry of a baby would sound within the mix of the morning light,* Elizabeth contemplated as she sat eating her morning meal. She pushed her plate away and got up to walk again. She wandered out into the garden, which was bare. The fruits were canned, and the rosebuds had now disappeared. It was a little cooler than she expected, and she drew her shawl closer around her shoulders. Rachel joined her outdoors, and they both walked in silence in the cool morning air. Elizabeth's walk was slow and labored. The pressure in her lower abdomen prevented her from singing. She, however, walked on breathing deeply. Her heart heard the sound, "Today, she will deliver her son."

She laughed loudly and asked Rachel to help her inside. Rachel held her hand and gently guided her back to the door. As she stepped into the room, her water broke and gushed down her legs. Rachel yelled for her mother, who came out of the kitchen and observed what was happening. Midge guided Elizabeth to the room, where she assisted her in cleaning up and made her comfortable in the bed. Elizabeth had no sooner gotten into the bed when she had the first contraction. Midge hastened Rachel to go find the runner who would go to get the midwife immediately. She believed the baby was ready to come out and there would be no delay in this delivery.

Zacharias was told his wife was ready to give birth. He came over and kissed her and left the house for the booth. There he prayed in silence and gave thanks to God. Midge vigilantly sat by the side of the bad, comforting her friend as the contractions came and encouraging her to breathe. Elizabeth laughed in between contractions as she recounts how painful the contractions were. "Can you imagine me doing this six times?" Midge chided. "I had loads of pain but was always swift with the delivery of the baby. Severe pain shot across her abdomen, and Elizabeth screamed, pulling awfully hard on her friend's arm. Midge instructed her to breathe; she had a feeling the baby would not wait and was getting ready to come into the world. Rachel returned to the room and helped her mother to put extra paddings on the bed and to place a pot of water on the fire, which Huldah would need when she got there. If she came on her donkey, she should be there in twenty minutes. Midge cleaned her friend and offered her water. Elizabeth clutched to her friend's arm as if afraid to let her go. A mild panic swept across her face, and she asked her friend to pray her favorite psalms. Midge, in her most soothing voice, repeated the words of David. "He that dwelleth in the secret place of the Most High shall abide under the shadow of the Almighty. I will say of the LORD; He is my refuge and my fortress: my God; in him will I…" (Psalm 91:1-2) Elizabeth bellowed out a scream almost pulling her friend down on her in the bed Midge checked her to be sure the baby was not yet coming. Rachel stood vigilantly in the doorway, ready to let Huldah in; she hoped Elizabeth would be well. She, herself, was still not a mother and have no idea what the woman was experiencing. She went to the door to see if Huldah was coming. Midge sang to her friend and rearranged her on the bed, propping her head up and moving her feet up to keep her legs open. She pulled her dress up and rubbed her abdomen with olive oil as she continued to sing,

> Surely he shall deliver thee from the snare of the fowler, and from the noisome pestilence. He shall cover thee with his feathers, and under his wings shalt thou trust: his truth shall be thy shield and buckler. Thou shalt not be afraid for the terror by night; nor for the arrow that flieth by day.

Psalm 91:3-5

Another contracted rippled across her abdomen, and Elizabeth cried out, holding on to her Midge's arms for consolation. Tears spilled from her eyes, and she asked her friend how long it would last. Midge did not have an answer for her friend but encourage her to take deep breaths during the contractions. From Midge's own experience, many women had their babies within the first two hours of labor, but some women could take the whole day with contractions coming and going for long hours. She hoped for her friend's sake it would be a quick birthing process.

Zacharias could hear the cries of his wife from the booth. Beads of sweat gathered on his forehead as he intensely prayed for the safe delivery of their son. He knew God would be faithful in completing what he started, but he knew her birth pains were real. His heart pounded every time he heard her cried. He felt so useless and was still speechless, so all he could do was stay in silent prayer and consternation. This day would soon be over, and he would get to see his boy. He picked up on the psalms Midge had started and prayed silently. "A thousand shall fall at thy side, and ten thousand at thy right hand; but it shall not come nigh thee. Only with thine eyes shalt thou behold and see the reward of the wicked" (Psalm 91:7-8). He heard the cries of his wife as the voice of the midwife sounded in the yard. She had arrived on her donkey and descended with a basket in her hand. Zacharias took the beast to the back and tied the animal to a tree so it would not wander away. He felt a peace settled on his heart, for he knew the help his wife need was now here. Huldah entered the room and gave out orders to the women. She took her outer coat off and requested Rachel take it to the dining area. Midge brought her warm water, with which she cleaned her hands and arms. She examined Elizabeth and told her it was almost time for the baby. She showed her how to breathe and how to push when she asked her to. Midge would stay by her head to encourage her to breathe, and Rachel would bring her fresh water when needed. Huldah positioned herself at Elizabeth's feet and watched for the baby's head. She knew the story of Elizabeth's miracle pregnancy, and this was the first time she had ever delivered a woman off eighty-eight years old. From her examination, the labor was progressing well. She was not deterred by her age because she knew she had divine help. Elizabeth did not seem to be having any complications. Her pelvis was fully opened, and the baby head was already down in the cervix and crowning. She would order her to push once the contractions started again. She was happy that the baby has not presented as a breach of birth. She believed that the baby would be out in the next few minutes. A wave of contraction swept over Elizabeth's abdomen, and she cried out in pain, but she followed the instruction of the midwife to push. She pushed as hard as she could and heard Huldah said the head was out. Another contraction followed by another, and the demand from Huldah to keep pushing increased. The pains were sharp, and Elizabeth felt like she was splitting into two halves. She grabbed her friend's arm and continued to push. She felt a release as her baby was delivered into the arms of the midwife. She cut the umbilical cord, and Huldah lifted the baby in the air and his little lungs filled with air. He let out the loudest cry Elizabeth had ever heard. "My son, my son," she laughed and cried as her abdomen continued to contract. The hardest part of her labor was over. Huldah quickly cleaned the baby as Midge washed her hands and took over the care of the baby. Midge continued to clean the baby as she counted ten fingers and ten toes; his eyes were a perfect blue, his ears, nose, and mouth were perfect. He was a perfect boy. She swaddled the baby, who would be given to his mother as soon as she delivered the placenta and was able to hold her child. Huldah massaged the abdomen of Elizabeth, and with a few more contractions, the placenta was delivered. Huldah cleaned up the bed. Her job was done, Elizabeth was stable. Her bleeding was normal for delivery. Midge took the baby and placed him on her chest. Elizabeth cradled the child in her arms loosen the cloth off his tiny body. She looked over every detail of his body, crying, "My son, my son! My male child from the Lord." She broke forth in thanksgiving, and every eye in that room held tears. She swaddled her baby again, and Midge assisted her to offer her breast to the crying child. With a few attempts, he latched on successfully and was bonding with his mother and his mother with him in perfect harmony. Huldah looked on in gratitude to God for a mother of eighty-eight who had birthed a perfectly healthy baby and producing breast milk to feed her child. She gave a few instructions to Midge, who had helped her before. Rachel helped the woman to clean up, and she fetched her coat; it would be her place to announce to Zacharias that his son was born.

Zacharias was still kneeling in prayer when Huldah found him in the booth. "Your son is born," she chanted. "He is perfect in every way, and Elizabeth is well also." He nodded at her and multiple times raised his hands to heaven in silent praise. Huldah collected her beast and told him he could go to the door to meet his baby boy. Midge brought the baby to the door. Zacharias kissed his son, then lifted him to the heavens in silent praise; he gave his son back to Yahweh. He then handed the child back to the woman and returned to his booth. He would see his child again in eight days on his circumcision, and then he would be able to see his miracle every day. Zacharias knelt in the booth and wept for joy before God. So, had concluded the message of Gabriel, the angel who stands in the presence of God. John was born. His promised seed was here. He wondered how soon he would receive his voice again. He hoped soon. The silence has been too long, and now that the baby was here, there was much to be said. Back in the room, Rachel assisted Elizabeth by putting the sleeping baby into his crib after he was fed. Midge washed her friend and changed her clothes, and remade the bed. Elizabeth was then ushered back into bed to rest. She quickly fell asleep; labor and delivery of the baby had been painful and exhausting. Midge took the dirty bedding outdoor, and as she washed the bedding, she gave worship to God, who had given everything he promised her friends. She was an eyewitness to it all. In eight days, there would be the circumcision and the naming of the baby. She had made all the plans, and all the people to assist her have been assigned their tasks. She would leave later today to announce to the neighbors that the baby was born. She had arranged with a runner to go into Nazareth to take a letter to Elizabeth's family so they could make arrangements to come down for the bris and naming of the baby. She would be sure to remember to have Zacharias write the letter to be delivered. This was the most important ceremony for the baby, and she was sure all her family had by now heard and would be attending, even if it was only out of curiosity. She was convinced that Mary's return to Nazareth with her surprising pregnancy may have led to a leak of Elizabeth's pregnancy to all her family. She doubted that Mary would return at this time since she had just left. The young maiden had to now get her life in order for marriage. Her thoughts came back to the present. There was much to be done. She hanged her washing out and returned to the room with basic instructions for Rachel to provide warm water for the compress for Elizabeth to use on the abdomen and the pubic area for pain. She would make lunch for everyone and take Zacharias's own to the booth in the back. She would have Elizabeth rest in bed today and have Rachel offer the baby for feeding whenever the baby was awake. The baby should be checked for urine and feces and should be cleaned with warm water and soap and swaddled in a new cloth. She was to be sure Elizabeth was frequently offered warm tea, milk, and water as she needed fluids to produce milk for her baby. She had to assess the baby often to be sure he was breathing properly and to be sure he burped before he was returned to his crib. She had to ensure that both baby and mother were kept warm by using extra blankets. Rachel was well capable; she had assisted her own sister and sisters-in-law with their new babies. She was happy she could be helpful to Elizabeth and the baby, and they were both still sleeping. She was sure the baby would be up soon and requesting food. Midge dressed and left the house for her mission in the village to make preparation for the upcoming ceremony. She would first stop by Benjamin's house and let him know that his friend's son was born. He would have to help his friend soon in rebuilding a larger booth in the front of the house for the naming party. As she hastened over the hill, she felt a melody of praise rising up in her soul. The hills came alive with the sound of the noontide. The sheep and the donkeys in the field seem to lift their heads to greet her. The wind and the birds seemed to whisper her name. Jehovah has looked on the nation and has birth forth a new season of grace and mercy. Yahweh has been faithful to the words of His prophets. Midge did not know what this would mean for her grandchildren. She would be asleep and silent in the grave. But born this day was the prophet of the Lord's child, and she had held him with her own two hands.

Benjamin was overjoyed on hearing of the baby's birth. Like Midge, he also celebrated the beginning of a new season. One that he, himself, had only read of and hoped to see as Isaiah prophesied,

> The voice of him that crieth in the wilderness,
> Prepare ye the way of the LORD, make straight
> in the desert a highway for our God. Every val-
> ley shall be exalted, and every mountain and
> hill shall be made low: and the crooked shall be
> made straight, and the rough places plain.

Isaiah 40:3-4

He wondered why the desert; the boy would be raised here in these hillsides where the air is clean, and the food is plenty and fresh. Midge left him in his thoughts as she rushed on to complete her errands to gather the women who would help her with the cooking and baking for the ceremony. Benjamin had agreed to help Zacharias with the booth for the ceremony. He still had all the material from the last dinner party they had. It was cooler now, so they would have to make a fire pit for the celebration to continue into the night and for those who would sleep over. He signed as he thought on how so many in Israel have fallen into a spiritual sleep and no longer look for the promised Messiah. He wondered at the grace of God in choosing simple hill folks to fulfill his divine promise of salvation. Peradventure, he should have any doubt he was reminded of God's choice for their second king of Israel, King David. He was but a young boy still freckled and ruddy on the cheeks from spending so much time in the sun taking care of his father's sheep. When Samuel came to anoint the next king of Israel, his father presented his other seven sons but forgot about David in the field. In his father's eyes, he was not qualified to be a king; he was but a little boy. But when the seven sons that he presented were rejected by God, he sent for his youngest child. David was anointed to be the next king of Israel to the amazement of his family. Nothing changed in his life immediately. He kept tending his sheep. But David knew he was different from the day that oil was poured on him by the prophet Samuel. He marveled at the supernatural strength he had when a bear and a lion came to take his sheep. He killed them both with his bare hand. He found himself writing songs and playing his harp with more fervor. His day of recognition came when his father sent him with food to his brothers in Israel's army. He found the giant Goliath talking against Yahweh and his people, and righteous indignation rose up in him; he offered to fight the giant to the shock of his own brothers. Saul knew the Spirit of God was on the lad and gave him permission to fight. David did fight the giant with a sling and a stone. The giant fell to the ground, and he cut off his head with his own sword. Israel did have the victory that day. Benjamin pulled himself back from his thoughts; he looked to the heavens and prayed, "Jehovah, I do know what you are doing, I know that this is the time you have chosen to bring salvation to Israel and to all who have ears to hear and eyes to see will both see and hear." He hurriedly dressed and went over the hills with his tools to see his friend's house. He hoped his friend had gotten back his voice. There was so much to talk about. So much had happened here in Judea, and in the politics, in Jerusalem, there was always something new daily. Jerusalem was brewing with all kinds of gossips and talks of threat. It was hard to find someone he could trust to talk with. There were so many views, and traitors have risen up all over the hill country and not to mention in Jerusalem.

One had to be careful to whom he talked and what he talked about. The nation was divided, and all kinds of false hope and belief were hanging in the air. How sad he thought that a baby, the prophet to the Messiah, was born today, and very few would even believe much more to celebrate this precious birth for what it truly was. He hoped that John's birth would stir the hearts of the people, even there in Ein Kerem. They forgot so easily an eighty-eight-year-old woman and a ninety-eight-year-old priest gave birth to a child. He wondered what greater sign a people could ask for, but his people were a forgetful people. They had forgotten who their God is, and they have forgotten His promises as written in the Torah and the books of the prophets. Life had become mundane and driven by Rome's aristocrats. The leader of the red coat army acted like he was a god, and his soldiers travel the earth collecting trophies for him. Israel has forgotten their God, but God has not forgotten Israel—"*the apple of His eye.*" Israel was missing off of its greatest moment, but as one of the prophets has spoken, "Thy have eyes but could not see, and ears but could not hear." Benjamin hurried up the hill and, as customary, found his friend in a booth in the back. He grabbed a log and sat on the ground, greeting his friend with a hug and congratulated him at the birth of his son. His friend was still dumb, so he rambled on about the reconstruction of the booth and the significance of his son's birth and about the season and era they were living in. He filled him in on the latest gossip in Jerusalem. Zacharias sat there and listened to his friend; he thought, *He is a good man, would have made a great priest or a rabbi. He so loved the things of God and a righteous living.* Benjamin caught himself rambling and stopped offering to assist his friend with starting the construction of the booth. Rachel heard the other man entered the yard and was talking to Zacharias. She had just completed lunch and brought a meal out for the men.

Meanwhile, Elizabeth was sitting up in bed feeding the baby.

She had completely eaten the meal and a drink Rachel brought her. She followed the instructions of Rachel not to get out of bed by herself today. She looked into the eyes of her precious boy as he drank his milk from her breast. *Who could have imagined Elizabeth giving suck by cradling a baby to her breast?* Tears sprung to her eyes, and the hot liquid splashed on the baby's face. She laughed, holding him with one arm and wiping the tears from his face. This was not a time for tears but for laughter and joy. John had strong jaws and pulled hungrily on her breast. She switched him to her other breast. She still felt a little pain in her abdomen and the pelvic area, and she was still a little tired from the morning birthing activities, but joy, abounding joy in her heart, was greater than the pain of child's birth. It was an amazing feeling of becoming a mother. She felt such intense love for the little one she held in her arms. She had never felt this way for anyone before. It was not like her love for Zacharias. This feeling was like she could die for this precious child than have anyone hurt him. It was a kind of possessive love that Elizabeth had never experienced. She now understood a "mother's love." This is the kind of love a woman experiences each time she brings a child into the world. She was so thankful to Yahweh that she got to experience this innate, built-in kind of love that surfaces at the birth of a child. It is truly a God-given kind of love. She had missed out on this all her life and now on reflection, how often she had seen the head of a mother spin in awareness to the cry of her child. Even in a crowded synagogue, a mother would immediately recognize her child calling for her. Elizabeth reveres this moment. She has gotten to be a mother. One so connected to her, bone of her bone, flesh of her flesh was lying here in her arms where he belonged, and he did, and only Yahweh could orchestrate this precious moment. The child she had carried for nine months was now her reality, a crying, feeding bundle of joy. She has now beheld with her own eyes that which has grown in her womb for nine months. While in her womb, all he did was kick her around. Now he was out; he could kick, swing his arms, and cry and turn red in the face. She laughed, looking up to the heavens, for that quickly the baby had fallen asleep again. Rachel entered the room and removed the sleeping child from her arms. She put the baby across her shoulder and lightly patted his back, waiting for him to burp. He was so tiny yet so completely equipped to start this new phase of his life. Elizabeth marveled at the wonder of life; that which was on her inside was now and the outside and was an active needy little energy who would now consume all her days. She was so thankful to have Rachel helping her at this time, and gratitude filled her heart. She knew Midge had gone into the village to make plans for the circumcision party in another eight days. She slid beneath the blankets feeling suddenly, completely exhausted again. Rachel had returned the baby to the crib, and he was sleeping peacefully. She missed not being able to see Zacharias and to see the expression on his face over his son, but these were the long-standing statutes and commandments. They would never break a commandment at this time. Such grace and mercy had been granted to them. Eight days was but a short time, it would pass by quickly, and he would share in the joys of parenthood. She fell asleep almost immediately. Rachel smiled at her mother's friend. Never had she seen such gratitude and awe in the eyes of a mother. Most women by the second child had become accustomed to the expectations. They were young and vigorous and are usually up and out of bed in a few hours after the baby. Elizabeth looked great for her age, but it was easy to tell she was not a young woman. She was an old woman and a first-time mother. A sense of honor and holiness hanged in the air. She knew this was a special moment and a special child. She would cradle this moment in her heart and hoped she would get some blessings by just participating in their care. If her mother did not return on time, she would start the evening meal.

Part 2: The Promised Child Is Born

Meanwhile, Midge hurried along the hill community of Ein Kerem to announce the birth of Elizabeth and priest Zacharias's baby boy. She invited their neighbors to come and celebrate the birth and the circumcision of the child in eight days. The neighbors all break forth in worship and praise to Yahweh. For it was with great joy that they received the news. They have never seen this in their lifetime, the sign of an old woman bearing a child. Even though they have seen the pregnancy, they have had doubts and have long-awaited the birth of the child. She had to also meet with the ladies who would be helping her with the cooking for the party. She needed to find a rabbi who also would perform the circumcision. Her energy was high, and her heart was merry from what she had just experienced. The birth of the Lord's prophet by her best friend. Who could imagine her friend Elizabeth giving birth at her age? She had never seen it this way before in all Judea; no, not in her lifetime. All those who heard of her pregnancy had marveled and were now happy to hear of the birth of her son. If it was even only out of curiosity, she knew that many would be there to see the mother and the child. She had first stopped by Benjamin's house and announced to him the birth of the baby. Benjamin was overjoyed. His friend was a dad, and all the promises of God were fulfilled. Tears sprung to his eyes on the unfolding of a great mystery, and he was blessed to be a part of it. They both stood there in worship to God, who had given them a chance to rejoice in a great miracle in these hills. Midge bade him goodbye and tackled the trail to find her helpers and to give the good news to all she met. Benjamin had hurriedly got dressed, grabbed some tools, and headed up the hill to congratulate his friend. He would help him to build the booth for the party of the naming ceremony. He was sure the whole community would be there to see this miracle. If not out of love, then it would be out of pure curiosity.

Not ever had an eighty-eight-year-old woman given birth in Judea; he knew it was for a sign and a wonder. He was particularly happy for at last that which some of them have believed and hoped for was now at hand. It was the birthing of a new season. The messianic age has come, and it has started right here in this hill region of Judea.

Benjamin was busy hammering with his friend Zacharias, the priest. He could not help himself. The historian in him was immerging above the hammer and the nail; his voice boomed in contrast to the silence of his friend. He voiced his thoughts as he heard the voice of the prophet Isaiah echoing in his soul,

> Comfort ye, comfort ye my people, saith your God. Speak ye comfortably to Jerusalem, and cry unto her, that her warfare is accomplished, that her iniquity is pardoned: for she hath received of the Lord's hand double for all her sins. The voice of him that crieth in the wilderness, Prepare ye the way of the Lord, make straight in the desert a highway for our God.

Isaiah 40:1-3

As he repeated the prophecy on his lips, again, he wondered why the desert. He voiced these thoughts to Zacharias. The boy would be raised in these hills where the air is healthy, and there was much fresh food to eat. Zacharias smiled at the mystery of God and knew it would be fulfilled just as it was prophesied. He himself had no answer for his friend but knew what God has spoken it was so. Benjamin continued to repeat from memory the prophecy of Isaiah concerning John the prophet and the Christ Lord fulfilling God's mandate on earth. He bubbled up the remainder of the prophecy while Zacharias listened in thankful adoration to God.

> Every valley shall be exalted, and every mountain and hill shall be made low: and the crook-

ed shall be made straight, and the rough places plain: And the glory of the LORD shall be revealed, and all flesh shall see it together: for the mouth of the LORD hath spoken it.

Isaiah 40:4-5

Zacharias nodded his head vigorously. His friend was such an enthusiast; he would certainly have made a great priest or a rabbi, even a prophet, he thought. He memorized and retained a large portion of the Torah and the scrolls of the prophets and believed it with all his heart as he also did, unlike some of the priests he worked with, they did not believe. They went through the motions of religious life but did not believe in the promises of Yahweh. Benjamin laughed loudly, catching himself rambling again. Within a short time, they had erected the booth and cover the roof with palm leaves. They also dig a fire pit since most people from Nazareth would be sleeping over after dark, and it was much cooler. The men were filled with so much energy; they did the job of four men in a short time.

Elizabeth was awake. She had eaten the lunch Rachel had brought her and all the extra liquids she had given her and encouraged her to drink. She was now sitting on the side of the bed, breastfeeding her son again. He had a strong sucking reflex for just coming into the world four hours ago. She looked deeply into his blue-colored eyes, unlike his father's hazel-colored eyes. He had perfectly formed fingers and toes, and he was a beauty to behold. She heard Zacharias and his friend in the yard working and missed sharing this moment with him. Within eight days, her husband will get to bond with their promised child, the prophet of the Lord. She switched the child to the next breast, and he fed him with content. It all came so naturally; she was overcome by a tender, calming, nurturing feeling of peace. Rachel watched the new mother in awe—her mother's oldest friend, a new mother by the divine will of God. She heard the story from her mother of all the happenings in Aunt Elizabeth's house, and she was glad she was here to participate. As she gave the child to the mother, she felt the tug of her own heart towards motherhood. Levi had waited on her long enough, and she now knew with all her heart that she wanted to be his wife and to be the mother to his two boys and even to have children of her own. She had helped to take care of the children of her sister's and her brothers' children and was present at the birth of some of the children, but this was so different. The labor was painful, but it was over so quickly. Elizabeth was an old woman but pushed that baby out like a young girl. Her face, at one time though in pain, seemed to glow as the baby was delivered into the world. She watched the new mother from across the room and knew that God had kissed her face and gave her great favor. She hoped her children would grow up and listen to the voice of this prophet and embrace the Messiah when he comes on the scene. It was at this moment when she knew she would instill in the hearts of her children the happenings she had heard and witnessed here that day. The baby had stopped nursing and had fallen asleep again. She went over to Elizabeth and took the child whom she cradled on her shoulder and patted his back until he burped. As per her mother's instruction, she instructed Elizabeth to rest. She placed the sleeping baby in the crib. She assisted Elizabeth to the toilet and tucked her back in bed. Her mother had instructed her that Elizabeth need to rest in between feeding the baby and should do no activities by herself today. She could give her a warm cloth for her abdomen and pelvic area if she had pain, and to be sure to pay attention that she had no heavy bleeding, Elizabeth thanked her friend's daughter. They were such a sweet blessing to her, and Rachel was such the perfect nurse. She was young but kind and decisive. She better listened to her little helper and get back in bed. Elizabeth fell asleep almost immediately. The delivery had certainly exhausted her.

Part 2: The Promised Child Is Born

Midge, in the meantime, had made her rounds around the hill and delivered the news of the birth of the baby to the neighbors. She spoke with the women who would help her to cook and found a runner who would take the letter to Elizabeth's sister in Nazareth. He could make the trip in two days and give everyone who wanted to come time to prepare and make the journey. She thought about Mary and believed she should be home by now. She prayed the girl would experience grace with her family. She doubted she would be making the trip back for the party. She would need to sort her life out and be married soon. Midge shifted her thoughts back to the present. She needed to find a mohel to perform the circumcision; she wondered why she had not thought of that earlier. If she could not find someone in Judea, she would have to go down into Jerusalem tomorrow. She suddenly remembered that Levi, her soon-to-be son-in-law, was a rabbi who was trained as a mohel also. She had been to a few ceremonies that he performed at, and he was good at what he did. She was sure he would be in Jerusalem today, but she stopped by his house as it was in the same yard as his parent's house. She would stop by and leave a message to see if he could perform the Bris for Elizabeth and Zacharias' son. She was sure Zacharias would have no objection. She hurried down the hill to their house and was surprised to see that Levi was home. He greeted the older woman with great affection. Surprised to see her visiting. He had a meeting scheduled with her in two weeks to present the dowry for his new bride. Midge set him at ease by voicing her need to find a mohel for Elizabeth and Zacharias's baby bris. He was also overjoyed to hear the news of the baby and informed her that he would be more than willing to take off from school next Tuesday to perform the ceremony. He has a deep admiration for priest Zacharias. The miracle of his aged wife's pregnancy had spread across the hills, and like most who heard in Ein Kerem, they knew it was a sign from God. He asked about Rachel and was glad to hear she was helping Elizabeth with the baby. He sent greetings to her and reminded Midge that he would be visiting in two weeks to offer his dowry. She smiled, bowed her head, and departed his house. She needed to get back to Elizabeth's house to cook diner and see about her friend. Levi watched her as she departed up the hill. She was such a good woman, and he was more than happy to marry her youngest daughter, who had chosen all these years to stay by her side. He loved the gentle-mannered girl who showed great kindness and affection to her mother. He knew she would make him a great wife and a good mother for his children. When his Miriam died two years ago, he thought he would never find love again, but as if by divine help, he spotted Rachel with her mother, and when he asked about her husband, his mother had informed her that the girl was twenty-six and unmarried. She had chosen to stay with her widowed mother and had rejected a few proposals. His heart had danced to an unknown melody, and he believed he would make a proposal himself to see if this woman would have him and his sons. He had approached her mother, who loved him immediately but stated she would have to talk to her daughter. He knew there had been some resistance from Rachel at the beginning, but the girl's heart had somehow softened towards him, and she had only agreed after her older brother told her that by right, the mother would live with him and his family when she could no longer care for herself. Rachel, herself, told him she had felt at peace living with her mother and being a companion to her. She confessed that this was her first time considering doing otherwise. Levi thought he caught a glimmer of affection in the girl's eyes. He had asked her to take her time with her decision, and he would be willing to wait for her. By the following week, the mother and older brother had approached him about her agreement, and the plans had been made for the dowry to be delivered. Since she was not so young anymore, he hoped she would not want a long engagement period but would agree on an early marriage. His boys really needed a mother, and he could feel affection already growing for this beautiful girl. He imagined even having more children with her. He would be glad to see her again and would take the boys over to the party, and she could meet them. He was also intrigued by the story of the older priest and his wife having a baby. She was eighty-eight years old. He could not wait to share this miracle with this class. Most of them were upcoming young rabbis who studied the history of their nation just for duty of study but lacked the true passion and connection of God's intervention in the lives of people. All Jewish boys by law had to study Thorah and know the laws and precepts by which they would govern their own household. He had a large class. Except for the well-known yearly miracle that takes place at the pool of Bethesda, where hundreds of people flooded yearly waiting for the angel to touch the water, and all who enters it at first would be healed. These young students treated this occurrence as a fallacy; he wondered what they would think of this story of an old woman giving birth to a son. He had passionately tried to stir faith in their hearts, but their hearts were far from the God that David knew. They were more interested in the politics of Rome and having an audience with Herod than with God. He was so sick himself of the apostasy of the nation. His father was a just and true rabbi who had taught him in school. He also believed and looked for the Messiah and an era of the days like unto King David's reign. He wondered who this special baby was and would be happy to talk with the priest Zacharias, but he also heard that he had gone dumb since his wife's conception. He was excited to go and perform the bris and was sure his boys would have a great time. He was also excited about seeing Rachel and hoped she would be happy to see him also.

Midge had made her way across the hills and was happy she had met good success with each task she sat out to do that day. She was surprised at her energy. Today she felt like a young girl bounding up and down the hills. She had made it back in time to start dinner. She would then rest and help Rachel half the night with the baby so that she could rest also. Rachel heard her mom entered the house and greeted her. Elizabeth and the baby were still asleep, and she gave her mother an account of the last four hours. Midge told her that she met with Rabbi Levi and that he sent greetings. Rachel blushed lightly as her mother explained to her that Levi would be performing the bris next Tuesday. She had thought lovingly of the man all day and of having his babies. She was glad that she would see him again soon. Midge started dinner while Rachel went to attend to the cry of the baby. Elizabeth was already sitting on the side of the bed to receive the crying child. Rachel bent quickly, retrieving the child while Elizabeth prepped her breast to feed the child. She handed the baby to his mother as she chatted away with Elizabeth about the news of Levi doing the bris. Elizabeth liked Levi and thought he was a good match for Rachel, and she could tell that Rachel was growing to love the man. She was so thankful for the friendship of Midge and her beautiful daughter, who were her angels in this season of her life. She knew she could not have done well this day without these beautiful ladies by her side. She watched her baby sucked and sang in a sweet, low melody in his ears. Mother and baby were now in their own world. Rachel withdrew to the kitchen to assist her mother with the meal. Benjamin and Zacharias were still working when Midge arrived. They made such good working buddies and had almost completed the booth and firepit for the party. Midge heard Benjamin shouting his goodbyes, for he would not stay for dinner. Later, when she took Zacharias his dinner, she would inform him of having asked Rabbi Levi to perform the bris. At dinner, she would get some time to talk with her friend. Rachel was doing a good job. She had discussed with Rachel that the baby needs to be fed every two hours and that she would rest half the night then take over from her to help Elizabeth while she slept. Elizabeth fed her son, who was now again asleep. She burped him and placed him in his crib. She wandered out to the kitchen to find her friend. She was hungry also. Midge greeted her and ushered her to the table, where they talk about the events of the day. Elizabeth expressed deep gratitude to her friend for all she was doing for them. Zacharias was still dumb, and it was easier for Midge to take care of the needs at this time. Elizabeth was happy she found a runner who was willing to start the trip to Nazareth today. The sooner they knew, the more time they had to prepare to make their plans to travel down to Judea. She had made a stew from dried meat and vegetables with herbs. The aroma filled the room, making Elizabeth more hungry. She arranged matza and beans, dried fruits, and nuts on the table. There was still fresh milk for Elizabeth. Midge had purchased this on her way home and had asked the neighbor to deliver milk twice daily until the baby was old enough. The neighbor had agreed gladly and said this would be his gift daily to Elizabeth until the baby was weaned. Midge shared a portion of the meal for Zacharias and took it to the back of the house, where Zacharias was reading and writing in his scroll. She informed him that she had asked Levi to perform the bris next Tuesday and he was pleased. He could not have thought of a better person himself; he had great respect for Levi's father and knew the young man was an honorable man. He hoped his dumbness would come to an end soon; it had limited him in so many ways, and what man does not want to be involved in the planning of his child briss? But he humbled his heart and waited on the grace of God to return his voice.

As Midge disappeared back into the house, Zacharias raised his head to heaven and gave thanks in his heart not only for the food but for this precious woman who has graciously served him and his wife these last nine months. While he ate his savory stew and bread, he contemplated the magnitude of the responsibility set before him in raising his son. He knew he was no longer a young man but if God had entrusted this prophet child to their care. He would give him years to enjoy fatherhood and prepare the child for service. He would ask Benjamin to be the sandek. He would hold the baby and assist in the circumcision ceremony. *What better person,* he pondered. He has been his amazing friend for many years and had stood by him even in this time of divine favor. He trusted no man like he trusted his friend Benjamin. He would write out the blessings to be read over his child and have Benjamin read for him. He already knew the destiny of his child and knew just what he would write. Putting away the dinner bowls, he lit a candle and took out his scroll, and began to write.

I want you to be happy; I want you to be strong. You came into the world, but to us, you don't belong. A prophet of the Most High you are called to be. I wish you contentment, I wish you joy, and above all, I wish you courage for the task to which you are called. I want you to know what a real gift you are. When we never imagined possible, we were given you. We will cherish and hold you dear and raise you the way God declares. A Nazarite chosen by God, announced to us by Gabriel, the great angel. We want you to know that we will treasure you dearly and groom you in the way our God explained. You are a dream and a treasure and, best of all, a gift to the world. You will forever herald a new time. May your arms be strong, and your feet be sturdy, may your voice resound and silent you will never be. May your faith be strong, and your words be sound for a prophet to God you are called to be and a blessing to your generation. Your mother and I will hold you near and care for you until our days draw near. Yahweh will provide and keep you always in His care until you have accomplished all you came here for. Amen.

Part 2: The Promised Child Is Born

He rolled the scroll together and put it aside. He hoped he would be able to speak soon, for, in forty days, he would have to take Elizabeth and the child down to the temple to perform the redemption offering of the first-born son in obedience to the Torah. He would search for a lamb without blemish. He would go to the shepherd he often used for his own family sacrifice. He smiled to himself, saying, "I have a son; I, Zacharias, am a father to a son named John." He would, for the first time, offer a sacrifice for a child. Though he had to redeem this child, yet he knew that this child was already committed to the service to God. He would have it no other way. He will not follow in his priestly duties, but according to God's divine order, he would be a prophet to the Lord. Zacharias already knew, and the angel Gabriel had told him how to raise this child, a Nazarite, unto the Lord.

Meanwhile, the ladies were sitting at the table eating and talking together. Midge updated Elizabeth on Levi's agreement to perform the bris. She was glad he had accepted. She really liked the young rabbi. The whole village had grieved when he lost his wife to childbirth. She was glad they would be like family soon. Elizabeth shared with Midge her desire to read one of the blessings at the ceremony. She knew Zacharias would ask Benjamin to take his place, but since he could not speak, she, at least, wanted to say one of the blessings. Midge agreed with her and assured her she would let Zacharias know in the morning. She assured Elizabeth that she had taken care of all the details of the food for the ceremony and on how gracious the neighbors had been to prepare and bring the food. She told her of the neighbor who pledged to bring her milk morning and evening until the baby was weaned. Elizabeth was moved to thanksgiving. Her husband, being a priest, has been given great favor by their neighbors. They always received generous gifts from the neighbor. Zacharias received his weekly supply from the temple, which was due to the priest as written in the Torah. The people were generous in their giving, and the priests were never without. The neighbors gave extra in the hope of extra blessings on their crops and live-stock. There was always fresh meat and poultry and eggs given in a daily supply to their house. Elizabeth had always kept a garden, but every other food came from the neighbor or from the temple. Zacharias got a monthly offering from the temple, and they did not have children, so he had saved some, and they lived modestly. They were never without and always had, in return, shared what they received with those in need. None had ever gone away hungry from their home. The ladies laughed and talked about the circumcision and naming ceremony. Midge promised to bring the white linen drapes used at her son's wedding. They would be used on the booth to form a canopy of welcome for her guest. She had gotten the local men to play the old songs, and there would be dancing, laughter, and joy in another eight days. Midge looked at her friend lovingly, "Who could have imagined my friend Elizabeth becoming a mother?" They both knew they were in the middle of a miracle, and she hoped all who heard would rejoice. The baby cried from his room, and Elizabeth arose with quick steps and walked to reach her child. Midge left the table to prepare for bed. She would sleep and then relieve Rachel at midnight to help Elizabeth with the baby. Rachel had out-walked Elizabeth and had the baby in her arms. She gave Elizabeth time to wash her hands and get comfortable in bed. She handed the baby to the mother and watched Elizabeth cradled the child as she placed her breast nipple into his mouth. The baby and mother fell into the rhythm of singing and feeding time again. Rachel watched in amazement. This woman was older than her mother, and this was her first child, and there they were in complete harmony, the mother and child. At that moment, it was as if nothing else existed. The mother and the baby have been swept away with their need for each other. The eternal bond formulated by God is now displayed in the mother and child. Rachel felt her own heart string tug with longings she had never known existed. When she chose not to marry but to stay with her mother, deep in her heart, she had made the commitment to remain celibate. She had gladly served her mother and her family members willingly and often submitted herself to prayer and good deeds. When Levi had asked for her hands in marriage, she was resistant to the proposal but was encouraged by her mother to rethink her decision. She remembered two years ago that her heart had broken for him when Levi's wife died in childbirth. He had two little boys to raised and would need a new wife to help him. She had prayed often for him and the boys but never dreamed he would cast his eyes on her. Most of the village had known for years that she had chosen to live a life of celibacy by choice. She had turned down two proposals, and it was known commonly in the village that she did not choose to get married but remain a companion to her widowed mother. Some had teased her, but others respected and honored her for her loyalty to her mother. Her mother had prayed silently for her that she would see the day her beloved daughter would be married and give her grandchildren. Her mother knew she had great compassion for Rabbi Levi and his boys and had always prayed for them. Her mother was not surprised when Levi came asking for her hands. She considered it a sign from God. Rachel had prayed about this decision and talked it over with her mom on going back on her words to care for her. Her mother had convinced her that she had never taken an oath and that she could do both since they would be living in the same village and when the time comes and if she was not able to care for herself, then she and her siblings could decide where she spent her final days. She was more worried about leaving her daughter in the world with no one to care for her. Rachel understood her mother's logic and had hugged her mother and agreed to accept the proposal. They had come to an agreement, and he would deliver her dowry in two weeks and then follow the usual one year of betrothal.

The Prophet

As she watched Elizabeth with the baby, her own desire for mother-hood was ablaze in her heart. She thought of Levi and his boys and imagined what a good mother she would be to them. She even prayed there and then that God would give her the joys of becoming a mother herself. She would love to have girls and maybe some boys and would be happy with whatever God chose for her. She would already have two sons, and she would be the best mother and wife she could be. She could hardly wait to see Levi. Where she was quiet and reserved, she now felt a new fire and passion burning in her soul. She had never experienced this before, and it was both exciting and scary. She knew he was a good man, and her heart felt warm and fuzzy all in this one moment of watching Elizabeth with her son. Rachel knew here and now that God was healing her heart of wrong thinking. He had never called her into a life of celibacy; it was her choice. Most women would go into celibacy after their husband died, but she had given up marriage on her own choice. Her mother had often begged her to reconsider her decision not to be married. Rachel had been the stubborn and the protective companion to her mother. It could not have been that way if her father had not died when she was six years old. He would long since have found her a suitable mate as soon as she turned fourteen, for this was the Jewish ways. She had grown up only having a mother, and she could not see herself leaving her mother. Her mother had completely encircled her with much love since she was the child of her old age. Her sons had insisted on getting Rachel married off, but she loved having the girl around and never pushed her against her wish. She, however, prayed and patiently hoped one day Rachel would change her mind. She had to agree that she spoiled her, and she was more strong-willed than most girls of her age. She was opinionated and had not had a father to affirm her, so she had always made up her own rules. Her sons had always financially taken care of them, but Rachel had always felt intense loyalty towards her mother, who remained a widow from the death of her husband. Midge knew that God was changing her heart to see His plans for her life, and she would have the joys of both love and motherhood. Rachel pulled herself out of her thoughts as Elizabeth attempted to burp the sleeping child. She took the sleeping baby out of her arms and encouraged Elizabeth to get washed and get some sleep before the next feeding time. Elizabeth decided that they would feed the baby on demand and see what their first night would be like. Rachel placed the baby in his crib and got the warm water from the kitchen for Elizabeth. She assisted her with her bath and helped her to bed, where she applied warm compresses to her abdomen and tucked her into sleep. Feeling exhausted, Elizabeth drifted off to sleep. Before she fell asleep, she gave Yahweh thanksgiving and worship for her friend and her little nurse, who has stood by her on this greatest day of her life. Rachel settled in the chair across from mother and baby. The night held a quiet stillness. From the window, she could see the moonlight filtering in, and the light in her own heart was shining brightly. She could hardly wait to see Levi next Tuesday. Her heart would now be open to sharing the dreams and the joys to become his wife. She knew he would be shocked but overjoyed. He had been a very patient man. He knew he saw in her the wife God wanted to be by his side. It has taken a little more convincing for her, but here in Aunt Elizabeth's house, God has opened her heart to see his grace and mercy in the human heart, and she knew the same miracle was happening in her life.

Rachel drifted off into a deep sleep and was awoken to the cry of the baby. She pulled herself quickly from the chair and reached for the baby as Elizabeth pulled herself in a sitting position and prepared herself to feed her hungry child. The baby nursed rather quickly and was asleep again. Rachel took the baby from Elizabeth's arms; she burped him, changed his diaper, and returned him to his crib. Elizabeth had settled beneath her blanket and had fallen asleep again. She resettled in the chair and prayed for her family and for Levi and the boys. She did not know how long before she drifted off to sleep but was awoken with her mother shaking her shoulder. She was here to trade places with her young daughter. Rachel took the cues from her mother and left the room to the guest room to finish her sleep. Midge settled in the chair and watched her friend and baby sleeping. Although she had watched this whole pregnancy and the birth of this child, she was still amazed at the miracle of his birth. Elizabeth had gained supernatural strength to carry the pregnancy and to birth the child. The baby let out a wail, and Midge arose from the chair to retrieve the child. Elizabeth sat up with groggy eyes and smiled at her friend, who handed her the baby after she sat up and made herself comfortable in the bed. "He already had a loud voice," Elizabeth retorted. "He is going to be a real loud mouth prophet!" Midge looked down at her friend lovingly and patted her head. She walked back and made herself comfortable as mother and baby bonded in the joy of feeding. Watching them has birthed increased faith and convictions in her own heart towards God and His favor to man. She knew of God, and the scrolls told of His relationship to Israel. She participated in sacrifices and daily worship, the giving of tithes and offerings in the temple and at the synagogue here in Judea. The priests and rabbi teach from the Torah, and the remembrance of God's goodness is celebrated at the great feasts each year, but here in the house of her own friend, she had witnessed the favor and grace of God in the birth of a child announced by an angel and born to a woman in her old age. This was the very prophet child who would one day proclaim the Messiah's entrance into the world. Only in the Torah were such stores recorded of these things now revealed. God was still among men and doing wonders. Having heard all the words spoken by the angel to Priest Zacharias, Midge knew that a holy moment had transpired, and she felt in that moment that God smiled on her friends and showed them great favor and love.

She smiled in return in that holy moment because she knew that her prayers would be answered no matter how long it takes. Midge prayed more fervently and with greater expectation. Her heart cry was that her Rachel would be a good wife and mother and would raise her children to fear God and honor the prophet and the Messiah when they are revealed to Israel. Tears gathered in her eyes and ran down her face unabashedly. Elizabeth lifted her eyes in time to see the tears on her friend's cheeks. "Weep not, daughter of Zion," she said. "It was a good day, a day when one of the greatest prophecies has been fulfilled, and you were a part of it." Midge shook her head in agreement. Elizabeth continued to nurse the child, and Midge reminded her that she would leave in the morning for home. Rachel would remain with her to assist with her needs, for she needed to go home to start the preparation of food for the bris. Before she left, she would talk with Zacharias concerning her request to read one of the blessings at the naming ceremony. The baby was asleep again. Elizabeth burped the child and handed him to Midge, who laid him in his crib. "The next time he woke up, he will have had his first day on earth," Midge said. Elizabeth smiled and tucked the blankets around her shoulders, and by the time Midge had changed the baby's clothing and got back in the chair, Elizabeth was sound asleep. She covered her own feet with a blanket and also fell asleep in the chair. She dreamed her daughter was dressed in a beautiful wedding gown and had the biggest smile on her face walking in the grass towards her. In the dream, there was a large crowd, and there was Levi standing with his two boys, watching her with pure joy in their faces. She broke out dancing with her daughter swirling around and around in happy abandonment. Her joy was complete. Her own heart was filled with laughter, for finally, her beautiful daughter Rachel was happily married. She awoke out of the dream smiling. She knew Levi would provide for her Rachel and make her a happy woman. She also had no doubt that Rachel, though hesitant, was a good match for him.

She rose from the chair, folded the blanket, and placed it on the chair. Elizabeth and the baby were still asleep. Outside, the day had dawned, and the cocks could be heard crowing in the distant hills. She could hear the barks of the dogs as the darkness quickly faded in preparation for the rising of the sun. She would start breakfast and make an early return to her house. There were supplies she needed to get in Jerusalem, and the food preparation needed to be started. She just had a feeling that many people would be coming out for the ceremony, and she had to get enough supplies in Jerusalem to distribute to those who would help her to prepare the meal. This would take time to coordinate, so she had to start early. In seven days, the child would be circumcised before the people, and his name would be announced, many blessings would be read over him, and he would be presented to the community. She washed and went into the kitchen. Rachel was also still asleep, so she would be quiet so as not to wake anyone. She stirred the fire and placed a pot of water on it. From this, she could make coffee and leave enough for Elizabeth and the baby's bath. She opened the door, and the neighbor had left the milk on the steps as promised. She retrieved the bottle and placed it in a cool place in the kitchen. She would warm some for Elizabeth now and the rest she could have later. Midge made eggs and strips of leftover beef. She made a flatbread and prepared some oats and nuts. She had fresh orange halves and some grapes. The cry of the baby was heard from the kitchen, and she heard Elizabeth responding to him. Elizabeth had always had such a sweet temperament. She was simply a sweet, gentle soul that has never raised children or had the need to yell or scream. Her life has always been rather peaceful, and been married to a priest, an incredibly good priest, made her life even more peaceful. Midge had always called her Princess Elizabeth. She was drawn to this beautiful demure woman who married

Part 2: The Promised Child Is Born

Zacharias and moved into their hill community when she was only a girl like herself. They were both young and married, and she had gone and introduced herself to her in the synagogue one day. They had become friends immediately and had complete love and respect for each other. They were opposite in personality. Midge was a tough girl who had helped to raise her siblings, so she was strong-willed and bossy. She had married a good man who gave her the freedom to be herself. She was a good homemaker and a good person to her community. Elizabeth was a gentle flower, the sunshine in a room. She was beautiful to look at and a gentle soul who gravitated towards the children. Elizabeth had stood by her through the birth of her six children and loved her and her children while she herself remained barren. Midge had never seen her frown, or had she seen her ever gotten angry. She had always believed that God would give her a child in his own time. However, as the years rolled away and the season to bear children passed. Midge watched her friend graciously surrendered to her fate of barrenness. Her hands had never stopped helping other or showing kindness to all the children in the village. That was just the kind of girl she was. She heard steps coming down to the kitchen, and there was Elizabeth with the baby cradled in her arms. She greeted her friend with buoyancy and joy in her steps. She walked towards the door with the baby and open the door introducing her amazing son to the rising sun as it came upon yonder hill. It was much cooler than she expected, so she closed the door and walked back to the kitchen, singing and cuddling the child to her breast. Such radiance shone from her face; it lit up the heart of her friend. Elizabeth has become a mother in complete harmony with her son. Midge ushered her to the table and offered her a cup of warm milk. She sipped on the milk while she cradled the baby in her lap with her other arm. Midge piled the breakfast onto the table and stepped outdoor to take Zacharias the breakfast she had prepared for him. She greeted the priest with a light bow and morning greetings.

She set his breakfast on the makeshift table and sat on a log to talk. She brought greetings from Elizabeth and the baby and assured him that mother and baby were doing very well. She also informed him that Elizabeth was requesting to read one of the blessings at the naming ceremony. He nodded his head in approval. He handed her a scroll on which he had written all the details of how he wanted the ceremony to be. He has assigned Benjamin to be the sandek. He would be wearing a prayer shawl and hold the baby while the mohel performs the circumcision. There was strict instruction not to put wine in the baby's mouth but to substitute water during the ceremony. His child was a Nazarite unto the Lord and should have no wine, not even at this age. Benjamin would also be officiating in the ceremony and would play the role of the father during the ceremony. He wanted Midge to give the scroll to Benjamin, who would talk with Rabi Levi before the ceremony. Midge bowed and bade him goodbye and left the booth. Back in the house, she showed the scroll with the instructions to Elizabeth and let her know that Zacharias approved of her doing one of the blessings. Rachel joined them at the table where the ladies ate in between the many small dialogues they had. Midge then collected her clothes and bade the two ladies goodbye. She would go home to start the preparation for the ceremony and would give the scroll to Benjamin on her way home.

Meanwhile, Rachel and Elizabeth sat at the table and talked some more into the morning. Elizabeth expressed that she wanted to care for the baby, and Rachel would be responsible for cooking, washing the clothes, and cleaning the house. Elizabeth insisted that she would pay Rachel for her time and service with them. Rachel objected, but Elizabeth expressed that she could save up the money, and at the end of the three months that Rachel had agreed to stay, she would then give her a lump sum of money which she could use to buy something she would need as a new bride. She was soon to be a wife and a mother to two young boys. Rachel had lost the argument. She had time to think about what she would use the money to buy. However, she considered it a great honor to serve Elizabeth, and already she had greater rewards than Elizabeth could ever pay her in coins. As she gathered the clothes to take outside to wash, her heart was filled with a happy song of thanksgiving. She wandered out in the yard where the morning sun was already high in the sky. The cool wind tingled her skin, and the clean, fresh air filled her lungs. She felt alive as she broke forth into a little twirl viewing the surroundings from where she was standing. For the first time, she realized that aunt Elizbeth's house was on the highest point on the hill. She could see all the surrounding hills and valleys from where she stood. Plumes of smoke arose from the many houses jutting out across the hillside. She could hear the voices of the children playing and the barking of dogs in the distance. The trees appeared to clap their hands in the wind, the birds' singing was just a little more enchanting to the ears, and the wind carried on its wings the sweet smells from the kitchens below. Her gratitude for this moment exploded into an outburst of the song in her heart.

> O Lord, our Lord, how excellent is thy name in all the earth! hast set thy glory above the heavens. Out of the mouth of babes and sucklings hast thou ordained strength because of thine enemies, that thou mightest still the enemy and the avenger. When I consider thy heavens, the works of thy fingers, the moon and the stars, which thou hast ordained; what is man, that thou art mindful of him? and the son of man, that thou visitest him? For thou hast made him a little lower than the angels, and hast crowned him

with glory and honor. Thou madest him to have
dominion over the works of thy hands; thou hast
put all things under his feet.

Psalm 8:1-6

She washed the baby's clothes and hanged in the sunshine, and
then she tackled the other clothing for Elizabeth and those she had
collected from Zacharias. From the house, Elizabeth listened to the
beautiful voice of the little songbird who reminded her of herself.
Zacharias listened to the young maiden and pondered on her expression of praise. She was usually a lot quieter and more demure
in nature. He could tell that the maiden was filled with the presence
of God. Sitting there in the hut, he bowed his head in gratitude and
thanksgiving to God. Today he would write out his personal blessings for the baby's ceremony. Rachel finished her washing and returned to the house. Here she cleaned and danced to the rhythm of
her own song. She now dreamed of been happily married and raising
her children in the love of God. She imagined spending happy years
with Rabbi Levi. She was so happy he was a good man who really
loved God and not just a teacher by trade. He was considered one of
the few that did not take a bribe or watered down the teachings but
believed every prophecy and writing of the Torah. Many had spoken
of him as been a good man. Many of the boys who went down to Jerusalem for school showed great respect for him as a teacher. Rachel
went in to check on Elizabeth, who was happily feeding the baby.
She raised her head from the baby and acknowledged the presence
of the maiden. "I heard your singing," Elizabeth said. "One day, you
will have the joy of motherhood and make Levi a wonderful companion." Rachel smiled and received the words of the older woman.
Who understood patience and faith like Elizabeth did? All her years
of growing up, she had never heard Elizabeth complained or had a
mean word in her mouth. Even though their promise was delayed,

it was not denied; a child was born to this beautiful couple in their old age. Elizabeth rose from the chair and place the baby in the crib. She had brought the crib into the baby's room. She explained that at night she would return to the crib to her bedside. But his room had the table on which to wash and dress him. Elizabeth then made her way to the kitchen to show Rachel what to fix for lunch and had Rachel bring the meal out for Zacharias. Elizabeth was happy that her strength had returned so quickly. She had very mild contractions in her abdomen as her uterus was trying to return to its normal size. She had a very small amount of bleeding, and caring for the baby has been wonderful. He was waking up and eating almost every two hours and would go back to sleep almost immediately. She was changing his diaper and washing him just as often. His little body was pink and healthy to look at, and his feet and arms were strong and firm. He was sucking well, and she had an abundance of milk. Her baby was perfect, and she knew that soon, in another seven days, Zacharias would be able to hold his son and bless him daily. Her joy was complete. She had never experienced such completeness of joy.

Benjamin's greetings resounded in the house. He had come to see Zacharias after receiving the scroll from Midge. He greeted his friend and settled down beside him on a log. He was so excited and could not contain himself. He was happy his friend had chosen him for the honorable position as the sandek and to officiate at the ceremony. Zacharias was known by many people, but they had always had a special bond. He was no priest but was deeply religious and faithful to the ways and worship of Yahweh. All these years being the friend of Priest Zacharias had enriched his life. He knew all the ceremonial blessings and had officiated at many of his children's and grandchildren's naming ceremonies. He bowed and thanked his friend for asking him to take this honorable position. There was nothing he would not do for his friend, not only because he was a friend but also because he has been a faithful servant of Yahweh and has brought many blessings to his life. Zacharias nodded his head and smiled at his friend in response. He knew he had to get ready for the great ramblings of his friend. He was the perfect storyteller and had a way with his words. Zacharias has never gotten tired of his friend's many speeches, so he made himself comfortable and smiled at his friend. Benjamin made himself comfortable and started his monologue. "I am so blessed to participate in history," he said. "Last night, I spent the time going over the scrolls of Isaiah, and I remembered the prophecy of Malachi and read it over and over again."

> Behold, I will send my messenger, and he shall prepare the way before me: and the LORD, whom ye seek, shall suddenly come to his temple, even the messenger of the covenant, whom ye delight in: behold, he shall come, saith the LORD of hosts.

Malachi 3:1

Benjamin vocalized how in reading this scripture, his eyes opened up to see that this was the second prophet that spoke of the prophet of the Messiah. Zacharias shook his head in agreement. He, himself, had read this scroll again a few nights ago and knew that Malachi had also prophesied about his child. Benjamin paused for a while and then asked his friend why he thought Isaiah spoke of the prophet in the wilderness. He believed that the Judean hills were a great place to raise a child. There was an abundance of food, sunshine, and plenty of fresh air. Zacharias smiled and shook his head at his friend's whimsical question. If he could speak then, this would be where he would interject that God never made a mistake, and it would be fulfilled as he spoke. He had no idea how John would go to the wilderness by the dead sea. He knew the Essenes had made it their habitation and had lived in that harsh land in isolation for years. He and Elizabeth were old and could not survive that harsh desert sun, but if that was what God wanted, then It would be fulfilled by God in His own time. Benjamin broke out of his reprieve and interrupted the thoughts of Zacharias. He had imagined the prophet bursting on the scene and having great power and was not afraid of the Roman assigned king. He envisioned John preaching against the atrocities of Israel and the corruption in the temple. He could even imagine this prophet been confrontational with Herod and with Rome. Zacharias bent over with laughter even though no sound came forth from his mouth. Like his friend, his imagination took a leap. He was a quiet man but could only imagine Elijah calling down the fire before four hundred false prophets. It was the hardest and worst season documented in Israel's history. Jezebel, the pagan queen, had brought the demon god Baal to Israel and Ahab, and most of Israel had traded their God for a lower demon deity. God was so angry with King Ahab that He promised that the nation would go into captivity and become slaves to their Babylonian captors for seventy years. Just as was spoken, it came to past. Today Israel did not worship a demon deity, but they still trivialized the worship of Yahweh, having reduced it to pure performance. Where was the purity and sincerity with which men of old wept and waited before God? Did not Samuel and the prophet lie before God as Yahweh appointed Saul to be King? Who watched as King Solomon prayed until the glory of God filled the temple, and God granted to him wisdom, knowledge, and understanding and added riches and glory to his name? Where was the call for justice, mercy, and the Glory of God? Who will weep like Jeremiah, with great Lamentations for a nation that had forgotten God, or who will lie in the streets of Jerusalem for three years and eat bread mixed with cow dung, but Ezekiel did? Zacharias shivered on the remembrance of these things, and a holy fear gripped his heart. Most of the leaders and priests were mere hypocrites, and it was over four hundred years since the voice of the prophet Malachi had been heard in their streets as documented by the scribes. Yahweh has been silent, and everyone did whatever was right in his own eyes. The Talmud had replaced the Torah, and they revised the interpretations of the laws in the Talmud yearly to satisfy their own inability to abide by the laws of God. Very few yearned for holiness and the old ways of living. Rome had held them captive now for so long that it had become normalcy, and many revere the king Herod and the governors, and Caesar himself was like a god. He agreed with Benjamin it was going to be an interesting time. *Just to imagine a prophet in the streets of Jerusalem again*, he got excited thinking about it and gave quiet worship. No teacher or prophet came out until his thirtieth birthday; it was just the way it was. A Jews became a man at thirty years of age. If he had anything to say, that was the time he would be respected, and his words accepted. He may never be alive to see it all fulfilled, but he was thankful to God for choosing to give him this special child. Benjamin promised that he would go to see Rabbi Levi so they could discuss the details of the bris before the ceremony. He bade his friend goodbye and started his journey home. Once he left, Zacharias sat down to write out the order of the ceremony and the blessings to be read.

Meanwhile, Elizabeth was showing Rachel what to get ready for dinner. She was happy that her second day as a mother was going well. She hoped by tomorrow the letter would reach Nazareth, and her sister and other family members would have time to plan and come to be with them for the ceremony. She thought of Mary and hoped she had also reached home safely. The baby had come so quickly after she left for Nazareth, and she had fallen into motherhood that it was the first time she had given thoughts of Mary, who had left three days ago. She said a quiet prayer and hoped God had made the provision for Mary to be accepted and not rejected on her return to Nazareth. To be an unwed pregnant woman was no joke matters in Israel. The penalty could be stoned to death if Joseph did not take responsibility for the pregnancy. *"Do not commit adultery"* was one of the ten commandments punishable by death for a woman. If the man agrees to the marriage, then they would be saved. However, they would still be shunned for breaking the law. Her prayer was that Joseph would have a message from God before her cousin Anne found out about the pregnancy. She had bought her new clothing, but of a certainty, Mary was filled out in her abdomen, and her thin form had gained some weight like that of a pregnant woman. She was sure her mother would sense almost immediately that something was different. It could not be just from three months in the mountains. She prayed the maiden would have great wisdom and get to talk with Joseph in privacy soon. She had Rachel share out some extra food for Zacharias that evening, and Rachel took the food to Zacharias with words of love and comfort to him from Elizabeth. Rachel smiled as she relayed Elizabeth's message to him. The old man's face lit up with a smile as he nodded his head in acknowledgment. Rachel had cooked his favorite meal as instructed by Elizabeth. There were lintels and wild rice with beef stew. One of the temple helpers had delivered a nice chunk of fresh meat that morning, and it was what he was now eating. Rachel had lost her father six years after she was born. She, therefore, had very little recollection of her father. Except for her six elder brothers, Uncle Zacharias, as she called him, was one of the few men who had always encouraged her and prayed blessings over her young life. He had always shown kindness to her mother in times of need and had shared many meals, gifts, and social times with her family. He was like an uncle, and she had always addressed him this way. She went back to the house, and she and Elizabeth ate their meal in the silence as the day surrendered to the fading sun. They were no sooner finished when the shrilling cry of the baby pierced the air. Elizabeth dismissed herself from the table to attend to the wailing child. Rachel stayed behind to clean up the table and the kitchen. While she worked in the kitchen, she could hear Elizabeth singing while she fed the child. She put some water on the fire. She was sure Elizabeth could use this. She was looking forward to a full night's sleep. Elizabeth had assured her she would take care of the baby by herself tonight and she should try to have a good night's sleep. She was more tired than she realized. It has been two remarkably busy but wonderful days and nights helping to care for Elizabeth and baby John.

Meanwhile, in Nazareth, the runner had gotten there safely and delivered the letter to Abigail, Elizabeth's sister. Excitement stirred in their household. They were so excited to hear that the baby was born and that the mother and baby were doing well. There were only six days in which to tell all her family the good news and prepare for a large group to go down to Judea. Travel by donkey would take then at least two days if they stayed overnight on the outskirts of Samaria. They would find lodging in Jerusalem and travel on the day of the bris up to Ein Kerem. Abigail and her children and grand-children would travel up with Nathan and his family and any other family member who wanted to come down to celebrate this memo-rable occasion with Elizabeth and Zacharias. It was only yesterday that Mary had arrived back from Judea, and she heard there were possible some questions about Mary been pregnant. This news had shocked her, and she cannot imagine Anne and Jacobed's dilem-mas. She had not gotten a chance to talk with her cousin but knew this was a terrible situation. She was rejoicing on the birth of her sister's first child in her eighties but troubled about her young cous-in's pregnancy out of wedlock. "What could have happened?" she wondered. Mary had spent three months with Elizabeth and return home just before the birth of her child. It was somehow sad that she was receiving both bad and good news together but prayed all things would work out for good. Tomorrow she would make her rounds to see all the family and see who wanted to go down to Judea with her after the Shabbat. They would leave early Sunday morning and should be in Jerusalem by Monday night. There they would rest and then travel to Judea for the ceremony at noon on Tuesday. Ruben, her husband, would not travel down with them; they raised cows and goats, and someone had to stay back to care for the animals. They had two sons who would also stay back, but her two daughters and the grandchildren could travel down with some of the younger men. In the morning, she would go see the others and determine how many were going down with her to Judea. That night as she laid in bed, she thanked the God of heaven who has blessed her sister and her husband with a son, and as they were told three months ago, this child was a special child. She still shuddered to think of Elizabeth giving birth for the first time at eighty-eight years old. It was an incredible miracle, and she would not allow any bad news to shroud the miracle that has come to the family. She, however, did pray for Mary and hoped Joseph was responsible for the pregnancy. Joseph was way much older than she, and she could not imagine why he could not have waited until the marriage. A year engagement was the norm, and if Mary knew she was involved with Joseph, why did she go down to Judea. She wondered if Elizabeth and Zacharias even knew of this thing. Pushing all the thoughts out of her head, she closed her eyes in sleep. Tomorrow would be a busy day. She had to reach everyone and make plans before sunset when Shabbat began.

However, at Mary's house, it has been quite a stir since she came home yesterday. Her mother was very happy to see her daughter but immediately knew something was wrong. Her little Mary looked like a woman. She was in nice new clothes which she said Elizabeth had bought her, but she had gained on so much weight that her mother looked curiously at her. It was not until she was changing her clothes that her mother commented on her breasts' size and the protrusion in her abdomen. "Mary! Are you pregnant?" her mother screamed. She has screamed so hard that her dad had come running to the door of the room. She quickly pulled on her house clothes which were too tight-fitting, and it was obvious from looking at her that she was with child. Anne ran into the arms of her husband, weeping. Her dad stood at the door, staring at her in horror as she tried to tell them it was not what they think. Anne screamed, "Shame! Shame!" She requested Joachim to go and get Joseph. Mary tried to talk, but her mother gave her no time to explain. She accused Joseph of disloyalty and wanting to know why Mary stayed in Judea so long if she knew this had happened to her. Anne's cries were inconsolable. Mary stood there in quiet assurance and felt great peace that God would see her through this moment. Would her mother even believe her story if she told her what actually happened? She was almost in a state of hysteria, and Mary completely understood her sorrows. Who would understand or even believe her story except God had given the revelation to them? What would she do if she told her that the Holy Ghost did this to her? Never in their history or lifetime had anyone gotten pregnant without a man. It was only Isaiah, the prophet, to whom this prophecy was given. She would wait for Joseph to come and prayed that God has somehow revealed to him that a virgin shall conceive in the womb and shall bring forth a son. Joachim reached Joseph's house and knocked loudly on the door. It was just after sundown, and he was not expecting company. He opened the door to find an angry Joachim, pointing his fingers and screaming vehemently at him, "What have you done to our Mary?" How could you have slept with her before marriage, and when did this happen?" Joseph stared at his father-in-law in complete bewilderment and was puzzled at the words that spewed from his mouth. Mary had left for Judea three months ago, and he awaited her return so they could be wed. He had not so much as kissed the girl. He tried to calm his father-in-law down, but Joachim grabbed him in the front of the robe and said, "You will have to marry her right away; I do not want my daughter to be stoned to death." Shaken by the statements of Joachim, he screamed out, "I did not touch your daughter," Joseph straighten himself and pulled himself out of the grip of the older man. He agreed to go back with him to the house to see Mary. He was deeply saddened by the news he heard. He knew he had not touched the girl. He could not believe Mary was pregnant. His thoughts troubled him, *Was the girl raped, molested, or did she fell in love in Judea and gave herself away? Did she not love him, and was she showing rebellion to the marriage?* This was rarely heard of in Nazareth; girls kept themselves until marriage, and so did the men. Stoning was considered the punishment for prostitution. She had taken up so suddenly and decide to go to Judea before their wedding to spend her final single months with her cousin Elizabeth. It had appeared somewhat haphazardly and when he heard of her departure to Judea, but he had pushed the questions aside because it was her final free months before she would be married to him. She was free to make her own decision. She was young but was always a good girl. They had spoken a few times after the engagement party, and she had confessed love for him even though he was much older. He did not know if she had a change of heart or had met someone else in the three brief months away. It was a highly unusual situation that he was presented with, and her father was in great wrath, thinking he was guilty of this great sin in Israel. Baffled, he walked in silence with his father-in-law. The dark unlit path to his house echoed the sound of the night. Not a star was seen in the night sky. Doom and forlorn like the night cloak of blackness gripped his heart for the ten minutes it took from his house to theirs. Joachim finally broke the silence and broke out crying about the shame that had come to the family and that they would be shunned for breaking the commandment of the Torah. He cried pitifully about accepting his dowry and for Rome, who had forced him to trade his daughter for money and for a man who could have desecrated the law in willful disobedience and brought shame in the land. He now suggested that they would be hurriedly married in shame instead of a beautiful ceremony he had dreamed of giving his youngest daughter Mary. Joseph was too troubled in his soul to respond to his angry father-in-law. He would wait to see the face of Mary to make some sense of what her father had accused him of. On approaching the house, he could hear the lament of her mother's cry. Her wails were sorrowful and soulful, bouncing off the silence of the night. The neighbors were in bed, and their doors were shut. The cry was of death and woe like that of a mother who has lost her child at birth. This was no easy sin for a girl to be caught in adultery. A betrothal is a marriage contract. She has broken a vow in lying with another. It was punishable with death by stoning, and he knew he was innocent. His heart became heavy; he knew from her cries that something was very wrong. The thing Joachim had spoken to him was true. On entering the house, he requested to speak with Mary alone while Joachim tried to console his wife. They had no objection because, in their hearts, they believed he had already unclothed her as man his wife. Joseph greeted Mary, who appeared calm and peaceful amid the chaos and the noise. She was beautiful and glowing. She was more beautiful than he could remember her. She had gained some weight, and she held herself like a woman with confidence and grace. It was difficult to tell if she was pregnant because he had no reference having been unwed himself. He just knew she was beautiful to look at, and he loved her more now with all his heart. An overwhelming sense of emotions washed over him. He wanted to hug her and protect her, but he had doubts and disappointments mingled with all the sweet sense of a lover and a defender. She held his hand and led him to the kitchen, where she sat him at the table. He could see that his little Mary had changed. Her abdomen protruded a little when she sat down on the chair, and her dress did not fit well anymore. "What happened?" he whispered. He was afraid even to hear her answer. His beloved, his beautiful bride-to-be, was pregnant with someone else's child. Tears spilled unchecked from his eyes and ran down to the table, forming a small pool where their hands met. Mary extended her hands to his and lovingly held his hands in hers. "Don't cry," she implored, looking deep into his eyes for understanding and acceptance. She hurt to know that she was the cause of his tears and that he thought she had caused him great sorrow. There at the table, she shared with him in a hurried speech the angelic encounter she had and the angel's suggestion for her to go and see Elizabeth. She spilled out all the accounts of what happened at Aunt Elizabeth's house and her journey in accepting God's will for her life. Joseph looked at her in awe and unbelief. Her face glowed like bright ambers of coals as she related the story. Her voice was pure and sweet and held a holy hush. She was so peaceful and convincing that it almost felt enchanted. Mary was making claims to be the girl chosen of God to carry the Messiah, but many girls waited and prepared themselves in Jerusalem; and why his Mary? And if Mary was chosen, why did he or anyone else not get the revelation? Greatly disturbed by her story, he pulled his hands away, told Mary blankly that he did not know how to believe her story. However, being a responsible man and still madly in love with this girl, he agreed that they would go back to her parents and see what they had to say. For tonight he agreed with her not to dispute the fatherhood of the child. He would go home and pray and see if God would give him some kind of revelation. He agreed with her, but in his heart, he was thinking of dissolving the engagement privately. If he did it openly then, Mary could be stoned to death for his denial of the pregnancy. If he did it privately, there is a possibility that her life and the life of the child could be spared. They returned to the seating area, and her mother was somewhat comforted by her father. Her father announced that they should be married in a quiet ceremony on Friday morning, and Mary would be moved to his house immediately. Not knowing what to say, Joseph agreed that in two days, he would be married to her, but deep in his heart, he knew that their lives would be forever marred by doubts and skepticism. How could he trust her story? He bade them goodbye and departed to his house broken-hearted and greatly disturbed. If the story Mary had told him was true, he wondered why God had not given him a revelation too. This was a heavy thing for a man to marry a pregnant woman who was not carrying his child. In truth, he was a simple carpenter, but he had kept himself celibate in all his fifty years. Once he accepted the proposal of her father, he waited patiently. He was in no hurry; he had waited fifty years and, for the first time, found the girl that captured his heart completely. He had faithfully worshiped Yahweh and faithfully followed the commands of the Torah. He would never put himself or the maiden in danger by disobedience. He would never consider touching Mary intimately before marriage, and now her parents thought he was an infidel. He felt betrayed and decided in his heart that in the morning, he would return and let her parents know he was not responsible for the pregnancy and would not marry her. Mary would have to share with them what she told him. For he knew he would not be made a fool of in Israel. He would put her away privately, and the parents had to decide what they would do with her. It would be a difficult choice for him. He knew he loved the maiden and had never felt this way for any other woman in all his years. His neighbors had always wondered if he would remain celibate all his life, and they were so happy when she had become his betrothed. The age difference was obvious, he was fifty years old she was only fourteen years old, but this was not unusual in Israel. They were happy for him, for the whole town also loved Mary for her life of piety and love for God and family. Joseph was their favorite carpenter and was perfect for her. Mary was the youngest and beloved child of her parents, and none had ever spoken evil of her. As Joseph knelt at his bedside that night, he prayed, pouring out his heart to Yahweh. His heart was broken into a million pieces, and his tears flowed unhindered. He has never given in to crying, but this thing has hurt his heart and his pride. He cursed the day he ever set his eyes on her and felt his heart bloomed in love like a flower unfolding. He would like Jacob had waited another seven years because this is the girl that had captured his heart. He was giving up the girl he loved, who now had betrayed his love and trust. This was more than he could have imagined, almost a year ago when he gave a generous dowry to her parents with the pledge of marriage in a year. Now forced on him was a pregnant girl he still loved, but he was not the father of the child she carried, and her parents had no idea he had not touched their daughter. This brokenness was too much for him. He surrendered his thoughts and his tears to God and crawled into bed emotionally exhausted. He drifted off into a restless sleep, and there he dreamed. A great angel of God appeared to him and said,

> Joseph, thou son of David, fear not to take unto thee Mary thy wife: for that which is conceived in her is of the Holy Ghost. And she shall bring forth a son, and thou shalt call his name Jesus: for he shall save his people from their sins. Now all this was done, that it might be fulfilled which was spoken of the Lord by the prophet, saying, Behold, a virgin shall be with child, and shall bring forth a son, and they shall call his name Emmanuel, which being interpreted is, God with us.
>
> **Matthew 1:20-23**

The dream ended, and Joseph jumped from his sleep, shaking.

This was the most profound encounter he had ever had. God had sent an angel to visit him and confirmed everything Mary had told him earlier that night. He did a dance while singing songs of praise around his room. Shouting praises to Yahweh Most High. His sorrow and his pain were immediately erased. His beautiful love had spoken in truth. He now regretted he had doubted her, but who was he to think Yahweh could have written him in His story of redemption and grace. He danced around his bed again and gave more worship to God. He was a happy man; he could still marry his love and get to participate in the beginning of a new era of God's love and grace. God with man. Mary, his Mary was chosen, and so was he; the angel had called him, the son of David, and so fulfilled the prophecy. His heart took on peace, and he knew he would treasure and cherish this woman forever. He always knew that she was special, but now he knew why—Mary—mother of God. He was elated that God had cleared up his doubt and gave him a place to be the earthly father of His Son. He would go early in the morning at the rising of the sun to see Mary and set her heart at rest. Joseph's heart was as happy as a young roe. The God of the universe has chosen him to be the earthly father for his son and has chosen his betrothed, Mary, to be the mother of His child. He, the carpenter, son of David, was born to be husband to Mary, mother of *God*. He and his soul mate would raise the Christ child according to everything God spoke to him. He sensed in his heart that they should not give an explanation to anyone for who would believe them. He had not believed the words of Mary, and God had to send an angel to convince him otherwise. Neither would her parents or anyone else believe them? They would only further accuse them of heresies. He would let God's will be done. He was sure they would be instructed along the way like he was tonight and that when the child was grown, he would fulfill the prophecy as Savior of the world. He made his breakfast in quiet contemplation. He now understood why he has had no previous interest in love and marriage. He had spent his apprentice years perfecting his skills as a carpenter and has served his community well both for charity and for pay. He built houses and furniture and repair anything they bring to him. He was the best in his trade, and when his parents were alive, they many times begged him to be married and give them grandchildren. He was content to live alone and poured all his energy into his work. A year ago, when his cousin Joachim had financial troubles, he came offering his youngest child in marriage for a handsome dowry that would save his cattle farm. It was almost as if immediately imprinted on his heart was the joy to accept the young maiden he knew very well. Now he knew he was chosen for a holy calling. Here, in his room, he humbled himself before God, and he pledged he would not be intimate with her until after the baby was born. He got dressed, and this time his steps were rushed as he traveled the same dirt road he traveled last night to get to Mary's house. He had to restrain his joy and bowed his head in respect as he approached the house. He knocked on the door and greeted her parents this time with a smile, but they were unsmiling and still angry at him. The parents shook their heads at him refusing to greet him. Joachim informed him that a priest had agreed to come in private to pronounce his blessing over their marriage; therefore, he should come prepared to get his bride tomorrow. He warned him that the whole community would eventually know what had happened and that they would be shunned until after the baby is born. Once the child was born, they would take him to the temple and offer the offering required for the child and themselves. There would be no singing and dancing and seven days of celebration as was expected for a wedding ceremony. There would be no blessing from the family and no princess attire for Mary. He felt great compassion for Mary but knew she had a greater treasure carrying than they could even imagine. They dismissed themselves and indicated that Mary was in the kitchen. He found her sitting at the table, eating with her head bent down. He approached quietly and tapped her on the shoulders. She turned to look at him with very sad, red eyes from crying. It has been a long night, and her mother had not made it easy for her. He smiled at her, and she offered him a half-hearted smile. He sat opposite to her and extended his hands towards her. She raised her head, and her eyes met his. This is the Joseph she remembered. The man she loved, the man whose deep brown eyes made her heart rolled over a million times. The kind, compassionate, gentle, mild-mannered carpenter whose muscles were made strong from all the hard work he had done. He was strong but yet so gentle when he called her name. This is the man she trusted and loved and believed God had given to her. He was her prince, provider, and her protector. She placed her tiny hands in his large, firm but gentle hands. He squeezed her gently and quietly said, "I am your companion and protector; I will stand by you all the days of my life." He recounted to Mary how sad he had been the night before, the prayer he had prayed and the dream he had that morning, and how blessed he was to be woven in the tapestry of her life and in the perfect will of God. Mary bowed her head in quiet worship to Yahweh. Finally, she was not alone. Her secret was now his to bear, the beloved king of her heart. He shared with her what her parents had said concerning their marriage, and he believed they should not try to tell the story but keep it in their hearts until God chooses to reveal his son through his prophet of which she already knew. They would wait to hear from God and give the baby a normal life and do what God told them to do. Mary agreed with his decision. He was her chosen one and protector of the seed of God. Tomorrow they would be married, and she would leave the house of her parents to join him as man and wife. She knew to be shunned by the community would make their lives difficult, but Joseph promised they would find all the prophecies and read them together. They had each other, and God was with them, so they would survive the scorn until the town had forgotten what they considered their forbidden act. They now smiled together with the evident love and respect that was now forged between them forever. They had a mission they would accomplish together. They were parents to the Son of God. Joseph bade goodbye and promised he would come to claim his bride on the morrow. He told Mary he was sorry she would not have the gallant wedding and the seven days of celebration that she had dreamed of having, but he knew she carried a gift more precious which would bless them tremendously and bless the whole world. He knew she would do well in this situation, for they were both born for this moment, and they would endure the pain and laughter together. Mary submitted herself to the wisdom of her husband. He would now rule over her and make the decision for their future. She now felt safe and was confident she was able to take on the task that God has placed on her and Joseph. They were parents to the Christ child. She hoped that Elizabeth would have a wonderful birth and that both parents and child would be safe and well. She went to her room, collected her few possessions, and place them in the bags she brought from Judea. She would only take the dresses Aunt Elizabeth had given her. She knew her mother and all her family would shun her for the next six months. She already started by avoiding her all morning. Joseph was now her world, and they would do what God has determined for them to do together. She heard the shouts of greetings from her cousin Abigail as she entered the yard. She knew this could only mean one thing. Aunt Elizabeth has had the baby. She smiled and stayed in the quiet of her room. She gently massaged her abdomen and whispered to her child, "Your prophet is born!" She heard her mother greeting the woman, and they sat in the sitting room across from her room.

Abigail shared the good news of the birth of the son of Elizabeth and Zacharias three days ago and the upcoming bris next Tuesday.

She expressed they would be leaving on Sunday evening to arrive for the ceremony on Tuesday at noon. Anne listened in silence, she seemed distant and cold, and Abigail paused to find out if all was well. Anne broke down crying, and Mary could hear her mother sobbing from the room. She shared through her tears with Abigail that Mary returned from Elizabeth's house yesterday, and she was found to be pregnant and was in her third month. The mother shared that she had possibly got involved with Joseph, and due to shame, she had chosen to go to Judea to visit Elizabeth and now return to them in the shameful state as a pregnant and unwed mom. Abigail was saddened by the news, so what she heard yesterday was true. Her good news was met by very bad news. Anne, however, rushed to tell her that Joseph had agreed to a hasty marriage tomorrow and Mary would go to live with him immediately. She would be shunned, according to the Talmud, until after the birth baby. Anne, therefore, would not be able to travel down to Judea, seeing she was grieving the sins of her daughter. Not knowing what to say, Abigail bade her goodbye. The news was very sad indeed. She has known Mary as from a little girl she was always a good child, and Joseph had waited long to be married but was always an honorable man. What could have possessed him to touch her nakedness before the traditional wedding? Occasionally, things like this happened, and the Torah had provision for such transgressions. Their family had never experienced this problem before. She shook her head in unbelief and deepest compassion for Mary and Joseph, knowing that they would be shunned for almost a year. She had experienced a blessing and what appears to be a curse all in one day. She hastened down the road to the brothers and sisters' houses. She would find those who would travel with her and celebrate the Joy of a male child in Judea, a male child added to their clan. Her thoughts quickly returned to the celebration and happiness that she would share in Judea. Her sister of eighty-eight years old has borne a male child to her husband in his old age. Despite what she perceived to be the folly of Mary and Joseph, she would gather a group and go down to celebrate the miracle of life in Judea. So little did she knew that the baby Mary carried in her womb was the Messiah and that her own sister, well great in age, had given birth to his prophet. As prophesied in the scriptures, a great double blessing has been given to her clan. But as Isaiah had prophesied:

> Who hath believed our report and to who is the arm of the Lord revealed? For he shall grow up before him as a tender plant, and as a root out of a dry ground: he hath no form nor comeliness; and when we shall see him, there is no beauty that we should desire him. He is despised and rejected of men; a man of sorrows and acquainted with grief: and we hid as it were our faces from him; he was despised, and we esteemed him not.
>
> **Isaiah 53:1-3**

The sun was high in the sky and blazing down upon her head; Abigail had amassed a band of seventy people, including men, women, and children. The news of Mary and Joseph shunning had also reached their ears. They all shook their head in disbelief, joy and sorrow mingled in the air, but nothing would stop the celebration of Elizabeth and Zacharias' newborn child. They would leave Nazareth by Sunday; they would go by donkey and horse carriage and bring gifts for the baby and plenty of food for the new parents.

Elizabeth awoke with great joy in her heart. It was the day before the circumcision, and the name was revealed of her son. It was also the day when she would be able to look into the eyes of Zacharias again and rejoice with him for the birth of their child. There was still the house to be cleaned and bed linen and drapes to be changed. Her baby had woken up every three hours for feeding and to be cleaned up, but she had drifted off the sleep each time immediately after feeding him. She felt rested and energized. She would instruct Rachel on what to make for breakfast and, then she could help her to decorate the house in clean white linen drapes and table cloth. While she waited for the breakfast, she sang psalms of praise to Him alone, who was worthy. Yahweh had looked on her and favored her in her old age. He had given her joy and gladness, and her cup was overflowing with love for Him. Rachel joined her in singing in the kitchen. Her singing had flowed over and into the ears of the maiden. She also awoke with happiness in her heart and with joyful anticipation of the day. Soon she would see Levi, and they would get to talk for a while and expressed their hearts' desire. Elizabeth scooped the oatmeal into a bowl and added goat milk and some dried nuts. She placed some flatbread in a platter with eggs made the way Zacharias loved them. She portioned it with love and for Rachel to take to her husband, "Tell him I can't wait to behold his face at breakfast tomorrow." Rachel shook her head and smiled. These two were a true pattern of enduring love. She brought the food to Zacharias and gave him the message of his wife. Zacharias' face lit up like a burning fire. He smiled, nodding his head to the maiden. There was so much he wanted to say, but he was still dumb. He had prayed and request God to return his speech, but he remained dumb. He surrendered his heart's cry to God and waited. As the maiden disappeared around the side of the house, his thoughts returned to the task on hand. Benjamin would come today and help him to arrange the yard for the ceremony. In the house, Rachel and Elizabeth ate a healthy meal, and Elizabeth shared with Rachel what they would do today. The large table would be placed in the center of the hall, the chairs would be pushed back to the walls, and the table would be covered with a white linen cloth followed by a pad and a smaller white linen cloth.

Part 2: The Promised Child Is Born

This would be where the mohel would perform the circumcision. The door would be open, and those in the booth would be able to observe the ceremony. The floor would be scrub with lye and lavender water, and the windows were to be draped with white linen. Dried lavender flowers would be placed in corners of the room to fill the air with a sweet fragrance. The bedrooms would also be decorated in white drapes and white bed linen. Elizabeth hurriedly ate her breakfast. She had two hours to work before he would be awake again. While Rachel wiped the floor, Elizabeth retrieved the white linen drapes she had stored away. With Rachel's help, they moved the furniture around. The air was fresh and clean. Elizabeth hanged long white drapes at each window. On her dining table, a white linen cover was placed with two smaller towels and a tiny pillow for the baby's head. This was where the circumcision would be performed. The room was completely transformed. Rachel tied the dried lavender flower in little bundles and arranged them subtly around the room. The fragrance burst open in the room and filling the air with a heavenly scent. A small table with the menorah was lit and glowing in the room; it was a constant reminder of the presence of God. The room was filled with a sense of peace, calm, and cleanliness. Tomorrow this time, a child would be welcome into the Abrahamic covenant with God and man. "Tomorrow, God will be present here," Rachel whispered to herself. Elizabeth washed her hands and headed to the baby's room but not before giving Rachel instructions to hang white curtains in her room and clean white linen sheets for her bed. While Elizabeth fed the baby, Rachel cleaned the floors in the room and hanged the drapes as Elizabeth had requested. She had great joy and worked with much speed and energy. She would then go out and wash the baby's clothes. By the time she had cleaned her room and hang the drapes and change the bed linen, Elizabeth had fed the baby and put him back to sleep. She was now cleaning her room and placing new bed linens on and hanging drapes at her bedroom windows. Elizabeth was softly singing as she worked and looked at total peace with herself. Rachel gathered the dirty linen from the baby's room and made her way outdoors to the washstand in the back. Zacharias and Benjamin were busy working. They had washed the walls of the house with limestone, and it was white and shining in the noonday sun. The men had made an arch with palm leaves, descending from the road to the booth in the yard. It was beautiful. They had platted a lattice of the leaves, and it formed one continuous arch. The yard was swept clean. The grass was cut, and the garden weeded and cleaned except for the shrubs and bulbs that lie dormant for next Spring. They had arranged seats in the booth. The fireplace had wood, and tables for the food were constructed and ready for use. There was also an area where chairs were arranged for the musicians to sit. She imagined the dancing and celebration after the circumcision and naming were completed. There were two big pitchers sealed with wines in the corner of the booth. The booth was enclosed with goatskin on two sides. White drapes would be hanged in the front, and the other end would be open facing the house. The men had even cleaned a large area in the back of the house where the animals could be tied, and there was extra hay stashed and water troughs for the hungry animals. It was going to be a lovely day. The house and the yard showed signs of celebration. Rachel washed the baby's clothes, and a melody escaped her lips. Her happiness was for the happiness of the moment. God has blessed this priest and his wife with the gift of a child in their old age. God was still doing miracles in her day, and she was an eyewitness to it all. She will have many wonderful stories to tell her children. She would let Elizabeth know she would go home to help her mother with any last minutes preparation she had and would help her in the morning to take the supplies up to their house. She could already imagine the men all dressed in white robes and their prayer shawls and skull caps. She could envision all the women dressed in their finest dresses and headcovers. She herself would wear a purple dress trimmed with gold that her mother had given her during Purim. She had a white head wrap with gold lace that goes with the dress. She had not worn it since she received it and had put it away for a special occasion. This was the perfect occasion, and she would be seeing Levi and the boys. She wanted to look her best for this fine rabbi. Rachel finished her washing and headed back indoors. The men were also finished with the work in the yard. She headed inside and brought them back the lunch she had prepared for them. While she had lunch with Elizabeth, she told her of the great work the men had done in the yard. Elizabeth was not surprised. Both her husband and Benjamin were great with woodwork and worked well together. Tomorrow before the ceremony, she would go outdoors and have a look at the booth and the landscaping of the yard. Rachel reminded Elizabeth that she would go home tonight to help her mother with the final preparation for the meal tomorrow. Elizabeth agreed readily. They both had done all that was needed to be done in the house; it was crisp and clean and visitors ready. She was more than able to care for the baby on her own tonight. She and the baby would be perfectly fine to be alone for the night, and Zacharias was just on the outside; however, she did not anticipate any problems. Elizabeth's heart rested on her husband. Tomorrow he would be free to return to the house. Her bleeding had stopped by day number three, and so has the pain in her abdomen. She had great energy and was producing a large amount of milk for her baby. She could see that her baby was already gaining weight. She was worried that Zacharias was still not talking. During her pregnancy reveal, they had told their family and friends that Zacharias was on a vow of silence until after the baby was born. What would they think if he still were not speaking at the bris? She, however, knew Yahweh was faithful, and whatever time he chooses to return his voice, it would be well indeed. She missed sharing these first few days of the baby with him. The baby had filled her heart with so much joy and love, and she wanted to share those precious moments with him. She would try to go to sleep early with the baby tonight to feel refreshed for the ceremony tomorrow. "For thou, Lord, hast made me glad through thy work" (Psalm 92:4). These were the words of the sweet psalmist King David that echoed in her heart. Tomorrow he would hold his son in his arms and look into his eyes and hear his cry and pray the blessing over his life. She smiled as she caught herself daydreaming over the prospect of seeing Zacharias in the morning. She rose from the chair and hastened to the cry of the baby. Rachel out-ran her and retrieved the baby from his crib. She washed her hands and prepared herself on the chair to receive the child. She smiled as she watched Rachel's interaction with the baby. She was swirling around and singing to the fussy child. She handed her the baby, and she attached his mouth gently to her breast. She smiled up at Rachel and murmured, "Next time this year, you will be preparing for your own baby." Rachel smiled at her, hoping her prophecy would be true. Rachel sat in the baby's room with her and chatted about her dress for tomorrow and her prospect of seeing Levi again. Her eyes sparkled like a true girl in love. Her voice was gentle and soft. Elizabeth watched her in wonderment. The once shy, reserved maiden has become a symbol of love and joy. She wondered at the wisdom of the creator to bury deep in each heart the potential to find and explore the human potential of love and family. Even her heart that has folded itself upon the possibilities of birth and had long dried up. However, she looked at herself in her old age giving her breast to a baby, her very own child. She had unfolded and become the perfect mother unwrapping all the motherly skills once laid dormant in the very fabric of her DNA. It was like she was awakened to spring, and the air was filled with new possibilities. She saw the potential in this maiden that had put off marriage until now, embracing the thought of love and motherhood. In the few days of helping her with the baby, Rachel had become a shining princess. She knew Rabbi Levi and his sons were very bless-ed to have found this hidden gem. The baby fell asleep, and she laid him gently in his bed but not before planting a dozen kisses on his forehead. She would now help Rachel to prepare dinner and give her enough time to leave before the sunset in the eastern sky. Tomorrow would be a beautiful day for them all. She was sure heaven would applaud as their son is brought in the covenant relationship God made with Abraham thousands of years ago. It was their right of passage into the world. At eight days after birth, each Jewish male child had to be circumcised and given a name. This was more im-portant than a bar mitzvah. This was a direct blood covenant as com-manded by Yahweh. They had celebrated with so many of their neighbors and families, and tomorrow they would celebrate her and Zacharias. What a great honor this would be. God had not forgotten them, and the curse of barrenness was forever broken.

While Rachel prepared dinner in the kitchen, the voice of her mother, Midge, was heard at the door; Rachel rushed to the door and greeted her mother with kisses and hugs. Midge had in her hands drapes to make the perfect entrance for the booth. Midge hugged her friend Elizabeth as she complimented her on the beauty of the house and the excellent job the men had done on the outside of the house and the landscaping in the yard. She explained that she would need the donkeys in the morning to transport the food. She wanted to bring the drapes over tonight so as not to get them soil in the morning during the transportation of the food. The ladies chatted as Rachel put the finishing touch to the dinner. Rachel set the table for dinner as the older women continued to exchange stories of bris and the décor used at these events. Both women have a preference for white decor as it was symbolic of cleanliness and purity. The men and the boys would all be dressed in white, and from their conver-sation, they would be wearing white dresses also. Rachel smiled;

these women shared so much in common yet so many differences. This was what made them great friends. Their similarities bonded them together, and their differences complemented each other. Rachel had spent hours listening to them and was always fascinated by their conversation. She learned so much just been in their presence, and she was glad she paid attention to their conversation. Now that she had decided on getting married, there were many tips she had gotten from them and stored in her head and her heart. She did not see her own father's intimate time with her mother since he died after her sixth birthday. However, having watched Zacharias and Elizabeth has given her enough skills to take into her own marriage. She hoped Levi would be a gentleman like Zacharias and that she would be as loving and kind as Elizabeth. She hoped the love that will be forged between her and Levi would even be a fraction of that which she had watched for years transpired between Elizabeth and Zacharias. Rachel shared with her mom that Elizabeth had given her the okay to come home to help her in the morning and also to get her dress for the ceremony. She discussed with her mother the dress she planned on wearing. "You will look amazing," her mother said. The purple would be a perfect match for her skin tone and a perfect blend with the white background. Elizabeth portioned out some food for Zacharias and reminded Rachel to tell him she will leave for tonight and that she was excited about having tea with him in the morning. Rachel smiled on hearing the sweetness in Elizabeth's voice and the warmth in her eyes. She nodded her head in acknowledgment and took the meal out for Zacharias. She relayed his wife's message to him, and Rachel observed the same warmth spreading across Zacharias's face at the mention of her name. He could not talk, but his smile got wider and wider, and he nodded his head vigorously. Rachel bowed in reverence to the priest as she departed but not before telling him that she would be going home tonight to help her mother. She also told him that Elizabeth wanted to assure him that she and the baby would be well until they see him in the morning. He nodded again in agreement, and Rachel took leave from his presence. Inside the house, she sat and had dinner with the ladies, and Midge went over the dinner menu for the ceremony with Elizabeth. As the sun crept down in the east, Rachel and her mother hugged and bade Elizabeth goodbye. If they walk speedily leading the donkey, they would be home before it was dark. Elizabeth decided on cleaning the kitchen; she would then take her bath and await her son's next feeding session. She hoped she would get enough sleep tonight, for tomorrow would be a long glorious day.

Zacharias, on the other hand, was anxious. He was disappointed that he still had not received his voice back. At his own child's bris, he would be speechless. He would be dumb on the most glorious day of his life. It was the day of presentation of his son to God in the covenant in the foreskin. He, however, humbled himself before Yahweh in reverence and surrender. He knew it was a curse caused by his unbelief that had led to him losing his voice. Yahweh had promised it would return, and he would wait humbly and patiently. He would humbly wait for the love and mercy of God to restore his voice. He had impregnated his aged wife and watched the baby growing on the inside of her up until his birth. If God had chosen him to be the father of the prophet to the Messiah, then he was assured his voice would return in the due season. He was pleased with the work he and Benjamin had done in the yard and on the outer walls of the house. He rolled over on his sleeping mat and gave thanksgiving to Yahweh. Tomorrow he would lift his son to heaven and offer him back to God in covenant relationship, as has been done for generations for all Hebrew boys in covenant as given to Abraham by God. His boy was already filled with the Holy Ghost and was the great prophet of the long-awaited Messiah. "The voice of him that crieth in the wilderness, Prepare ye the way of the LORD"

(Isaiah 40:3). He whispered the words of the prophet Isaiah and fell into a peaceful sleep. He dreamed the house was filled with men all dressed in white and dancing around the fire pit while sweet music was played by happy men. The women then danced, followed by the children, and he was singing and dancing with the men also. He awoke from the dream startled, but when he checked himself, he still had not gotten back his voice. It was yet dark and early in the morning. He had hoped he would be speaking again soon and even so at the presentation of his son. He gave silent worship to God and drifted off into another peaceful slumber.

Midge and Rachel had gotten home safely the night before. Rachel chatted all the way home about her excitement of seeing Levi again soon. She wanted to know if she could be married in the next six months or if she needed to wait a whole year as customary. Her mother assured her that it could be discussed with Levi since she was his second wife and he needed help with the children, and she, herself, was not a teen but already a twenty-six-year-old woman. Levi was in his mid-thirties, and he was the rabbi and should know all the teachings and laws. She was pleased that her daughter had warmed up so much to the prospect of marriage. Midge could sense that in the few days her daughter had cared for Elizabeth and the baby, a miracle had taken place in her heart. She was warm and filled with great joy, wherein time past she would not speak of the marriage but was afraid and hesitant. Today she was filled with great passion and joy as she spoke of Levi and his boys. Midge held back her tears. Her daughter had received the gift of joy. Midge had very little to do that night. She had spent the whole day baking cakes and pies. The desserts need to be packaged to be transported in the morning. Both ladies worked in silence. They would both go to bed early. It would be a long day tomorrow. They would have to be awakened early in the morning to cook the beef stew and bake some flatbread.

Part 2: The Promised Child Is Born

The dough was already prepared and would be placed in the oven in the morning. The other neighbors were doing the larger bulk of the cooking. She was a great pastry maker, and so was Rachel. The ladies completed the packaging and got ready for bed. They took their baths and fell in bed, completely exhausted. Tomorrow they would celebrate with their friends.

The cock crowed loudly, and Midge stirred. It was still dark, but flatbread had to be baked and stacked, and she had to make a large portion of beef stew with potatoes and carrots. She knelt to pray and gave Yahweh thanks for the event of the day and for the opportunity to serve her friends well. She gave thanks for all her children but especially for Rachel, who had become a fine woman filled with joy. She was thankful to God for the strength to work even at her age and for the gift of a child to her friends even in their old age. "It is going to be a good day," she murmured as she donned her working clothes and headed to the kitchen. The brick oven was on the outside, along with a large fireplace for a large quantity of cooking. With a lantern in hand, she went out and rekindled her fireplace, adding more wood and coal to the oven. She placed her meat and vegetables on the fire in a large pot to slow cook. She would go in and start rolling the dough. There was a lot of flatbread to be made. The oven could bake three flatbreads at a time. If Rachel woke up soon, they would be able to work faster. She stoked the coals in the outdoor brick oven and added more coals. She then returned inside to her kitchen, where she portioned her dough in equal parts and started rolling the dough to shape the bread. She had three flat pans in which they would be placed the dough and put in the oven. "Good morning, mom," Rachel chirped. She was wide awake and dressed in her working garb. Midge smiled, extended her arms, and gather her youngest child in an embrace. She then put her to work rolling the dough, and she would put in and retrieve the bread from the oven. They had always

197

worked well together, and Rachel matched her mother with both speed and dexterity. With her helping hands, the bread would be all done before the sun came up. Both women worked in silence. Midge was in and out of the kitchen, taking new batches of flat dough to the oven and piling the already cooked bread in a basket. The bread was thin, so they took a short amount of time to bake. Midge was busy removing and putting bread in the oven, and Rachel had to keep up with rolling and shaping the bread. They had a hundred flatbread to make. They had done this before. The fragrance from the stew roses up to their nostrils. Rachel paused to make some coffee. She needed to stay alert, for it was going to be a long, beautiful day.

Zacharias rose from a restful sleep and remembered his dream. He opened his mouth again, but still, no words came out. He was disappointed, but nothing could squash the joys of today. The sun was just beginning to climb over the hill. He would see his wife and baby again today. He knelt in an earnest, heartfelt prayer of thanksgiving and worship to Yahweh. He washed his face in the morning light, and the cool air tingled his skin. The day was awake with the sounds of the morning creatures rising to worship. The birds flew by, chirping with all their hearts; the dogs barked incessantly in a distant hill evoking a sound of urgency. The cock crowed with a burst of delight to the awakening of the day. "Yahweh has created all things for the delight of his heart," he voiced inwardly. Lightheartedly, he made his way to the front door. He quietly opened the door, and he heard the sweet voice of Elizabeth singing softly to the baby. He approached the kitchen cautiously and hugged his wife from behind. "Zacharias!" Elizabeth turned at his touch, and he planted numerous kisses on her forehead. He looked lovingly in the eyes of his tiny son, and his heart was flooded with overwhelming joy. He was perfect, and he was in love. Elizabeth handed the baby into his arm. He cuddled the child to his chest and continue to stare into his perfectly formed face and beautifully shaped brown eyes. Zacharias paced back and forth in the room, cradling the child. Elizabeth was disappointed that he still could not talk, but she knew he was praying blessings over the child. She turned to the kitchen to make breakfast, and her heart flooded over with joyful adulation to Yahweh that had allowed her to give a boy child to her husband. She would have breakfast with her king and their prince today. From the kitchen, she watched him walking around the sitting room and down to the bedroom with his son as if enraptured. When she was finished making breakfast, she went to get him. She took the sleeping child from his arms and placed him in the crib. She turned, and they embraced for a long time, looking down on the sleeping child, their perfect gift from God. Hand in hand, they walk back to the kitchen, where they ate. Zacharias remained silent while Elizabeth talked about the house, the yard, and the anticipation of the ceremony. Zacharias nodded his head in pleasure. After breakfast, he took her hand and led her to the door and out into the yard. The arch from the palm leaves was intricately designed and loomed across the gateway. The limestone-painted exterior wall of the house reflected the sunlight as the beams of the rising sun hit the whitened surface. The men had done an amazing upgrade with the yard. It was perfect for the ceremony of their prince. She remembered the drapes Midge had brought, so she went indoors and retrieved them and, with the assistance of Zacharias, she hanged them to the front entrance of the booth. She tied back both sides with the golden sash. A mild wind sprung up, blowing the drapes mildly in the wind. It was like a sweet breath from God. The open drapes were a symbol of a sweet welcome of their families and friends into their home. He walked her to the back of the house, where he had stashed hay for the animals to eat. They walked back to the front of the house with the morning sun and wind kissing their faces. They raised their hands to heaven, and Elizabeth broke out in thanksgiving, "This is the day that the Lord

199

hath made; we will rejoice and be glad in it" (Psalm 118:24). He held her in a sweet embrace, and they walked back into the house. His heart was overflowing with love and thanksgiving to see the child that the wife of his youth has given him in their old age as predestined by Yahweh. There was not much work left to be done. They depended on their neighbors to prepare the food; all they had to do was take their baths and get dressed. By noon the celebration would begin. Zacharias went back to his booth and retrieved his scrolls and the blessing he had written out. There was one for his Elizabeth and two for Benjamin to read. Elizabeth had arranged his clothes on the bed. There was a nice new robe, yarmulke, and a prayer shall. She even took out his new sandals. He would get a good scrub today and be ready to present his boy to the Lord.

Elizabeth heard the sound of her friend's voice, and she opened the door to welcome her. She had the two donkeys with hampers laden with food. She and Zacharias went out to help them unload the food onto the table. Gratitude and love poured out of their hearts for their loyal friend and her daughter, who had served them graciously these last nine months. It was a worthy sacrifice of love to work so hard to make today special for her friends; Midge and Rachel were thrilled with the overwhelming blessings that came from having spent this time with them. They unloaded the stew beef with carrots and potatoes off the donkey and placed it near the fire pit. There was the basket with the bread; there was butter, jellies, cheese of different types, which were placed on the table and covered over with clean towels. There was a large basket with a large assortment of desserts, and these were placed on one of the serving tables also. There were stocks of serving plates, bowls, and spoons. Everything looked amazing and smelled wonderful. Benjamin had also arrived behind them and was setting up washing stations in the yard. There were many barrels of water and juices made from berries that he set up for the feast. The large pitchers with the wines were inside the booth. Benjamin also had a large variety of nuts and dried fruits which he handed over to the ladies. It already looked like a meal for a king's feast; they all chimed in as they observed the display. They all went indoors, where the men relaxed and had tea for an hour. Benjamin hassled his friend, the priest. While Elizabeth and Midge exchanged thought about the expectations of the day. The sense of happiness filled the air, and Rachel reveled in it. The men first went to take baths and got dressed and came out ceremonially attired and looking handsome for the holy occasion. The women always seemed to take a little longer to dress, so they wanted to be finished with the bathhouse. The men sat in the sitting room to await the arrival of their guests. Zacharias handed the scrolls with the blessings to Benjamin along with the order of the ceremony. Zacharias had given the blessings to Benjamin and the instructions before on how he wanted the ceremony to be done. Benjamin, having to stand in proxy, went over the details with him, and Zacharias nodded his head in agreement with the details he discussed. The woman had disappeared to make themselves pretty. Soon their family and neighbors started trickling into the yard. Benjamin, with his booming voice, was making everyone welcome and directing the men with the animals to the backyard. They brought more food and gift for the baby and the parents. The gifts were handed to Benjamin while the food was piled on the tables in the yard. There was then the arrival of the band of Elizabeth's family from Nazareth. They had slept over in Jerusalem last night and rose up early to avoid the midday sun. They all made themselves comfortable in the booth except for Nathan and Abigail. They left the younger boys to take care of their animals, and siblings entered the house, where they hugged and congratulated Zacharias. Abigail wandered into the room, where she found her sister dressing the baby. She hugged her sister and looked into the eyes of the precious baby boy lying on the bed, all dressed in white. Tears of joy moistened her eyes. She took the baby from Elizabeth and took him out to meet his uncle Nathan. Nathan's eyes welled up with tears. He has known of the years of waiting and the miracle that was presented to him today was unimaginable. He bowed his head and blessed the child. They were sure the day would be a mixture of tears of joy and loads of laughter for everyone who knew their story. Rabbi Levi arrived; he was dressed in black, and with his prayer shawl on, he also had a bag with his tools for the ceremony. He greeted the host Zacharias with kisses, offering blessings and congratulations for his great blessing from God. He perceived the man had not gotten his voice back, so he greeted the other men in the room. He spoke at length with Benjamin, who would be assisting him in the ceremony, while Zacharias listened in. Benjamin prepared water for the washing of the hands and a pitcher with extra water to be used that day to wash his hands several times during the ceremony as instructed by Rabbi Levi. The rabbi had left his boys in the care of his mother, Miriam. Midge had asked his mother, Miriam, to be one of the volunteers to arrange the food brought in on the table and later to assist with serving. Many children had already arrived and were talking or playing with each other. Men with their fiddle trumpet, harps, and cymbals had already arrived and were fine-tuning their instruments. There was a man with a shofar, and he gave three loud blasts. Abigail returned the baby to his mother and settled in a chair. She was receiving the gift the people brought for the baby. Rachel later came into the sitting room; she was going to help Abigail with the gifts received by taking them and storing them away in the baby's room. She was a beauty to behold. She greeted the men in the sitting room and locked eyes with Levi for a brief second before bowing. She collected the gifts and took them back to the baby's room. She made multiple trips and caught Levi's eyes on her several times. She gave him a quick smile, not wanting to openly show affection in public, seeing they were not yet married. Levi was pleased to see the beautiful maiden. She had a sweet glow and appeared so different from when he first requested her hand in marriage. His heart felt bold and confident; he had made the right choice. *This girl was beautiful and charming and would make a pleasing bride and mother,* he contemplated. After the ceremony, he would have time to walk and talk with her and to hear what was in her heart. It was time for the Ceremony. Rabbi Levi addressed the people as they drew near to the door. The fragrance of lavender mixed with the sweet odor of food heightened the sense, and the occasion produced joy among the people. The crowd that had gathered in the yard was unbelievably large. The air was filled with expectancy; everyone was excited and anxiously waiting to meet the miracle baby. Benjamin and Zacharias went back into the bedroom with Elizabeth and the baby. The baby was handed into the large arms of Benjamin at the instruction of the mohel; Benjamin walked before the parents with the baby while Zacharias and Elizabeth walked hand in hand behind him. They entered the room, and Zacharias stood to the right of the mohel while Benjamin moved to the left with the baby and Elizabeth standing behind him. A large sound of praise and cheering erupted in the yard as the baby and parents entered the room. There was not a dry eye in attendance as they all pushed to get closer to the door to have a look at the mother and child. Rabbi Levi's voice echoed above the noise, "With the permission of my teachers and the community!" The crowd responded, "To life." Rabbi Levi continued, "Blessed are you, Lord, our God, King of the universe, who has sanctified us with His commandments and commanded us concerning circumcision." Benjamin handed the baby to the rabbi, who placed him on the table, and the mother undressed the baby's lower body. Zacharias took up the knife and handed it to Rabbi Levi, who started the circumcision process with Elizabeth and Zacharias holding on to the baby's arms and legs. Benjamin recited, "Blessed are you, Lord, our God, King of the universe, who has sanctified us with His commandments and commanded us to enter him into the covenant of Abraham, our father." Those present were surprised that Benjamin, not Zacharias, was repeating the blessing, but the questions could be asked later. They, therefore, responded, "Just as he has entered into the covenant, so may he enter into the Torah, into marriage, and into good deeds. May the father merit to fulfill his obligations throughout the child's upbringing, to educate him, marry him off and raise him with acts of kindness." Benjamin recited, "Blessed are you, Lord, our God, King of the universe, who has granted us life, sustained us, and enabled us to reach this occasion. Blessed are you, God, guiding Spirit of the universe, who sanctifies Your beloved from the womb and has placed Your law in his body and marked this offspring with the sign of the holy covenant. For to the merit of this covenant living God our portion, our rock, protect this beloved child from misfortune, for the sake of this covenant that you have placed in our flesh. Blessed are you, God, who establishes the covenant." The baby cried as the incision was made. The Rabbi extracted the blood from the glands and washed and wrapped the penis. Then Elizabeth collected her child; she cleaned him, dressed him, and comforted him with her breast. The child settled down to nurse, the crowd cheered and worship as the minstrel sang a psalm of thanksgiving, and the musicians played in accompaniment. Midge and Rachel removed the soiled bedding from the table, and Rabbi cleaned his instruments and washed his mouth and his hands. Following the singing, Benjamin called the people to order for the naming ceremony. They all cheered as they awaited the name of the child. Chairs were placed in front of the table, and both the mother with the baby and the father sat and also Rabbi Levi. Benjamin asked Elizabeth to read the blessing Zacharias had written for her to read. Elizabeth read, "May you, my son, live to see a world that you create with your words, and may your future be a time we cannot yet imagine. May your purpose span the generations of your time. May your heart learn to understand and give wisdom to all who will hear. May you speak words of life and sing songs of joy and say what Yahweh says. May your vision be clear before you. May your eyes shine with the light of the Torah and your face glow with the radiance of heaven, and may you run to unfold the words of the Holy Ancient One Yahweh." Her eyes were filled with tears as she handed the child to her husband, who arose with the child and held him above his head. The people's cheers reached a crescendo as the priest thrust his son up to the heavens. Benjamin read loudly the blessings that Zacharias had written out, and a hush fell on the crowd. "John, my beloved, I want you to be happy; I want you to be strong. You came into the world, but to us, you don't belong. A prophet of the Most High you are called to be. I wish you contentment, I wish you joy, and above all, wish you courage for the task to which you are called. I want you to know what a real gift you are. When we never imagined possible, we were given you. We will cherish and hold you dear and raise you the way God declares. A Nazarite chosen by God, announced to us by Gabriel, the great ark angel that stands before our God. We want you to know that we will treasure you dearly and groom you in the way our God explained. You are a dream and a treasure and, best of all, a gift to the world. You will forever herald a new season and a new time. May your arms be strong, and your feet be sturdy; may your voice be strong and silent you will never be. May your faith be indelibly firm, and your words be sound and true for a prophet to God you are called to be and a blessing to your generation. Your mother and I will hold you near and care for you until our days draw near. Yahweh will provide and keep you always in His care until you have accomplished all you came here for. Our beloved son, John! For surely Yahweh had been gracious. Shalom." Benjamin continued to read from the scroll, "Our God and God of our ancestors, sustain this child for his father and mother and may his name in Israel ever be called John, son of Zacharias. May the father rejoice in the fruit of his loins and the mother be glad in the fruit of the womb. As it is said, your father shall rejoice, and the one who gave birth to you will be glad." The people clapped and cheered as the ancient blessing was read. The wine was brought out, and the people all drank after Benjamin recited, "Blessed are you, our God, guiding Spirit of the universe, Creator of the fruit of the vine." The people responded, "Amen." They drank and cheered as the music started, and the men danced and shouted for joy. Elizabeth and Zacharias took the baby to the room, where she cleaned him and put him to bed. Zacharias having forbidden wine to be put in the baby's mouth as was customary. They have a Nazarite's vow to keep as given to them by Gabriel the angel; instead, tiny sips of water were placed on the baby's tongue. On the outside, Elizabeth's family suddenly started to ask about the name—John that was given to the baby, and not Zacharias like his father or any other family name. Nathan's oldest son Ruben questioned his father about the baby's name. He was in training to become a rabbi, and he voiced the name had no resemblance to the priestly tribe of Zacharias. The family gathered themselves together and discussed the name of choice. On returning to her family, Elizabeth heard the debate about the baby's name and responded that his name was to be called John. They argued that none from their tribe or Zacharias's tribe had that name, and they requested the presence of Zacharias in this matter. They were already very skeptical that Zacharias was still not talking, and his baby was eight days old. Zacharias stood in their midst, and their loud arguing had by now attracted the attention of everyone present at the ceremony. The music stopped, and the people gathered around to hear what the father had to say. They gave him a writing scroll, and he wrote, "His name is John, which means 'Yahweh is gracious.'" They were all surprised and continued to murmur among themselves. Suddenly Zacharias's mouth was opened, and his tongue was loosed, and he began to speak and praised God. He was filled with the Holy Ghost and began to prophesy.

> Blessed be the Lord God of Israel; for he hath
> visited and redeemed his people, And hath raised
> up an horn of salvation for us in the house of his
> servant David; As he spake by the mouth of his
> holy prophets, which have been since the world
> began: That we should be saved from our ene-
> mies, and from the hand of all that hate us; To
> perform the mercy promised to our fathers, and
> to remember his holy covenant; The oath which
> he sware to our father Abraham, That he would
> grant unto us, that we being delivered out of the
> hand of our enemies might serve him without
> fear, In holiness and righteousness before him,
> all the days of our life. And thou, child, shalt be
> called the prophet of the Highest: for thou shalt
> go before the face of the Lord to prepare his
> ways; To give knowledge of salvation unto his
> people by the remission of their sins, Through
> the tender mercy of our God; whereby the day-
> spring from on high hath visited us, To give light
> to them that sit in darkness and in the shadow of
> death, to guide our feet into the way of peace.

Luke 1:68-79

The people wept and cried, and great fear came upon them all at the words of Zacharias. The people spoke among themselves, "What manner of a child is this? A prophet of the Highest?" The people questioned, "The dayspring from on high? He speaks of a new heavenly era." They said, "We will mark this day and tell it unto our children's children." Holy awe permeated the air as the older women cried, and the older men looked at each other in wonder. They were old enough to know that the gift of a child given to an elderly priestly couple was no ordinary thing; it was for a sign and a wonder, and as spoken by the father, this child was the prophet of Yahweh. The musician played, and the youths and children danced around the fire in a circle. It was time to eat and celebrate. A now quiet Zacharias sat in the booth, still shaken by the presence of the Holy Spirit that had overtaken him. Benjamin, Nathaniel, Rabbi Levi, and all the men, women, and children had gathered outside when Zacharias prophesied. Elizabeth looked at her husband in amazement. God has given him back his voice and allowed him to prophesy things so beautiful to the ears and hearts of everyone present. God has remembered His people; he has remembered all men to show grace and mercy. The Messiah has come, and his prophet was born. Elizabeth walked to the side of her husband, who held out his hands and embraced her. The men gathered around them, and Rabbi Levi spoke a blessing but was almost at a loss for words on what he had just witnessed. He promised he would write it down and would follow the life of John and reiterate it in the ears of his boys that they would remember this day forever. The men drank wine, and their hearts were merry. The musician played on the fiddle, and the men danced, followed by the women, then the youths and the children. There was an overflowing of joy at the house of Elizabeth and Zacharias. They remembered the words of the angel, "Many shall rejoice at his birth." They walked among their guests and greeted them, thanking them for coming out to celebrate with them. Midge insisted that the couple come to sit down and eat. She had shared out some food for them to eat and had placed it on the table inside the house. Hand in hand, a very happy couple returned to the house and sat side by side, and shared their second meal of the day. Zacharias blessed their meals, and they ate, discussing over the meal the mysteries of God to return his voice at such a pivotal time. "God's doings are never without witnesses," he said. "Everyone here today will remember this moment for our son's life is marked, and they will proclaim what they saw and heard today and watch for the fulfillment thereof. They will teach it to their children. It is only now beginning to unfold," he said. Elizabeth was so happy to hear the voice of wisdom again. Her priest and her king was talking again. She smiled at him and squeezed his hand gently. "How did we get so blessed?" she murmured in his ears. He knew they had nothing to do with it but that God had favored them and allowed them to participate in an era of love and grace on earth as promised to Abraham.

Rachel made her way over to Rabbi Levi and offered to make his meal, and they would eat at the table with Zacharias and Elizabeth. The event of the day and the utterance of the prophecy had imprinted on both their hearts. Levi agreed and joined the elders at the table. The beautiful princess brought him his meal and sat across from him with her mother sitting by. She placed the food before him, and he prayed over the food and ate. His boys were with his mother. "It was a beautiful ceremony," Rachel whispered. "It certainly was," Levi agreed. He then rushed on to voice how amazing the prophecy was and how Zacharias's voice was returned by the Holy Ghost for the prophetic utterances. He vowed that he would never forget this moment for as long as he lived. For him, this was an epic moment in history of mankind as Zacharias has prophesied of the birth of the Messianic age and of his own son chosen to be his prophet. It would be a day he would share with his students for a long time to come. He voiced that he would have them trace the ancient prophecies concerning the Messiah and his prophet and the promises as written in the holy scrolls. Rachel looked at him in wonderment; he was a true teacher and also believed in the prophecies of the Messiah. There was no guesswork, they were all eyewitnesses of these things, and it will be their responsibility to share this story with everyone they know, including their children. She had the joy of serving the elderly priest and his wife these last eight days and had visited with them with her mother over these last nine months that Elizabeth had carried the baby; she had learned so much from them. Levi listened intently to Rachel as she recounted her time spent with Zacharias and Elizabeth. She was so well-spoken and had an amazing glow and softness about her. She had such calm and peacefulness about her that he was mesmerized by her presence. How did he get so blessed in choosing the correct girl to marry the second time around? When he lost his wife, his heart felt it would never be whole again. But when he first cast his eyes on Rachel and spoke to his mother about her, it was the first time in two years his heart felt hope and the anticipation of love again. Now sitting across from this beautiful woman, he knew that God had also favored him to give him joy again. He had great doubt when he first approached her mother and proposed. She had actually rejected him, but her mother had insisted that she would talk to her and then get back to him. When she finally agreed, he was happy but also a little apprehensive. He had heard she was stubborn and self-willed and had resisted getting married up until now. He hoped he was making the right choice, for he needed a good mother for the boys. Today was a great day granted to him to sit with this maiden and had a heart-to-heart talk with her, and he was impressed. She was a girl of deep faith and convictions and even more so than what he was told. She wanted to teach her children the Torah, and they will learn about the Messiah and his prophet. "I know you are a good man, and I will not be afraid to walk with you." Levi smiled at her, "You should meet the boys after dinner." Rachel agreed to this, so they dismissed themselves from the table and walked to the booth outside in search of the boys and their grandmother. Levi's mother was a petite older woman with kind eyes and a welcoming embrace. Miriam was also a widow and lived next door to Levi and helped him with the children. She had failing health and was anxious for Levi to be married again. David and Jonathon were a year apart. David was three years old, and Jonathon—two years old. She greeted the boys who hid behind their grandma. "They are extremely shy,"

Levi interjected. Both boys had no recollection of their mother, for they were still so young when she died. Rachel bent and touched their little heads, looking into their deep brown eyes. She greeted them and promised to come to visit with their grandma soon. The boys nodded their heads at her. Her heart immediately felt a tug of love and compassion towards these young boys who had lost their mother so early in their lives. This was what she was born for. She was going to be a good mother to the boys. "You have to promise me that you will talk to me when I come to visit," she chimed. The boys nodded their heads in unison, still clinging to their grandma's dress. She offered to go and get them dessert from the table. When she returned, she had cranberry rugelach, two each for the boy. She explained to the boys that she helped her mother to make these, and she would be more than willing to make some exclusively for them. The boy's eyes lit up as they bit into the sweet treat. She bade them goodbye and promised to visit them soon again. As they walked back to the house, Levi opened his heart and shared how hard it has been for the boys. He spoke of his hope that his next wife would be able to love the children of another woman and someday give him children of her own. Rachel expressed to him for the first time that she can't wait to be his wife and the mother of his children. He stopped in his tracks and turned to look deep into her eyes. Her convictions were evident. "You will make me a happy man," Levi said. He could have hugged her and swept her off her feet, but the custom was there should be no public show of affection between the unwed. "We do not have to wait a year," Rachel said. "The boys need a mother, and you need a wife." Levi was elated. She explained to him that she had discussed it with her mother, and if he and his family were in agreement, they could be married as soon as her service with Elizabeth was over. Levi promised he would discuss the matter with the elders, but he did not know of any law that would oppose them getting married earlier than a year of betrothal but that he would have to discuss it with the elders. "You make me a very happy man today," he said. "I have gotten a miracle here today." For he himself had thought of an early marriage and to hear her voice the same. "We have all gotten miracles here," Rachel said. He had come to perform the bris and only to discovered that the woman he had proposed to was in love with him and his boys and wanted to have an early wedding. It was a miracle indeed. They parted in the house as Rachel went to find her mother, and Levi joined the men in the sitting room. The party continued outside as the wine and the food flowed. The sun had begun to set. The red-orange glow settled in the sky. The fiddler played, and the children danced around the crackling embers of the dying flames. Someone stoked the fire and added more coals. Midge brought two large lanterns to the booth to add more lighting to the yard. Groups of women and men were gathered in the booth and across the yard, talking about the events of the day while the children danced and played. It has been a beautiful ceremony. A mild wind rustled in the trees bringing in a chill in the air as the fading sunlight disappeared in the west. The food and the wine were almost gone. Midge had asked the people to take home whatever food was left.

Zacharias came to the booth and thanked everyone for coming. He prayed the Aaronic blessings over them all, "The Lord bless you and keep you and cause his face to shine upon you and lift up his countenance upon you and give you his peace" (Numbers 6:24-26). He wished them a safe journey home. Elizabeth's family would travel back to Jerusalem tonight. They had secured rooms at the inn since it was so many of them. They wanted to make an early departure to Nazareth in the morning. They all had enjoyed the ceremony and were amazed by the sign and wonder God has given to their family. Elizabeth had a small window to ask about Mary's return. Abigail's facial expression was a wave of sadness, but she told her she was quickly married off to Joseph, but that she had no need to be a concern; they have come to celebrate with her. Elizabeth's heart rejoiced. She knew God had spoken to Joseph, and that was all that matters. One day there would be no silence to these boys as their voices and their names will echo throughout Israel as salvation will come to those who will believe. She bade goodbye to her siblings. They were immeasurably blessed, having come to celebrate with Zacharias and Elizabeth. They would all return to Nazareth and tell of the Prophet of the Most High God that was celebrated tonight and of the prophecy that the Messiah was here. Israel has not had a prophet in over four hundred years. The kings had killed all the prophets and did with them what they pleased when they spoke the council of Yahweh against the wickedness of the kings. The wicked kings of Israel had done evil and were exiled from the land and the temple destroyed. Since their return from the Babylonian captivity, the last prophet Malachi spoke of the messenger that comes before the Messiah. Many have held on to the ancient prophecies and waited for the promise of a king from the lineage of David. They promised to remember this day, and all they had heard for of a certainty, the spirit of prophecy came on Zacharias today. In his old age, he was called to father the next great prophet in Israel. They had no doubt about what they heard and saw for why would God give an old couple a baby except it was for a sign and a wonder, for was it not Abraham and Sarah who conceived a child in their old age as a sign and a wonder and the birthing of an era of God's covenant with man, and that the Messiah would come from their lineage? God has spoken, and they receive the gift of the son he has given to the world. As the men saddled the horses and donkeys and hooked their carts up, the women collected leftover food and water. They would have enough food to eat in the morning and for their journey back to Nazareth. Nathan and Abigail hugged Elizabeth and Zacharias. It would be another long time before they would come again. They were not so young anymore, but they would come down for the next feast days to Jerusalem as God gave them life and strength. They bade goodbye. "Take care of Prophet John," the men said as they patted Zacharias on the back as he accompanied them up the road. He waved as they got on their animals and cart and started their descent in the dark shadows. It was a new moon, and the sky was clear. They should be in Jerusalem within two hours. The neighbors were also taking their leave, asking for personal blessing from the priest as they departed.

Back in the house, baby John was awake and calling for his mother. Rachel hurriedly gathered him from the crib, planting kisses on his forehead. "Hello, John," she said. "Welcome into the world and to the men of Israel and to Yahweh Most High!" Elizabeth smiled at her words; she washed her hands and prepared to breastfeed the child. It has been a wonderful day filled with many miracles. Rachel handed her the baby and left her to feed and bond with the child. In the yard, the guests were departing. Levi came to say goodbye, promising that he would talk to his kinsmen and that her mother should talk with her family and to be sure all the family was in agreement for an early wedding. He shook her hand; holding on a little longer, she felt the firmness and strength of his hands, but they were also soft and reassuring. They were both experiencing the miracle of love. For Rachel, this was first love, and for Levi, this was a second chance at love. They were both mature, and both knew what they wanted. Rachel bade Miriam and the boys a good night and waved as they left in the falling darkness. The crescent moon rose over the hill and making it a perfect night for romantic excitement. "Good night, my love," she murmured. This was more to herself than to him. He had made her the happiest girl alive tonight. The families were all leaving. They collected their bowls and pans they bought with food. Rachel went to the tables to help her mother with the cleaning up. She did not want to soil her dress, but very few things were left. This would be a good opportunity to talk with her mother alone. Her mother watched her as she approached. She was such a beautiful young woman. She wondered when her little girl grew up and became so lovely. Her face glowed in the moonlight. Midge knew her daughter was in love, and for the girl's sake, she was happy. "I see your happiness, my child," Midge nudged her. Rachel threw herself into her mother's arm and blurted out all the emotions she felt in her heart that night. She was enthralled with all the senses of love for Levi and the boys and share with her mother that she wanted to get married as soon as she was finished serving Elizabeth. She shared with her what Levi had said about an early wedding, and her mother agreed that she would speak to her brothers, and she was sure they would all agree they could get married sooner than later. Rachel confessed to her mother that she never imagined being in love could evoke such wonderful feelings. Midge knew it was the time to share with Rachel the joys of intimacy, romance, and sexuality. These were gifts innately given to humans by Yahweh, and for Rachel, these emotions were awakened. When she chose a life of celibacy, there was no need to have this conversation, but now that she had decided to be married, she needed to share with her from her own experiences that she will be well equipped to make her husband a happy man. She also encouraged her to talk with Aunt Elizabeth, who had what her mother described as a perfectly beautiful marriage. The ladies talked under the crescent moonlight until the only person left in the yard was Benjamin and Zacharias, also deep in conversation.

Benjamin assisted Midge in loading the pots and pans on the donkey. Midge bade her daughter goodbye and got on the donkey. Benjamin bade his friend goodbye and took off with Midge. It has been a long but glorious day of God's favor and grace. They were all exhausted to the bones but too happy in their hearts to give in to the weakness of the flesh. Zacharias waited until they disappeared down the hill and joined in the company of the happy neighbors going home to sleep with hope and dream again for the Messiah and his prophet to come.

He entered his house and locked his door, and went in search of his wife and child. John was sleeping, and Elizabeth was already lying in bed. She watched him as he hovered over the sleeping child, praying blessings over him. He got washed and came and lay beside his beautiful wife, cuddling her to his chest. "It is so good to be in bed with my princess again," he murmured softly in her ears. His voice and kindness had always been the key to her heart. He was always such a gentleman. He laid there kissing her gently on the forehead and praying blessings of strength and long life over her. He wanted her and himself to live long enough to see their son come to age. He wanted them to be his teacher and to instruct him in the ways of Yahweh. As they laid there, they knew how truly bless-ed they were. Comforted by each other's presence, they fell into a blissful sleep. Elizabeth awoke to the cry of her son, the prophet, who was ready to be fed again. She pulled herself quietly from the arms of her husband and retrieved the crying child. She escorted him to his room, where she nursed him and changed his diaper, and rocked him gently back to sleep. She went back to her room and laid him gently in his crib and crawled quietly back in bed. Zacharias was still soundly asleep in his feather bed. He had spent seven nights on the hard ground with only the stars for his companion. "He must be in a dream," she murmured as she looked into his peaceful face. She herself drifted off only to dream of a field of yellow daffodils and her searching for her son on the hillside. She was yelling his name over and over again. She awoke to his cry and got up smil-ing. He was still in his crib. In the dream, he was about two years old and running around in a garden of daffodils when he suddenly disappeared. She got him out of his crib and kissed him on the forehead. "You are the prophet to the Lord Messiah, and no one will not take you away from me. You will fulfill your God-given destiny," she murmured in his ears. Again, he was fed and cleaned up and returned to his crib, and Zacharias was still fast asleep. Elizabeth crawled back to bed and was soon asleep. The next time the baby cried, the day was dawning, and the cock was crowing in the distant hills. Zacharias stirred in his sleep and sat up. He was finally hearing the cry of his son. "He has great lungs; he will be a great prophet one day." He got up and picked the child up from his crib and handed him to his mother.

He then kissed his wife and went to the sitting room to spend time in prayer and worship. He had to go down to Jerusalem to report to the High Priest, Joseph ben Caiaphas. He has been out of commission for nine months. He had to return to fulfill his religious duties. God has been gracious to him and Elizabeth, and there is nothing more he wanted to do but to serve in the temple until his time came to an end. He would report in on Thursday. He opened the scrolls and read from the writings of King David. He chanted the songs of thanksgiving, knelt, and bowed his head in prayer for his family and his nation. When he had completed his petitions, Elizabeth had made breakfast, and the sun was rising and filling the house with golden rays. His voice was like music to the ears of Elizabeth. "Don't ever go quiet on me again," Elizabeth whispered as he entered the kitchen. "No, my love, never again," he murmured in her ears, giving her a hug and kisses on the cheeks. She had missed his voice, and he had missed teasing her. Rachel was awoken to their talks and playful laughter and joined them for breakfast. She ate in quiet contemplations, listening to the voices of Elizabeth and Zacharias as they throw playful banters at each other. There was such deep friendship between them; even at their old age, they still enjoyed the company of each other above anyone else. She now understood the words of Yahweh that said, "Therefore shall a man leave his father and his mother, and shall cleave unto his wife: and they shall be one flesh" (Genesis 2:24). He had really become one with Elizabeth. She hoped that she and Levi would have this oneness and harmony she saw with Zacharias and Elizabeth. After breakfast, Elizabeth went to tend to the baby. Rachel cleaned up the house. There was extra work to be done to return the house to normal now that the bris was over. She removed the white drapes and the tablecloths she would wash them today. The drapes she folded and put on the table for Elizabeth to put away. She replaced the drapes and tablecloths with the original ones she had removed a few days ago. She then went out and washed the baby's clothes. The air was crisp and clean. Thin white clouds spread across the deep blue sky. She was sure there would be no rain today, but it was cool, so she pulled her shawl more tightly across her chest. She stood in the washing stand and washed with her hands while she bellowed out the song Moses and the people sang when they crossed the Red Sea after leaving Egypt.

> The LORD is my strength and song, and he is become my salvation: he is my God, and I will prepare him a habitation; my father's God, and I will exalt him. The LORD is a man of war: the Lord is his name.
>
> **Exodus 15:2-3**

The anthem filled the air and blessed the heart of those who heard it. Zaharias had tackled the booth to dismantle it. The maiden's voice filled the air, and he joined in joyful praise and was so grateful to God to hear his own voice again in songs of joy. He was a priest, a man of liturgical utterances, he had so missed the sound of his own voice, but Yahweh has been gracious.

Rachel's singing came to an end as her thoughts went back to the events of yesterday. The miracle of yesterday still lingered in the air, she had heard the priest joined in the song, but now her thoughts were somewhere else or rather on someone else. The joy of spending time in the presence of Levi yesterday brought on feelings of loneliness. She really missed him and hoped she would see him again soon. She chastened herself for such thought but realized that they were natural and that these were feelings and thought that makes love significant. If she did not have such thoughts and feelings, she would not know what love was like. She also knew that she could not abandon herself to these thoughts because it would be some time before they would be married. She loved this new sensation and feeling of being in love. Her heart was as light as a feather in the wind, and without thinking, she started to softly sing the songs of Solomon as she hanged the clothes on the line.

> Let him kiss me with the kisses of his mouth: for thy love is better than wine. Because of the savour of thy good ointments thy name is as ointment poured forth, therefore do the virgins love thee. Draw me, we will run after thee: the king hath brought me into his chambers: we will be glad and rejoice in thee, we will remember thy love more than wine: the upright love thee.
>
> **Song of Solomon 1:2-4**

Elizabeth listened from the bedroom window and chuckled. "Oh! To be young and in love," she whispered. She was glad this beautiful young girl that called her aunt was experiencing the treasures of heaven given by the Father above, the love of a man the way God intended. She decided she would release her each evening, for she will need to go home to make plans with her mother for her wedding day. She had removed the remainder of white linen and drapes from the rooms and return the house to normalcy. She was enjoying being a mother and still find the energy to do the things she loved to do. As they sat for lunch, Elizabeth discussed with Rachel that she would relieve her to go home each day. "You will soon have a wedding to plan," she said. She further told her that with Zacharias now in the house with her; she could go home once her daily chores were done and have time to talk with her mother and plan out her big day. Rachel quickly agreed, seeing that her evenings would usually be free. There were so many things to talk over with her mother, and Elizabeth was getting more independent every day. She thanked them for having her and expressed how her service here with them and the baby has been a blessing for her life. She shared how her heart had opened up and was filled up with love where once she had held back and not wanting to let anyone in. She spoke to them of how their story of remaining pure in heart towards God when they did not get what they prayed for but how God had rewarded them even in old age and gave them a baby boy, John the prophet of the Lord. "This story has changed my life," Rachel told them. I will tell it to Levi's children and my children. They will be taught to acknowledge the prophet and the Messiah when they come out among the people. Elizabeth had tears in her eyes. This maiden had also seen the face of God. Their story has become her staircase to heaven, and she would forever be changed into the glorious person God wanted her to be, a wife and a mother and a woman who truly feared the Lord.

Part 3:
The Prophet John: His Life and Legacy

Zacharias had returned to temple duty in Jerusalem for almost two years following his son's birth. The news of the child's birth had caused quite a stir among the priesthood when the child was brought into the temple to be given back to God according to the Torah. "Sanctify unto me all the firstborn, whatsoever openeth the womb among the children of Israel, both of man and of beast: it is mine" (Exodus 13:2). He and Elizbeth came with the child and offered a lamb without blemish. As the sacrifice was made, the child was consecrated to God. Those in the temple that day stood in awe and wondered at the miracle of the old priest and his wife, who presented their first child to God. In their heart, they all knew it was a sign and a wonder. They all speculated on the mystery of a child given to him in old age. However, Zacharias held his tongue, refusing to share the events of the things surrounding the child's birth. He feared they would try to tamper with the destiny of the child. The excitement and wonder about the child soon waned and died and temple duty continued as usual. Zacharias was an old man now and had marked his one-hundred years on the earth. By the divine grace of Yahweh, his natural strength has not failed, and he still had the rigor to run around with his son and continue with periodic temple duty. His son John was two years old and kept his mother busy running around the house and getting into everything as an energetic toddler did. These were strange times in Israel and especially in Jerusalem. King Herod had been extremely agitated since three Magi showed up in Jerusa-

221

lem looking for the baby king of the Jews. They were stargazers and astrologers who had seen a bright star over Jerusalem, and according to old prophecies, they have come to see God's child. Balthasar was from Arabia, Melchior from Persia, and Gaspar was from India. They had all converged in Jerusalem and had all followed a special star that burst out in the galaxy more brilliant than all the stars in their scope of sight. The prophecy had stated,

> I shall see him, but not now: I shall behold him, but not nigh: there shall come a Star out of Jacob, and a Sceptre shall rise out of Israel, and shall smite the corners of Moab, and destroy all the children of Sheth.
>
> **Numbers 24:17**

They had come with an entourage and bare great gifts for the infant King. They understood that each child born in the earth is marked by a shining star as ordained by the Great God of the heavens, and so they have come to search for the child in Israel whose star so brilliant had pulled them to the ancient land of mystery, the land of the God of all gods. They were taken to Herod's palace, where they discussed the purpose of their visit. Appalled by this great mystery, King Herod called for Caiaphas, the high priest. He questioned him concerning such prophecies as recounted by the wise men. Caiaphas marvel and responded to the question with the quote from the scroll of the prophet Micah,

> In Bethlehem of Judea: for thus it is written by the prophet, And thou Bethlehem, in the land of Juda, art not the least among the princes of Juda: for out of thee shall come a Governor that shall rule my people Israel.
>
> **Matthew 2:5-6**

The high priest discussed with the king that it was an ancient prophecy that they waited for, the coming of a Jewish Messiah, like unto King David, and that they had virgins prepared and waiting in Jerusalem but knew of no virgin pregnancy in Israel. Zacharias carried out his priestly duty with a smile, for he knew that the Virgin Mary should have given birth and has caused a stir in the heavens and in Jerusalem. He kept quiet through the whole discourse and the strange visitation of the stargazers. He knew Yahweh's promise could not be thwarted. Unknowing to him and all else in Jerusalem, the wise men did find the infant king with his mother and father in Bethlehem in Judea as was prophesied. However, Yahweh had warned them severely in a dream not to return to King Herod because his intention was to kill the child. Totally overcame by fear, they secretly got up in the night and hurriedly left Judea, fearing the wrath of Yahweh more than the wrath of King Herod. It was now over a year and a half since the Magi came and had promised King Herod that they would report back to him when they found the star again and found the child king. Herod knew something significant had happened in the galaxy that has brought a revelation to earth. He had enough knowledge of ancient mysteries to know something of significance had happened and that a king child was born. The Magi had ignored his edict and had returned to their countries under the covers of the night. These wise men were no ordinary people. Their giftings of looking into the mysteries of the heavens were revered, and they were honored in their own country and sought after for their accurate predictions of times and seasons by gazing at the stars and communicating with the watcher angels that had fallen out with the God of Israel. The gift of divination was important to the pagan nations, and its wisdom was highly sought after. God had forbidden the nation of Israel to seek after and communicate with demons and false deities. If they reported that a king was born, then a king was born. Not only one but three seers from different countries had come as if by divine guidance and had met the same day in Jerusalem with a similar request to see the child king. Herod swore that he would find the baby and destroy him off the face of the earth now and forever. He had great ambitions for his own son to sit on the throne in his place after his death. So, long as Rome remained in power, his son would sit as the only king of Judea. His own father was Herod The Great, who had ruled with great terror. His father had converted to Judaism and was appointed by Rome to be the resident king of Judea and other regions in Palestine. He had made himself great by painting the landscape of the Middle East with great infrastructures and aqueducts and brought great glory and wealth to Rome in that region. He had great political ambition and had worked himself up from Governor of Galilee to becoming king of Judea under Rome occupation. He was a fearless leader and ruled with a hand of iron. He, Herod Antipas, now ruled with terror, and he wanted his son to sit in his stead. *Who dared these Magi to defy his orders?* "No one defies the king," he bellowed when the search parties were unable to find the Magi. He would not sit by idly and allow a prophecy planned to dethrone him come to past. He would find the child and kill him even if he had to kill all babies born in his territory at that time. The edict went out, "Every boy child under two years old in all Judea must be killed." His soldiers would go from house to house, killing all these infants to fulfill the wish of the wicked king.

Zacharias hurried home to Ein Kerem in Judea. He must get his baby out of the region, for the edict of the king called for the massacre of all boy babies in Judea. The high priest discussed the matter after the morning sacrifice, and they all believed Herod was over-zealous and foolish to think he could kill the plan of Yahweh, but none had the power to stop him. The High Priest Caiaphas had earlier that day declared that if the child was born, then the actions of King Herod was also according to the prophecies of Jeremiah, "Thus saith the Lord; A voice was heard in Ramah, lamentation, and bitter weeping; Rachel weeping for her children refused to be comforted for her children, because they were not" (Jeremiah 31:15). He did not think there was much he could do, so he dismissed Zacharias and all those who had young children from temple duties in order for them to go home and see if they could go and save their own children, who were two years old and younger for they also who would certainly not escape the edict of the king. The pain of the impending doom mingled in the air. "Has God forgotten them as His children?" people murmured as the morning sacrifice ended. "Who kills babies?" the heart of the people mourned and cursed the wicked Roman monarchy with its wretched reach of evil to bring death and destruction to the innocent babies. They were reminded of Pharaoh's decision while in Egypt's bondage to destroy all boy babies and how the midwives in fear of Yahweh disobeyed the order of the king, who then further instructed all Egyptians to throw all the baby boys born to the Israelites into the river Nile. History was repeating itself, and the groans and sighs of the people could be heard as the incense and smoke faded into nothingness. Zacharias got home by high noon. Elizabeth was surprised to see him home so early from Jerusalem. He was anxious and agitated and asked about his son. John was still taking his afternoon nap. "Hurry up," he ordered his wife. "You must take the baby and escape to the wilderness by the Dead Sea. Stay with the Essenes for Herod has determined to kill all babies two years old and younger. Our child must be saved to fulfill his God-ordained destiny. This tyranny must not prevail against the will of Yahweh." Both Zacharias and Elizabeth had discussed the child's safety in the past should in case anyone of them should die and because of the prophecy of Isaiah, which said that John would come out of the wilderness preaching the gospel of the kingdom of God. They had made an arrangement with an Essenes family that they would raise the child should any evil befall the parents. The Essenes lived in caves in the harsh desert by the Dead Sea. They had made themselves the protector of the written words of the Torah and the prophets and have given themselves to the study prophecy and waited patiently for the coming Messiah. When they heard the story of Zacharias, they had come in search of answers and swore to protect his child if he ever needed their help. They have built themselves secret bunks and covenanted with Zacharias to protect the covenant child. It was determined that the soldiers would start the massacre in Bethlehem and then throughout all Judea.

The Journey was twenty-three miles from Ein Kerem to the Dead Sea region. It was a dry, acrid, and treacherous wasteland. But with their gentle surefooted donkey, it was manageable. Elizabeth would go by donkey to Ein Gidi where she could refresh the beast at the oasis and possibly arranged for a camel to take her down the rough terrain. She had rehearsed this several times with Zacharias and was familiar with the territory and its customs. She would travel alone to avoid attention, and it was however too urgent a matter to get others engaged in. She would start the journey immediately to give her two days' head start before the centurion bands came to this region. She padded the hamper in which she would put the sleeping child, and on the other side, she loaded with his clothes, water, and food supplies. Life and energy flowed through the couple as Elizabeth prepared to flee with her child. Zacharias kissed and blessed his child, then loaded him into the hamper. He held his wife in a long, tender embrace, and he kissed his bold, beautiful wife, who still had a fire in her eyes. She was dressed in layers of clothes to protect her from the harsh desert sun, with her face completely covered, only revealing her eyes. She mounted the beast and started on the trail that led to the desert by the dead sea. Zacharias watched until the beast disappeared from his sight. He sighed in sadness and was overcome with weariness. He knew he might never see his son again, but he knew his son was not only a gift to him but a gift to the world to usher in the Messiah. For God will not do anything on earth unless He tells it to His prophets, and this was an old statement know in the priesthood and in the scriptures. King Herod may not be pleased when he hears his son had disappeared. Like Moses, his child was a proper child chosen by Yahweh to carry out a special assignment on the earth. John was born to be a prophet to Christ. He had no doubts that Yahweh had already protected his son and that this massacre would cause great grief, but the mighty duo—children of prophecy would be saved. He must return to Jerusalem to complete his tour of duty. As he walked back down the hill with his face set towards Jerusalem, he prayed Elizabeth would get safely to the Dead Sea and that angels would watch over her and the precious child she carried. He prayed over Jerusalem and the whole region of Judea and for all the innocent blood of children that would spill in the streets. He prayed for the mothers whose children will be snatched mercilessly from their arms and their sucking breasts and pierced through with the sword or slashed in the neck because of the wrath of the wicked king. He prayed for the helpless fathers of Israel who would stand by powerlessly as the blood of their seeds spill to the ground and desecrate the land. He prayed for the brokenness in humanity and for a world ripe for the Messiah to arrive. The one to give light to the gentiles and to give glory to Israel. The Comforter, Counselor, Mighty God, Everlasting Father, and the Prince of Peace as prophesied. Rome had plundered and caused worldwide bloodshed and the millions of carcasses of men left in battlefields unburied or burned with fire. His soldiers were so ruthless that they live to carry out the edict of the king, even to the killing of innocent children. "May the blood of the innocent rise up to speak to you great Yahweh, and may you vindicate these your children and bring this bloody Roman Empire down," Zacharias whispered as he made his descent into Jerusalem. The sun was going down as he entered the Eastern Gate. The shofar blew a woeful sound as the people gathered for the evening sacrifice. There was much to pray about and to petition the God of heaven about. He quickly washed and dressed in his robe. It was his place to offer the lamb on the altar of sacrifice. As the knife sank into its neck and the body yielded up its strength and its blood, he prayed that Yahweh would look upon the sons of Israel and have mercy for the wretchedness and the folly that would take place in the land. The smoke from the altar arose. The aroma of the burnt flesh yielded its fragrance to the skies. He knew that not even a million lambs could appease the sins that would take place in the land. For Herod would desecrate the land with the blood of the innocent children two years and younger. A whole generation was wiped out because of the folly of a man thinking he could defy Yahweh. He hoped that some of the mothers had already fled, and he hoped his Elizabeth was well on her way to enter the hiding place of the Essenes. He knew his son would be protected and become the prophet God ordained him to be. A faint smile lighted his eyes. "My son, John," he murmured, "God has remembered my wife and me and used us to usher into the world the prophet to His child." The lamb was consumed by the fire, and another priest came by, and he had gathered live coals from the altar, and he made his way to the Altar of Incense. Soon the aroma from the perfumed oil erupted in the air, and the people worship Yahweh and bring their petitions to Him. Their children would be taken and killed, and they were powerless to stop this slaughter. The women were especially tearful, and the men were somber. The Aaronic blessing was released as the people bowed with contrite hearts. "The Lord bless thee, and keep thee: The Lord make his face shine upon thee, and be gracious unto thee: The Lord lift up his countenance upon thee, and give thee peace" (Numbers 6:24-26). The crowd wandered away in the setting sun. They neither felt the peace of God nor was His face shining on them. The will of King Herod would be done. The cleaning team descended upon the temple, and an exhausted Zacharias made his way to the sleeping quarters, where he collapsed on the floor weeping. The weight of the sorrow that would flow tomorrow tore his heart apart. *Can this deluge be averted? Yahweh! Can King Herod be stopped?* He washed and prepared for bed. He had no desire for supper, for his appetite had fled away, and his soul was bathed in sorrow.

Meanwhile, Elizabeth had made it successfully before dark to the Judean desert region. Thankfully, she had met one of the sect leaders traveling with a team from Jerusalem. She explained her mission, and they happily provided a canopy of safety for her to travel in. She was blindfolded and taken into the labyrinth of the caves deep into the depts of the earth. It was here that she met with Rabbi Ruben Sid, with whom Zacharias had agreed to care for his son. The room was warm and lit with many torches. The walls were lined with multiple scrolls of the sacred writings. Their voices echoed off the walls, but it has been a safe place to live. The Romans had not penetrated this harsh land. They had settled for the comforts of Jerusalem and neighboring occupied towns in Israel. The child was handed over to Ruben's wife, Eve. Elizabeth handed the scrolls containing John's life that Zacharias had started since his angelic visitation. Rabbi Sid knew part of the story and promised that he and his clan would take care of the child and raise him in the ways of Yahweh. Should they survive the wrath of King Herod, then they were free to return and claim the child, but he doubted it was going to be easy. The child's life, he thought, would be safer hidden away in these caves until God chose to release him into his destiny. Exhausted from her long trip, Elizabeth was offered a place to refresh herself. She was given a meal and a warm place to sleep. Tomorrow she would make her way back to Judea if Rabbi Sid thought it was safe. If not, she would linger among the Clan until the edict of the king was completed. The Roman Soldiers had never ventured out into the harsh desert and had never penetrated the secret places of the Essenes.

So, Elizabeth knew her son would be safe. As she laid quietly in the dark, she prayed to Yahweh for the protection of her husband. She knew he would travel back to Jerusalem that night to finish his rotation of priestly duties. She prayed for every mother who would watch helplessly as their child would be taken and killed. Many of the younger women lived in fear of the wrath of the king and would readily give up the lives of their babies than fight for their lives. The men felt powerless against the training and violence of the Roman soldiers. They could only pray. While Yahweh sometimes did not intervene in man's violence against his fellow man. She still offered her prayers. She knew the prophecy would be fulfilled but knew her child would live. She cried for the lost souls and the innocent blood of the children that would be spilled on the ground; it was too hard to bear. The prophecies would be fulfilled because the dark prince of the world who stand in constant opposition against the redemptive plan of Yahweh for humanity was again trying to thwart the plan of God. He would fail, but the merciless spilling of the blood of the innocent children would appease his wrath against Yahweh for trying to save the souls of the wretched man who sold their souls to him for the apple of the knowledge of good and evil. She fell into a fitful sleep and dreamed of great doom over Jerusalem. She woke up wailing for the babies whose blood would be spilled in Judea but knew prophecy would be fulfilled.

Meanwhile, in Jerusalem, Zacharias arose from his cot. He had slept but a few hours, for his night was filled with lamentation and prayers to Yahweh. Today his assignment was to again kill the morning sacrifice and place it on the altar of burnt offering. He washed and prepared himself and solemnly and made his way into the temple. The atmosphere in the temple was somber. Sorrow and pain marked the faces of the priesthood. They nodded and bowed their heads in acknowledgment of each other but not a sound of chatter or laughter was heard that morning as they prepared for the morning sacrifice. The fire was stoked, fresh wood was applied to bring it to a roaring blaze. The blackness of dawn disappeared, and the rustling of feet could be heard entering the Outer Court, where Zacharias stood at his post to appease Yahweh for the sins of the people. A spotless lamb was securely tied up and placed by the altar by the temple helpers. He raised his eyes and looked over a crowded room, and tears spill from his eyes as he beheld mothers huddling with their babies. More people had turned up for the morning ceremony than usual, and he immediately realized that a multitude of young families was huddled in the courtyard. They were seeking a sanctuary, a place of refuge away from the wrath of King Herod. Zacharias grabbed the knife and plunged it into the heart of the lamb. He did it with more intensity than was usual, for he knew no animal blood would change the edict of the wicked king. The people had rejected the ways of Yahweh and accepted a wicked king that placed burdens on them that was too hard to bear. Today he chose to kill their children. He, seeking to kill the Messiah and his prophet, had committed a wicked deed. His wicked plan would fail but at the price of the many innocent babies whose blood would spill out on the ground in Israel today. The priesthood chanted the morning prayers and a soulful song raised to Yahweh. He knew the sacrifice would not avert the calamities of the hour. They have been going through the motions, and for years, they have had no Jewish king, no prophet, and the high priests were appointed by a stranger, a Roman resident king. The nation had played the harlot and had rejected the laws of Yahweh. God desired a holy people and not just a ceremonial act. He gave them the laws in the Torah, and they have chosen to live their own way. The animal was placed on the altar, and its burnt flesh gave off a pleasant aroma that arose with the smoke and the flames. Yahweh would not respond today, for the hearts of the people were tainted. Their sins still separated them from God. They have forsaken his ways. He, however, had sent his son and his prophet, and in time redemption would come. But today, the blood of their babies would spill. The prayers and chanting increased, and the wailing and the weeping of the people reached a crescendo. The babies cried as the Outer Court became overflown with all Jerusalem crying out with one voice to Yahweh. The prophecy was fulfilled. "A voice was heard in Ramah, lamentation, and bitter weeping; Rachel weeping for her children refused to be comforted for her children, because they were not" (Jeremiah 31:15). He felt powerless, but Zacharias knew the lamb of God was here, Israel's redemption was safely hidden away to be revealed in God's own time, and he had sent his son the prophet to the caves by the dead sea. The sacrifice burnt to ashes, and the priest assigned to the Altar of Incense, approached the fireplace and collected live coals from off the altar. The people watched as he entered behind the veil, and the priesthood continued to sing and read from the Torah one of the psalms of David.

> The Lord is my shepherd; I shall not want. He maketh me to lie down in green pastures: he leadeth me beside the still waters. He restoreth my soul: he leadeth me in the paths of righteousness for his name's sake. Yea, though I walk through the valley of the shadow of death, I will fear no evil: for thou art with me; thy rod and thy staff they comfort me. Thou preparest a table before me in the presence of mine enemies: thou anointest my head with oil; my cup runneth over. Surely goodness and mercy shall follow me all the days of my life: and I will dwell in the house of the Lord for ever.
>
> **Psalm 23-28**

The fragrance from the incense erupted, and its intoxicating aroma filled the room, and the cries of the people erupted. The priest returned from the Outer Court and pronounced the Aaronic blessing. *"The Lord bless you and keep you and cause his face to shine upon you and lift up his countenance upon you and give you his peace.* Their prayer ended, and the people echoed an amen. Screaming was heard from the rear of the Outer Court. The snarl of the horses was heard, and Zacharias turned to see that the soldiers had invaded to courts of the Lord. They were in their full regalia. They were dressed in a red cape and red-feathered helmet and brandishing swords. They wore breastplates of iron and armor of fine brass glistening in the rising sun. It seemed like a whole band of soldiers had surrounded the temple mount. "Not in the temple," Zacharias cried, rushing to the front entrance in an effort to forbid the soldiers to come in. The people scattered, running in every direction. Zacharias felt righteous indignation, and he screamed at the soldier who appeared to be leading the band. "This is God's house; there is no reason to spill innocent blood in this holy place." A fierce-looking soldier pushed him out of the way as the soldiers entered the court. They pulled babies from the arms of the screaming mother while the helpless fathers looked on. Their butchery had begun, and they have started in the house of the Lord. Some of the women ran towards the Inner Court, and Zacharias ran back and stood before the entrance forbidding them to enter. All the other priests had disappeared. "Run to the mountain," he screamed above the noise and chaos. The mockery and the laughter of the centurion echoed in his ears as he turned to see the giant of a man standing before him brandishing his sword. "So, you are Zacharias," he snarled. "You are the one who, we heard, had a boy child in your old age. We were told to kill your son, so where is he? Are you hiding him behind the veil?" He moved closer to the vail, and again Zacharias resisted, screaming, "This is holy ground! Sacrilege! sacrilege!" His shouts ignited the rage of the soldier who turned and plunged the sword into his heart. Zachariah crumpled to the ground, and his blood spilled out between the altars. The irate soldier withdrew his sword and commanded his soldiers to withdraw from the temple. The people had scattered and were chased all over the temple mount by the soldiers. There the broken bodies of babies pierced through the heart were scattered everywhere with blood running in the streets of Jerusalem. The priests on duty that day came out of their hiding. They wept as they got help to gather the body of Zacharias and removed him from the temple. A son of Aaron had died on duty defending the temple he was born to serve. The sons of Levi were forbidden to touch the dead but today was a day of great grief. The men in Jerusalem had returned to the temple mount and collected the bodies of babies strawed all over the mount, and a mass grave was dug, and the bodies were placed in the grave and out of the burning sun. Zacharias was also buried, and the people who had returned lamented, for there was a great dirge in the land. The soldiers had disappeared in search of babies all over Judea. The people could not be comforted.

Elizabeth arose from her sleep and remembered she was in the caves by the Dead Sea. Her sleep was plagued with dark dreams; she dreamed Zacharias had died. She wept as she prayed to Yahweh. She knew her son would be safe but wonder at the fate of her husband. She would make her trip back to Ein Kerem. Her baby would be safe with the Essenes. She must return to see the calamities in Judea. She quickly dressed and requested Rabbi Sid to arrange for an escort to take her to En Gidi, where she would collect her donkey and then make her way home. She kissed her boy goodbye. He was playing with the children and was oblivious to the decisions that were made for him. Eve had gentle eyes; she believed her baby would be protected and cared for. Her sorrows had caused deep lines to appear around her eyes. She was not a young girl; the stressors of the previous night had left her tired and worn. She had fulfilled her part in Yahweh's great plan. She that was called barren has had two years of great laughter. She has seen her husband and her son expressing great joy and happiness. Yahweh has given them great joy in a baby boy filled with the Holy Ghost from her womb. She knew his destiny—prophet to Christ. She knew her task was done. The prophet would come out of the wilderness one day and proclaim the kingdom of God to Israel. Zacharias had shown her all the prophecies concerning the Messiah and his prophet... She had no fear; she knew their destinies were sealed in heaven. She smiled, climbed on the beast, and allowed the young man to take the lead. She was tired and just wanted to get to her own bed. They came into Ein Kerem at sunset. Because of her fatigue, the escort had given her several rest periods. Midge has heard of Zacharias's death and had gone to the house looking for Elizabeth. She knew of their plans so decided to wait until her friend return. This would not be easy. Zacharias was dead. Midge saw the beasts coming and came through the door and walk with long strides to her friend. Elizabeth descended off the beast and collapsed in her friend's arm, crying. "I know he is dead," she whispered. "My Zacharias is gone." Midge waved the escort on and took her friend into the house. She laid her in the bed and changed her clothes. It was a long trip, and her friend was tired and broken-hearted. She fed her lintel soup and bread. Elizabeth ate very little and fell asleep telling her friend she loved her. She rose not from her bed again. She went on to the light to meet her Zacharias in paradise.

And thou, child, shalt be called the prophet of the Highest: for thou shalt go before the face of the Lord to prepare his ways; To give knowledge of salvation unto his people by the remission of their sins, Through the tender mercy of our God; whereby the dayspring from on high hath visited us, To give light to them that sit in darkness and in the shadow of death, to guide our feet into the

way of peace. And the child grew, and waxed
strong in spirit, and was in the deserts till the
day of his shewing unto Israel.

Luke 1:76-80

John grew well in the wilderness. He learned to gather locus and wild honey for meal. He was a Nazarite, and by the time he was old enough, Rabbi Sid separated him for the life he was called to. He studied the Torah for ten hours daily and learned the secrets of separation for service to God. The boy was wise beyond his years. The Holy Ghost was upon him. At thirty years old, he arose out of the desert a mighty prophet in words and power. He was a loud-mouth, undaunting, uncompromising prophet. His speech was like no other; he was so ignited with power that the people came by the droves to the River Jordan to listen to him. He was scantily dressed in a loincloth of camel's hair. It has not been seen this way in Israel in a long time. They have read about the schools of the prophets in the Torah and the books of the prophet. He was a new wonder in Judea. They said he was Elijah's reincarnation. Men came and joined themselves to him. His message was commanding and pricked the hearts of the people. The temple leaders hated him; he was unconventional and unabashed. He quoted Isaiah the Prophet concerning the Messiah.

The voice of one crying in the wilderness, Prepare ye the way of the LORD, make his paths straight. Every valley shall be filled, and every mountain and hill shall be brought low; and the crooked shall be made straight, and the rough ways shall be made smooth; And all flesh shall see the salvation of God.

Luke 3:4-6

He was dressed in weird clothing made from animal hair and spent a lot of time by the Jordan River. He started a new ritual of baptism. This was never seen in Israel. He caused such a stir that the people came out to see him. The message was filled with cries for Israel to repent and return to God. He teaches of impending doom and judgment. He preached kindness and piety and offered them baptism on the repentance of sin. The tax collectors came, the Roman soldiers also came to observe his activities; they wanted to know who the up-setter of the season was. They, however, were convicted of their sins and were baptized. For six months, Israel experienced a revival. The prophet prophesied of the coming Messiah. "I indeed baptized you with water; but one mightier than I cometh, the latchet of whose shoes I am not worthy to unloose: he shall baptize you with the Holy Ghost and fire (Luke 3:16). For six months, he preached and baptized the people as they came out to the Jordan River. He had men coming out to be discipled by him. They were amazed by his doctrine. The people had long waited for the Messiah, and they were curious, "Would the Messiah come in their lifetime? Was he the Messiah? And if not the Messiah, why was he changing the rules and baptizing in a river?" He ate wild honey and locust, drank no wine, and his hair was long and uncombed. A Nazarite, he was unto God. The people were drawn as by a supernatural force. They had to hear him. They were tired of the liturgy in the temple. It was dead and empty and did not make them think or change their way of living. This prophet breathed life and freshness about God and was unafraid to speak what God spoke to him. Six months into his preaching, the most amazing encounter occur for in the crowd by the river walk a man; John stopped his baptism and placed his gaze on this man. His voice rose and, his right hand extending, he cried, "This is he of whom I said, After me cometh a man which is preferred before me: for he was before me…Behold the Lamb of God, which taketh away the sin of the world" (John 1:30, John 1:29). "The Messiah," the people murmured as Jesus descended the riverbank and requested to be baptized by John. Overwhelmed by the presence of the Messiah, John refused to baptize the son of God. He has never seen his cousin before, but the Holy Ghost alerted him to the Messiah's presence. He felt so unworthy but was reassured by Jesus to fulfill this act of righteousness. The prophet laid his hands on the lamb and immersed him in water. Suddenly there was a wonder in the heavens, and the people stared into the heaven as it thundered in the midday without rain clouds in sight.

> It came to pass, that Jesus also being baptized, and praying, the heaven was opened, And the Holy Ghost descended in the bodily shape like a dove upon him, and a voice came from heaven, which said, Thou art my beloved Son; in thee I am well pleased.
>
> **Luke 3:21b-22**

God had spoken from heaven, and the people shook as the dove rested on his head. The lamb and the prophet stood side by side. John has fulfilled his purpose. He has presented the Messiah to the world. He watched as Jesus was led by the Spirit. He would go to the wilderness from which he came. He was to be prepared for his assignment. He knew that he would increase in influence and that he would decrease in influence. He pointed some of his disciples to the Messiah, and some followed him. While Jesus returned to Nazareth to begin his ministry, John the Prophet continued to preach the kingdom of God, repentance, and baptize by water. He preached another two years by Jordan, and he even dared to condemn King Herod's relationship with his brother's wife. He was charged with treason and cast in prison. He had hoped to see the Messiah ministering, but now he was incarcerated. His disciples came and told him about Jesus' work and ministry. He was downhearted and discouraged in prison. He doubted his prophetic gift; he doubted he had identified the correct men. He sent his disciples to ask him hard questions.

> Art thou he that should come, or do we look for
> another? Jesus answered and said unto them, Go
> and shew John again those things which ye do
> hear and see. The blind receive their sight and
> the lame walk, the lepers are cleansed, and the
> deaf hear, the dead are raised up, and the poor
> have the gospel preached to them.

> **Matthew 11:3-5**

His disciples returned to him and told him the words of the Messiah.

The lamb reassured the Prophet John that he was the promised one, and he was comforted. Jesus passionately spoke about the prophet, the one called John; He stirred the hearts of the people to think.

> What went ye out into the wilderness to see? A
> reed shaken with the wind? But what went ye
> out for to see? A man clothed in soft raiment?
> Behold, they that wear soft clothing are in kings'
> house. But what went ye out for to see? A proph-
> et? Yea, I say unto you and more than a prophet.
> For this is he of whom it is written, Behold, I
> send my messenger before thy face, which shall
> prepare thy way before thee.
> **Matthew 11:7-10**

John would not live much longer; he went on to suffer the martyr's death. The Herodian Princess Salome dancing had pleased King Herod so much that in his soulish satisfaction, he promised his stepdaughter to give her up to half of his kingdom. Her mother, Herodias, still angry at John for speaking against her and the king, pushed her daughter to ask for the prophet's head. John was beheaded and his head placed on a charger and given to the maiden. His spirit and soul rose to rest in paradise. A bloody mess it was as his disciples came to retrieve his body and buried him. The word came to Jesus that the prophet was dead. Jesus withdrew himself away to a desert place. But his work must go on. He had spoken these words earlier concerning John. "Verily I say unto you, Among them that are born of women there hath not risen a greater than John the Baptist" (Matthew 11:11a). He was a prophet, son of Zacharias and Elizabeth, the prophet to the Messiah, and prophet to all Israel. He was set in place to announce the new era as ordained by Yahweh, the kingdom of God with men again, the redemptive plan of Yahweh for salvation. He had touched the living word, the Lamb of God—Jesus Messiah. He had spoken of His coming and of His kingdom; he had baptized Him and had seen the heaven open. Where others have only spoken of him, he got to usher in the Messiah and to touch him with his own hands. Certainly, there was no greater than the Prophet John.

About the Author

Marian Kerr Bahin was born on the Island of Jamaica, the West Indies. She is the third of four children to Rupert and Merlene Kerr. At the age of fourteen, she had an encounter with the person of Jesus and was born again. She has an intense love for Jesus and the church and always knew she would spend her life telling others about Him. By the age of eighteen, she became the youth president for her church, the Petersfield Church of God Mountain Assembly. She would continue to serve for ten years, in which she was promoted to youth director of the small church denomination. She served intensely, raising up the youths of her denomination to serve God passionately and holy. In 1993, at the age of twenty-eight, she migrated to New York City with a desire to attend Bible School and launch into full-time ministry. However, in an inner audible voice, the Lord spoke to her to pursue nursing, which was a childhood dream. All the doors to attend college opened, and within a year of been in New York, she was enrolled in the Bronx community College of Nursing.

She was the first of her family to graduate from college and went on the pursue a career in nursing for over twenty years. It was in 2015, at the age of fifty, that she started feeling a tug back to full-time ministry and evangelism. She had actively served in all the churches she attended in whatever capacity she could, including missions, women's ministry, being a mentor to youths, and street evangelism. She was hungry to give more time back to the Lord and be actively involved with winning the lost at any cost. However, as her dreams of ministry sparked, she began to experience health challenges. Her health took a spiraling fall and left her debilitated and home-bound with no medical answers for over five years. She prayed and sought the prayers of others. It was during this season that her marriage began to fail. She lost everything during this season, including her finances, her husband, and even the tragic death of her youngest sister, who was very dear to her heart. She learned to intensify her prayers, poured over the scriptures daily, and spend time in worship, believing that the God who saved her at fourteen years old was able to deliver her out of her dilemmas. It was during this season that the small videos on Facebook and YouTube appeared as *The Jesus Storyteller*. It was in this season that the book *The Prophet: A Story of Love and Grace* also emerged. In her own pursuit to find the grace of God, she rediscovered two women, Mary and Elizabeth, whose lives were bonded because of the grace and favor of God on humanity. It was a story that had captured her hurting heart in a fresh way that she picked up her computer and could not stop writing as she took the imaginary journey of what it could have been like in the unfolding of Yahweh's love to humanity.

Marian is mother to son, Aaron Bahin, who currently serves in the Navy and is presently deployed to Bahrain in the Middle East. She is currently enrolled in the River University School of Ministry after getting healed miraculously by Jesus on November 1, 2020. She started Bible school in January 2021 and is thrilled to know it is never too late to pursue the plans God has for your life. Her dream is to win the lost to Jesus Christ because this is truly the hope of the world.

CPSIA information can be obtained
at www.ICGtesting.com
Printed in the USA
LVHW051650201021
700977LV00013B/409

9 781637 695760